GLOBAL EDUCATION REFORM

Global Education Reform documents the ideologically and educationally distinctive approaches countries around the world have taken to structuring their education systems. Focusing on three pairs of case studies written by internationally acclaimed experts, the book provides a powerful analysis of the different ends of an ideological spectrum—from strong state investments in public education to market-based approaches.

An introductory chapter offers an overview of the theories guiding both neoliberal reforms such as those implemented in Chile, Sweden, and the United States with efforts to build strong and equitable public education systems as exemplified by Cuba, Finland, and Canada. The pairs of case studies that follow examine the historical evolution of education within an individual country and compare and contrast national educational outcomes. A concluding chapter dissects the educational outcomes of the differing economic and governance approaches as well as the policy implications.

With contributions from Michael Fullan, Pasi Sahlberg, Linda Darling-Hammond, and Martin Carnoy, *Global Education Reform* is an eye-opening analysis of national educational reforms and the types of high-achieving systems needed to serve all students equitably.

Frank Adamson is a Senior Policy and Research Analyst at the Stanford Center for Opportunity Policy in Education.

Björn Åstrand is Senior Lecturer at Karlstad University, Sweden, where he serves as the Dean for the School of Education.

Linda Darling-Hammond is the Charles E. Ducommun Professor of Education Emeritus at Stanford University and President of the Learning Policy Institute. She is author of more than 500 publications, including several award-winning books, and is a former president of the American Educational Research Association.

GLOBAL EDUCATION REFORM

How Privatization and Public Investment Influence Education Outcomes

Edited by Frank Adamson, Björn Åstrand, and Linda Darling-Hammond

Routledge
Taylor & Francis Group

NEW YORK AND LONDON

First published 2016
by Routledge
711 Third Avenue, New York, NY 10017

and by Routledge
2 Park Square, Milton Park, Abingdon, Oxon, OX14 4RN

Routledge is an imprint of the Taylor & Francis Group, an Informa business

© 2016 Taylor & Francis

The right of Frank Adamson, Björn Åstrand and Linda Darling-Hammond
to be identified as the authors of the editorial material, and of the authors for
their individual chapters, has been asserted in accordance with sections 77
and 78 of the Copyright, Designs and Patents Act 1988.

Library of Congress Cataloging in Publication Data
Names: Adamson, Frank, editor. | Astrand, Bjorn, editor. | Darling-
Hammond, Linda, 1951- editor.
Title: Global education reform : how privatization and public investment
influence education outcomes / edited by Frank Adamson, Bjorn Astrand,
and Linda Darling-Hammond.
Description: New York : Routledge, [2016] | Includes index.
Identifiers: LCCN 2015034324| ISBN 9781138930551 (hardback) | ISBN
9781138930568 (pbk.) | ISBN 9781315680361 (e-book)
Subjects: LCSH: Education--Finance--Case studies. | Educational
change--Economic aspects--Case studies. | Education and state--Case
studies. | Public schools--Finance--Case studies. | Privatization in
education--Case studies.
Classification: LCC LB2824 .G55 2016 | DDC 371.2/06--dc23
LC record available at http://lccn.loc.gov/2015034324

ISBN: 978-1-138-93055-1 (hbk)
ISBN: 978-1-138-93056-8 (pbk)
ISBN: 978-1-315-68036-1 (ebk)

Typeset in Bembo
by Saxon Graphics Ltd, Derby

CONTENTS

1

PRIVATIZATION OR PUBLIC INVESTMENT?

A Global Question

Frank Adamson and Björn Åstrand

In August of 2011, student dissatisfaction with education in Chile culminated in a massive multi-day demonstration by hundreds of thousands of people[1] who marched, chanted, and threw sticks, rocks, and paint while police fired back with tear gas and water cannons. The source of this large-scale protest was surprising: The intense fracas was about education, a topic that rarely takes people to the streets. But this was not the first such occasion in Chile: huge protests had also erupted in 2001 and 2006.

Why was Chile in such distress about its schools? The short answer is that, in 1980, the country had instituted a set of market-based education reforms that privatized primary and secondary education by creating a voucher system, expanding the private sector, allowing tuition fees for many students, and reducing funding to public schools. Over time, these moves increased segregation and inequality and reduced quality in most schools.

Chile was the prototype for what has since been called the "neoliberal" education agenda, which has spread to other countries and is currently advocated by a number of international organizations and governments worldwide. There is an ongoing global dialogue about whether and how to institute similar market-based approaches in both developed and developing nations.

The specifics vary by location, but the underlying principle is that market-based systems deliver education better than governments. This idea was popularized by University of Chicago economist Milton Friedman, who championed privatization as a market-based "solution" to the state "monopoly" on education in the 1970s and 1980s. He theorized that free markets—with little government oversight or ownership—would promote competition, improve efficiency, and lead to higher quality goods and services. This theory later became identified as neoliberalism.

IMAGE 1.1 Chilean Student Protestors[2]

In the 1970s, the dictator of Chile, Augosto Pinochet, who met with Friedman, put the market-based theory into practice, privatizing social sectors and publicly owned enterprises, from banks to the education system. In 1980, Pinochet followed the education plan of Friedman and his students, implementing a nationwide voucher system.[3] Contrary to his theory, however, Friedman's neoliberal, free-market approach exacerbated educational inequalities, erupting in massive student protests and the election of student leaders to Chile's parliament.

Friedman's arguments, rooted in the efficiency of markets, have since evolved into a number of private and profit-centered approaches around the world. In 2015, the president of the World Bank voiced support for private, for-profit companies providing public education, a strategy that channels public money into private profit.[4] That public education is now seen as a new and profitable market is evident. At a recent meeting of the International Finance Corporation, for example, one venture capitalist called education a 4.65 trillion dollar market, identifying global expenditure on public education as an untapped reserve of profit.[5] With only a fraction of those funds currently providing profit streams, there are substantial incentives for private companies to seek to capture market share in education.

Neoliberalism, Privatization, and the Global Education Reform Movement (GERM)

The theory of action associated with privatization—that better performance will result from transfer of government functions to private entities who own or manage them—has become more widely discussed and implemented in the education sector over the last two decades.

One way to understand the political manifestation of this privatization push is through a term popularized by an author in this volume, Pasi Sahlberg. He refers to a set of market-based policies that have strong advocates in the educator sector internationally, referring to them as the Global Education Reform Movement, or GERM. As Sahlberg defines it, this set of policies includes: school choice and competition, high-stakes testing, narrowing of curriculum, and the use of under- or unqualified, and therefore cheaper, teachers.[6] He notes that the idea of the GERM evolves from the international exchange of education policies and "best practices" among education systems. This kind of "policy borrowing"[7] is made possible by greater international communication and comparative tools such as PISA (Programme for International Student Assessment) and the conversations it generates within and across countries. Sahlberg observes:

> GERM is not a formal global policy program, but rather an unofficial educational agenda that relies on a certain set of assumptions that are used as education reform principles to improve quality and overall performance in education[8] ... GERM has become accepted as "a new educational orthodoxy" among international development agencies, consulting firms and private philanthropists. As a consequence it has shaped many recent education reforms throughout the world, including those in the United States, Australia, England, many parts of Latin America, some Scandinavian countries, and an increasing number of countries in the developing world.[9]

Interest in these ideas can be viewed as stemming, on the one hand, from disappointment with the performance of some public education systems and beliefs about what may lead to better outcomes, and, on the other hand, from the amount of potential profit available, which has stimulated advocacy efforts from private providers of education services, venture capitalists, technology firms, and others.

While some countries have adopted these principles to varying extents and in different ways, others have resisted market-based approaches and have instead pursued public investment strategies, including developing and maintaining a professional teacher labor force and ensuring that resources reach students equitably.

This book examines countries of both types—those pursuing the market-based privatization model and those using strategies of public investment in education. On one end of this spectrum lie countries such as Finland, which takes a public investment approach that privileges the provision of high-quality, equitable opportunities for students to learn. On the opposite side sits the privatization approach most accurately typified by Chile that distributes vouchers to families (discussed below). Figure 1.1 shows this spectrum, including all six countries included in this study.

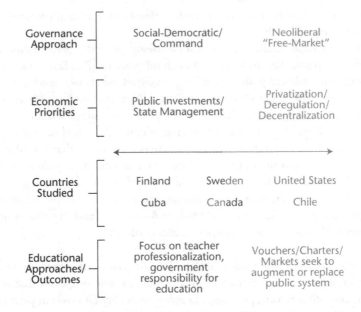

FIGURE 1.1 Spectrum of Selected Countries, by Approaches to Governance, Economics, and Education

Toward the middle of the spectrum, some countries have changed their approaches, while others have developed blended models that rely, to different extents, on publicly governed and managed choices versus privately owned and governed approaches. Sweden shifted towards privatization, turning its social-democratic approach to a market-based model that became increasingly dominated by privately owned, including for-profit, providers. Ontario, Canada changed in the opposite direction, from incentives for private provision to a strong public investment model. Cuba has consistently invested in public education since the 1960s, while the United States has implemented both privatization and public investment models in various places, with approaches to chartering schools that have varied across states in the ways they have emphasized their public versus private management and governance.

We have selected and organized these six countries into three pairs, with each pair connected by geographic and cultural proximity, but each country within the pair pursuing opposite educational strategies (see Figure 1.2). Pairing these particular countries allows for three types of analysis: (1) examining the historical evolution of education within an individual country; (2) contrasting the different approaches of neighboring countries; and (3) comparing countries that pursue similar education strategies in different geographic locations.

	Scandinavia	North America	Caribbean/South America
Public Investment	Finland	Canada	Cuba
Privatization	Sweden	U.S.A.	Chile

FIGURE 1.2 Country Pairs, by Region and Type of Education System

Hayek and Keynes: The Original Privatization versus Public Investment Debate

The birth of the GERM principles goes back to the first iteration of neoliberalism (call it neoliberalism 1.0), proposed by the Austrian economist Fredriech Von Hayek. As a veteran of the destruction of World War I, Hayek harbored great suspicions about governments wielding too much power, both politically and militarily.[10] Therefore, he recommended a return to market liberalism (hence the *neo* in neoliberalism) as a response to centralized economies, state-based socialism, and fascism. Hayek proposed neoliberalism 1.0 in the 1930s as a "middle way" between classical liberalism and these centrally planned economies.

In the 1930s, however, the world economy was in the midst of the great depression caused by the market failure in the late 1920s. John Maynard Keynes then offered a public investment plan, called the New Deal in the United States, which saw governments regulate markets and invest heavily in labor and infrastructure. The New Deal worked and the United States saw increased growth through the 1960s.[11] The New Deal included many of the public investment approaches now used successfully in Finland, Canada, and Cuba, and detailed in the next section.

Despite the success of Keynesian economics and the New Deal, Hayek and others formed a group in 1947 called the Mont Pelerin Society. This group aimed to promote the tenets of liberalism and free trade instead of the Keynesian approach, which they viewed as state-sponsored and Marxist.[12] Their neoliberal 1.0 ideas lay mostly dormant for decades, according to Hayek, but found an incubation nest at the University of Chicago, the home institution of Milton Friedman.

The situation changed in the 1970s. Ideologically, the geopolitics of the Cold War replaced alliances from World War II, creating fear in some Westerners that central state planning by the United States would result in Soviet-style repression. On a practical level, the combined expense of expanding social services, military expenditures (especially the Vietnam War), and the 1973 oil crisis all strained the U.S. economic system. A new phenomenon of higher interest rates combined with higher unemployment and lower growth developed, termed stagflation. These economic and political contexts combined to create an opportunity for neoliberalism 2.0 to develop in theory in the United States and in practice in Chile.

Neoliberalism 2.0 and the Birth of the GERM

In the 1970s and 1980s, neoliberalism 2.0 had not yet solidified as an economic or political system. While Hayak's neoliberalism 1.0 focused on opening markets using liberalization policies, Friedman and other leaders in the 2.0 version emphasized privatization and deregulation as their main policy drivers for making decisions.[13]

In Chile, Pinochet, with the help of Friedman and his students, changed the course of Chile's system and created the blueprint for market-based education reform. Most importantly, Pinochet overthrew the democratically elected Salvador Allende in a 1973 coup. Allende had supported investment in education and social justice, similar to Cuba, Finland, Sweden, and the United States in the 1960s and 1970s. He even declared 1971 the year of the democratization of education, two years before being deposed by Pinochet.

Pinochet rolled back these reforms when he established a dictatorship with political and military controls that focused on privatizing social programs and public infrastructure (such as copper mines), liberalizing trade, and deregulating the market. Pinochet *privatized* the education system in 1980, based on Friedman's main idea of markets that provide *choice*, implemented in education through the *voucher* system.

Thus, Pinochet realized the goals of neoliberalism by using privatization as the underlying principle, or *policy driver*. He then used choice as the main *economic rationale*, based on the theory that parents' choice of schools would increase competition among schools, thus motivating them to provide better education. Finally, Pinochet adopted Friedman's vouchers (explained below) as the *education mechanism* for translating the policy driver and economic rationale into schools. Figure 1.3 shows how the features of Pinochet's approach—privatization, choice, and vouchers—relate to each other in the policy sphere.

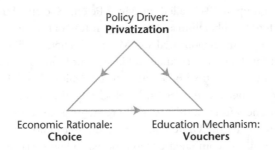

Policy Driver:
Privatization

Economic Rationale: Education Mechanism:
Choice   **Vouchers**

FIGURE 1.3 Primary Elements of Chile's GERM Approach to Education

Key Elements of National Education Systems

Figure 1.3 reveals a framework for understanding how privatization took hold in Chile. In addition, it serves as a model for understanding education policy and practice in general. This framework is especially important because market-based reform has neither taken hold at the same time, nor in exactly the same way, in different countries. Figure 1.4 shows the more general framework of policy drivers, economic rationales, and education mechanisms that we then apply to every country in this study. These figures reveal the main features that countries have used in pursing either the privatization model or the public investment approach in education. While we do not present the figures for each country, we do discuss the different elements that comprise each level: policy drivers, economic rationales, and education mechanisms.

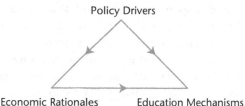

FIGURE 1.4 Key Elements of National Education Systems

Policy Drivers

When politicians pursue different models for their economic and education systems, they try to answer, either implicitly or explicitly, some fundamental questions. These questions concern ownership, legality, and government oversight. Table 1.1 shows these questions, along with the neoliberal and public investment policy drivers used to address these fundamental issues.

TABLE 1.1 Policy Questions and Drivers (Top of Triangle see Figure 1.4)

Policy driver questions
1. Who decides issues of ownership and investment?
2. What processes and actions are defined as legal?
3. At what level of governance do decisions happen?

Neoliberal policy drivers	*Public investment policy drivers*
Privatization	Public ownership
Deregulation	Public responsibility
Decentralization	Equity
Liberalization	Democratic decision-making

Neoliberal policies respond to the question of ownership by increasing the levels of privatization. In the case of education, privatization refers to the transfer of public-sector responsibility to privately owned or operated organizations or companies, for example non-governmentally run schools such as private or charter schools. Often, the result is that the public pays taxes to private or quasi-private organizations for services, but the organizations have little public accountability because they are not elected bodies or politicians. A public investment approach retains public ownership over education by keeping politically appointed people in decision-making roles of responsibility, subject to public vote.

The neoliberal approach to the issues of legality is commonly called "deregulation," which is somewhat of a misnomer. Deregulation is still regulation in the sense that all rules are regulations, even the rule that says, "there are no rules." Therefore, deregulation really describes a process of changing regulations in a way that usually favors private interests, especially when they stand to benefit from having fewer rules, responsibilities, and public accountability.

Often deregulation occurs in concert with decentralization and market liberalization. In these cases, national governments cede control over and responsibility for education to local governments that often lack the requisite capacity to provide high-quality education. These local municipalities then outsource education to private or quasi-private entities, turning deregulation, decentralization, and liberalization into more pathways leading toward privatization. These terms, especially decentralization, are vastly overused, creating an unfortunate situation in which the words are bereft of meaning while politicians still use them to make fundamental changes to economic and political structures.[14]

On the other hand, public investment approaches to legal questions and governance focus on the government's responsibility to provide high-quality education through democratic decision-making. The democratic aspect includes the possibility of voting out politicians who fail to provide adequate public education, as occurred in Ontario, Canada. While a public investment approach certainly does not guarantee effective education systems, it offers the key possibility of democratic redress that disappears when private companies do not have the same mandates of regulations and public accountability. Cuba stands as an exception to the democratic aspect of the public investment model because it maintains a command economy. Nevertheless, Cuba still manages schools in close relationship to their communities and has produced excellent results, using education strategies similar to those in Finland, including investing in teacher preparation.

Economic Rationales

With any large public sector, taxpayers always want to know how well the system functions, and rightfully so. In the case of education, the key questions include: Who's responsible for providing education? What's the best delivery mechanism?

And, how much do different approaches cost? Table 1.2 shows these questions and the corresponding answers to them in the context of neoliberalism and public investment.

To build public support for their approaches, neoliberal proponents focus on three organizing economic rationales: (1) efficiency; (2) the axis of competition–choice–quality, and (3) the apparent scarcity of resources.[15] On the supply side, neoliberals aim for efficiency in education systems, arguing that private firms deliver goods and services more efficiently than the government. On the demand side, neoliberals promote competition as a means to deliver more consumer choice, which theoretically leads to higher quality products.

While neoliberals use economic theories as the main source of their rationales, proponents of public investment consider the social benefit of their economic approaches as the primary rationale for delivering education. In the public investment model, the main goals of education are providing universal access to students, as opposed to competition models that create winners and losers among schools and students. The government is primarily responsible for providing education instead of outsourcing it to third parties. This does not preclude the use of contractors; rather, it places primary political responsibility with public entities to ensure equitable opportunities and accountability to the public.

When it comes to cost, countries like Finland spend a little bit more but receive quite a high return in better education performance. Over the last 45 years, Finland has averaged spending 5.8 percent of GDP on education, while the United States has averaged 5.1 percent of GDP over the last 35 years.[16] This difference is not trivial, but it also does not explain the differences in international assessments discussed in the conclusion of this volume between Finland and the United States, for example. Instead, countries emphasizing different economic rationales end up creating education systems that also perform quite differently.

Both neoliberalism and public investment lay claim to equity as a driving principle, making it a contested term. In the United States, education reform supporters cite a lack of equitable outcomes for low-income and minority children as a rationale for privatizing schools. On the other hand, proponents of

TABLE 1.2 Economic Questions and Rationales (Bottom Left of Triangle see Figure 1.4)

Questions that economic rationales address
1. What are the main goals of education systems?
2. Who's responsible for providing education?
3. How much do different approaches cost?

Neoliberal economic rationales	*Public investment economic rationales*
Efficiency	Universal access
Choice/Competition/Quality	Preparing citizens for economy and
Scarce resources (apparent)	democracy
Equity	Equity

public investment point to the chronic poverty and underfunding of schools as reasons for inequitable education outcomes. They maintain that increasing investments wisely and targeting them toward high-need populations will better serve students than introducing private entities as middlemen in an education marketplace. One main question addressed by this book is how equity has been approached by countries using distinctive models and with what results.

Education Mechanisms

If the policy drivers are the engines of education reform and the economic rationales are the vehicles, then the education mechanisms are the tires, where the rubber hits the road. The main questions for decision-making address the delivery mechanism (usually the type of school), the type of curriculum, and the content and learning targets for students. Table 1.3 shows the questions and neoliberal and public investment approaches to education.

Proponents of privatization have proposed at least five different tools, some of which overlap: vouchers, charter schools, school markets, market-based approaches to teaching, and test-based accountability. Vouchers and charter schools are defined and utilized differently from country to country but both enable private management (and sometimes ownership) of schools utilizing public funding. They have two main differences. First, voucher money follows a student to the school where he/ she registers, with both public and private schools as options. By contrast, governments give contracts, or "charters," to a school that has proposed to operate a particular kind of program in a specific way, using the per-pupil funding that would have otherwise gone to a government-run public school. Charter schools are essentially privately managed public schools that have been deregulated to varying degrees, depending on the jurisdiction they are in and how they are authorized.

A second important difference between vouchers and charter schools is the role of religious schools, which can receive vouchers but are not part of the charter universe. The separation of church and state in the United States has

TABLE 1.3 Education Questions and Mechanisms (Bottom Right of Triangle see Figure 1.4)

Questions that education mechanisms address
1. What's the best delivery mechanism for education?
2. What curriculum gets taught?
3. How do we know if students learn?

Neoliberal education mechanisms	*Public investment education mechanisms*
Vouchers	Well-prepared teachers
Charter schools	Equitable funding of schools
School Markets	High-quality infrastructure
Market-based teaching	Whole-child curriculum and pedagogy
Test-based accountability	

limited the use of vouchers in education (with the exception of experiments in a few cities like Milwaukee). On the other hand, charter schools generally operate as independent, non-religious, "public" schools and serve as the main vehicle for developing markets, or portfolios of diverse schools, in U.S. districts.

The third mechanism is markets, which applies to Sweden in particular, where students can theoretically attend any public or private school for free. (Milwaukee's market featuring both vouchers and charters approaches this model, although not all schools are free to all students.) Although all of Sweden's schools are included in a market model, in practice, students do not attend any school of their choice. Ultimately, the distribution of students in this market system reveals a similar type of stratification as found in Chile and the United States.

The final two neoliberal education mechanisms—market-based approaches to teaching and test-based accountability—affect the nature of teaching and learning in schools. Creating a market for teachers by lowering standards for entry and allowing broader access to the occupation can reduce costs, as can greater attrition (produced by evaluation focused on terminations or creation of less desirable working conditions) that typically substitutes more inexperienced for more experienced teachers. Increasing class size is, of course, another way to reduce costs. Because personnel salaries usually represent around 80 percent of education expenditures, cutting teacher costs is the easiest way to increase profits under a privatization model.

Test-based accountability systems are used to inform the market and sometimes to base decisions about such things as school closure, teacher pay, and teacher retention on test results. The use of "high-stakes" testing can both incentivize schools and teachers to "teach to the test" because their jobs depend on scores, and to seek to recruit higher-scoring students while avoiding or eliminating lower-scoring ones.

For decades, psychometricians (test experts) have cautioned against misusing test results for punitive decisions instead of using them to gather information about what students know and what they still need to learn. Nevertheless, testing is viewed as a way to inform and motivate the market. In addition, providing tests and test preparation materials to schools, districts, and states is a highly profitable endeavor and receives political support from testing conglomerates.[17]

The incentive of profit functions at all levels in the education reform movement and has become an important motive in many contexts. Private companies that operate schools inexpensively can pocket the differences between what the state provides and what the companies spend. Governments may also outsource education provision, thus reducing their responsibility for education management and outcomes. Outsourcing then opens doors for profit-making by private companies in testing, curriculum delivery, facilities maintenance, transportation, school management, and other areas. The approach often shifts the language of education to one of markets in which companies and teachers produce schooling, and students and families become consumers and products instead of learners and partners.

In contrast to the privatization model, the public investment approach tends to value four different mechanisms for improving education: (1) well-prepared teachers; (2) equitable funding of schools; (3) high-quality infrastructure; and (4) whole-child curriculum and pedagogy. A common thread between Finland, Cuba, and Canada is the high level of investment in teachers. Each country values their teacher labor forces and makes teaching a profession and a priority, from funding to training, both pre-service and in-service. These countries then provide the necessary infrastructure for teachers and students to succeed (strong curriculum, reasonable class sizes, materials, and supports). Finally, because these countries do not use tests for high-stakes accountability, their teachers have more latitude in and more capacity for helping students learn a broad array of skills that prepares them for life, instead of just for workforce participation.

The GERM Spreads: Who's Infected and Who Resists?

This book focuses in part on the historical spread and application of neoliberalism, captured within the sector of education using Sahlberg's concept of the GERM. We first discussed its roots in neoliberalism and presented a framework of its different features, as well as different approaches used in models of public investment. But how did the GERM influence countries around the globe? And how did public investment strategies evolve along the same timeline?

Figure 1.5 shows the major moments when three of the countries in this study incorporated the rationales and mechanisms of market-based reforms into their education systems. The figure also shows when and how the three public investment countries began and evolved their models, using different strategies to avoid privatization of education.

	Chile	U.S.	Sweden	Finland	Canada	Cuba
1980s	GERM begins: Pinochet's voucher system			Public Investment approach: Equity-based system		Public Investment approach: Investment in teachers
1990s		GERM case: Milwaukee voucher program			GERM resisted: Voucher program overturned in 2003	GERM protection: Trade sanctions/ command economy prevents neoliberal ideas and policies, until 2015
2000s		GERM case: Charter school movement and New Orleans reforms	GERM case: School system marketized	GERM immunity: High int'l test scores		
2010s					Public Investment approach: Professional capacity building	

FIGURE 1.5 Tracking the GERM: Susceptibility and Resistance in Recent Decades

The figure reveals that the 1980s–1990s saw an influx of neoliberalism in governments, accompanied by the influence of market-based reforms on education. Chile served as the experimental petri dish for neoliberalism, privatization, and the formulation of the GERM model. The United States and Sweden exhibit different but related strains, illustrating how the model has adapted to the context of its host nation (through vouchers, charters, and markets) while still expressing the fundamental building blocks of neoliberalism (privatization, deregulation, etc.). Conversely, the three public investment countries demonstrate how, although the GERM has spread to many countries, it has not necessarily influenced education everywhere.

In the 1970s, Finland actually changed its education system to focus on equity through public investment. A generation later, Finland reaped the benefits of its initiatives and created a level of "immunity" by scoring highest on international tests, beginning in PISA 2000. The Finnish business community had been pressuring the government to privatize the education sector, but once Finland had the highest international test scores, those arguments disappeared.

In Canada, the province of Ontario actually became "infected" with the GERM, adopting austerity measures in the late 1990s and tuition tax credits for private schools. However, by the early 2000s, Ontario developed "resistance" in the form of public backlash after conservative politicians called for greater investments in private schools, only to be voted out of office. Ontario's new public investment model, grounded in collective professional capacity building, has performed well in both outcomes and public opinion since the change.

Finally, Cuba has received an unusual form of "barrier protection" from the GERM through U.S. sanctions that have somewhat insulated it from globalization and neoliberalism. Unfortunately for Cuba, despite having "off the charts" high achievement scores compared to Latin American countries, the recently lifted embargo will likely mean a flood of commerce and ideas, including, potentially, the global education reform movement.

Organization of this Book

In what follows, we present case studies of each of the six countries, presented in the order of their geographically proximate pairs. Based on the research from each country, we can also identify the primary policy drivers, economic rationales, and education mechanisms that accompany privatization or public investment.

In Chapter 2, Abelardo Castro-Hidalgo and Lilian Gómez take up the story of Chile, beginning well before the Pinochet takeover and following the story through years of protests and recent efforts to redirect the system. Martin Carnoy contrasts the case of publicly oriented tiny Cuba with the Chilean approach to reform in Chapter 3. In Chapters 4 and 5, Björn Åstrand and Pasi Sahlberg describe the very different strategies taken by Sweden and Finland as they diverged from what were common democratic commitments in the post-war period. Sweden's embrace of privatization has contrasted with Finland's commitment to an entirely public system. Over the course of the subsequent decades, they switched places in terms of education status.

In Chapter 6, we look at the competing impulses within the United States and how those have played out in the most noteworthy sites for privatization—Milwaukee and New Orleans—as well as how high-achieving states like Massachusetts have managed a more successful public investment strategy. In Chapter 7, Michael Fullan and Santiago Rincon-Gallardo pick up this thread and describe Ontario's development of a comprehensive public education improvement strategy that followed the rejection of a government that was actively disinvesting in public education and planting incentives for privatization.

The book finishes with a cross-case policy analysis that synthesizes the most important lessons within and across countries. These lessons can inform educators and policymakers around the world as they consider policy strategies associated with investments in both public improvements and private alternatives, as well as the possibilities for a choice of models that might be able to meet democratic needs.

Notes

1 Franklin, J. (August 5, 2011). Chile student protests explode into violence. Retrieved from http://www.theguardian.com/world/2011/aug/05/chile-student-protests-violence; Long, G. (August 11, 2011). Chile student protests point to deep discontent. Retrieved from http://www.bbc.com/news/world-latin-america-14487555; Nacional (August 18, 2011). Minuto a minuto: Autoridades cifran en 40 mil los asistentes a marcha y organizadores en 100 mil. Retrieved from www.latercera.com/noticia/nacional/2011/08/680-387032-9-minuto-a-minuto-pese-a-la-lluvia-empieza-a-agruparse-manifestantes-en-la-alameda.shtml.

2 Retrieved from www.theatlantic.com/photo/2011/08/student-protests-in-chile/100125/.

3 Carnoy, M. (2002). *Lessons of Chile's Voucher Reform Movement*. Rethinking Schools. Retrieved from www.rethinkingschools.org/special_reports/voucher_report/v_sosintl. shtml.

4 In his speech leading up to the 2015 World Education Forum, Jim Yong Kim specifically praised a private, for-profit company, Bridge Academies, as a publicly funded solution for public education in some African countries. Kim, J. (2015). Ending Extreme Poverty by 2030: The Final Push. Retrieved from www.worldbank. org/en/news/speech/2015/04/07/speech-by-world-bank-group-president-jim-yong-kim-ending-extreme-poverty-final-push.

5 Global market estimate provided in speech by Rob Hutter, Managing Partner at Learn Capital, at the International Finance Corporation's "International Private Education Conference," San Francisco, 2014. The IFC is the private arm of the World Bank Group.

6 Sahlberg, P. (2011). *Finnish lessons*. New York: Teachers College Press. p. 99.

7 Steiner-Khamsi, G. (2014). "Cross-national policy borrowing: understanding reception and translation". *Asia Pacific Journal of Education*, 34(2), 153–167.

8 Hargreaves, A., Earl, L., Moore, S., and Manning, S. (2002). *Learning to Change: Teaching Beyond Subjects and Standards*. San Francisco: John Wiley & Sons; Hargreaves, A., and Shirley, D. L. (2012). *The Global Fourth Way: The Quest for*

Educational Excellence. Newbury Park, CA: Corwin Press; Sahlberg, P. (2011). "The fourth way of Finland". *Journal of Educational Change,* 12(2), 173–185.

9 Sahlberg, P. (2011). *Finnish Lessons.* New York: Teachers College Press.

10 Samuels, W. J. (2011). *Erasing the Invisible Hand: Essays on an Elusive and Misused Concept in Economics.* Cambridge: Cambridge University Press.

11 The New Deal was not the only factor in American growth. World War II contributed heavily to the U.S. manufacturing sector. Also, American growth sometimes came at the expense of others, including citizens in a number of Latin American dictatorships orchestrated and supported by U.S. involvement, including Pinochet's autocracy in Chile.

12 Samuels, W. J. (2011). *Erasing the Invisible Hand: Essays on an Elusive and Misused Concept in Economics.* Cambridge: Cambridge University Press.

13 Friedman, M. (1962). *Capitalism and Freedom.* Chicago, IL. University of Chicago Press.

14 Mintzberg's full quotation: "The words *centralization* and *decentralization* have been bandied about for as long as anyone has cared to write about organizations. Yet they represent probably the most confused topic in management. The terms have been used in so many different ways that they almost ceased to have any useful meaning" in Mintzberg, H. (1983) *Structures in Five: Designing Effective Organizations.* Upper Saddle River, NJ: Prentice-Hall International, p.95.

15 Mundy, K. and Murphy, L. (2000). "Transnational advocacy, global civil society? Emerging evidence from the field of education". *Comparative Education Review,* 45(1), 85–126.

16 OECD (2015). *Public spending on education* (indicator). Retrieved from https://data. oecd.org/eduresource/public-spending-on-education.htm.

17 Cave, T. and Rowell, A. (2015). "'Reform': Creating opportunities to profit", in *A Quiet Word: Lobbying, Crony Capitalism and Broken Politics in Britain.* London: Vintage.

2

CHILE

A Long-Term Neoliberal Experiment and its Impact on the Quality and Equity of Education

Abelardo Castro-Hidalgo and Lilian Gómez-Álvarez

The Long Battle for "Inclusive, Tuition-free, High-quality Education"

> Tonight at 9:30 P.M., some students were in a university education building, while outside others did a "cacerolazo," a form of popular protest during which people make noise by banging pots and pans, even from their own homes, to call for attention ... The electricity went out everywhere on campus so we went to the building entrance. Some of us lit candles to light the place ... At 12:20 A.M., we could see special forces of around 30 police officers deploying. When we tried to go back into the building, they were already on us. When we managed to shut the doors behind us, they broke the entrance windows with sticks and stones, and—without provocation— they released three tear gas containers into the building. This created quite a commotion as some students choked on the gas. Some of them passed out, while others threw up.
>
> *Student, Universidad de Concepción*

This is how a student from the School of Education at Universidad de Concepción describes the scene on Friday night, August 5, 2011, while students occupied the School of Education building as part of the student activist movement. This student movement, which has become a social movement, broadly rejects the privatization of education and the inequality of education that privatization produces. The protests have peaked at several key moments since the 1990s, rooted in Chilean students' longstanding interest in social welfare and education rights. This chapter first provides a short vignette detailing the long struggle by students for education equity, including the failures and successes of their movements. The discussion then turns to the systemic and policy issues that have continued to galvanize student protests.

Historically, Chilean students have actively engaged in social issues and participated in decisions about policy and university management. Since its foundation in 1906, the Federation of Students of Chile has served as a significant force that contributes to democratization processes, with a clear focus on building a welfare society. Moreover, during Pinochet's dictatorship, the student movement was one of the first organizations to organize resistance against his policies.

The first stage of the student movement against these privatization policies began in 2001. At the time, Education Secretary Sergio Bitar agreed to grant loans, guaranteed by the state, to students of private universities. Students perceived the Chilean state as strengthening private universities at the expense of traditional universities, which were grouped in an association called CRUCH. The movement succeeded in securing Bitar's commitment to increase loans and scholarships to students from lower-income families at CRUCH universities. More broadly, the student movement put the need to revise the system on the political agenda, including the increasing privatization of higher education.

A second stage of the student movement came in 2006. Called the "Penguin Revolution" after the design of uniforms worn in public schools, it began in the city of Coronel as a protest against the failure of authorities to rebuild a school after flooding. It quickly spread to the capital of Chile, Santiago, where students protested about lack of funding for transportation and school lunches for poor students, although students at private "voucher" schools received these benefits. From there, the movement spread across the country, drawing attention to the fundamental inequity of the educational system.

The students created a list of demands, including improving the quality of public education; ending the inequity in education; reversing decentralization (putting the state in charge instead of the municipality); stopping student selection for private voucher schools; and eliminating profit from schools receiving state money. The strength of the movement forced the government to create an Advisory Board for the Quality of Education, eventually resulting in draft legislation that included student demands. However, opposing interests sought to preserve profit making and student selection, proposing an alternative draft law that, instead of including the central points of the Penguin movement, consolidated and gave legal support to the existing system.

The next round of student movements addressed these "pending" issues in different ways. In 2009, students at the University of Concepción created a general strike (supported by teachers), taking over buildings across the university, demanding more food scholarships, reduced university fees, and elimination of enrollment fees. Other student federations followed this movement closely, aware that students and families pay 78 percent of the costs of higher education, even though the higher education system often produces students who graduate straight into unemployment—sometimes with degrees that do not have a corresponding labor market and with debts they cannot pay.

Other groups have aligned to form massive demonstrations in the streets, culminating in 2011 with hundreds of thousands of protestors in Santiago. Images of violent clashes between protestors and police, including tanks, water cannon, and tear gas spread around the world. At this point, students demanded:

- free education throughout the educational system;
- elimination of profit in schools;
- transition of education into the hands of the state;
- participation of teachers, students, and workers in university management to ensure transparency in the use of resources;
- democratization and provision of high-quality education

At present, the student movement is still active, with the latest iteration resulting in four student leaders being elected and currently serving as "student legislators" in the House of Representatives in the Chilean parliament. In January 2015, a new education law restricted, but did not eliminate, profit and selection of students. It also phased out the co-payment (fee paid by parents) for private voucher schools, but did not end the voucher program. While several bills have been passed leading to some improvements, several laws will also require review for the changes to take place. In the meantime, the student struggle for educational rights and equity will continue, even if it remains highly contested, as detailed in this chapter.

Chapter Overview

Chile's original constitution promised a democratic state that cares for its people and builds strong social institutions. Important investment did occur during the 1960s and 1970s towards the development of a modern state, providing greater equity and opportunity for everyone. However, the coup d'état on September 11, 1973 began a process of dismantling this progress by changing the constitution and privatizing key institutions originally managed by the state, including much of education. Evidence now clearly points to US influence both militarily on General Pinochet's rise to power and economically through Chile's adoption of the neoliberal ideas of the University of Chicago's Milton Friedman, implemented by his Chilean students, better known as "the Chicago Boys."

When Pinochet was finally unseated in 1988, the educational system had changed dramatically— it was much more unequal, less professional, and more driven by standardized tests. Subsequent efforts in the 1990s to redress some of these problems did not entirely uproot the neoliberal system. Instead, the government introduced relatively small, incremental changes from time to time to address equity issues, but they were either insufficient or inadequate to turn the ship around. Hence, student-generated revolts arose in 2001, increasingly involving more and more students, with the crescendo in 2006 with the so-called Penguin Revolution (municipal high school students are called 'penguins' owing to their black-and-white uniforms). The student movement has gained momentum at different times, with another massive equalizing effort in 2011 that gathered together over hundreds of thousands of people from all sectors, not only education. The battle continues even with the new socialist government elected in 2014—Michelle Bachelet's second term in office. Current education reform aims at reducing segregation, eliminating selection, banning profit, ensuring universal gratuity and coverage, and securing quality and accountability at all levels.

The goal of this chapter is twofold: to review the main changes in the Chilean educational system as a product of policies introduced by different governments and constitutions; and, within that context, to analyze how the neoliberal system has influenced government operation of the education sector and resulting public opinion. We discuss the evolution of the Chilean education system during four main eras in the history of Chile: (1) the Welfare State (1938–1973), (2) the Neoliberal Experiment (1973–1989), (3) the Return to Democracy (1989–2010), and (4) the Continuing Tug of War (2010–present). These stages are marked by important political transitions, such as the 1973 coup d'état and the return to democracy in 1990. These stages also present education policies adopted by different governments, either resulting in increasing or decreasing the quality of education in the country.

The chapter begins with a brief introduction to the main characteristics of Chile in different areas. The second part, the Welfare State, presents a promising nation taking care of its people's social rights, including education. The third section details the neoliberal turn under Pinochet and Friedman's acolytes. The narrative continues with a description of the return to democracy followed by the present situation, supported by figures and data to illustrate the main consequences of almost 90 years of political, economic, and social change.

Chile: A Land of Contrasts

Nestled in one of the world's most unusual landscapes, with a population of just over 16 million, Chile is characterized by its sharp contrasts. It is the longest, narrowest country in South America, flanked by the Andes mountains on the east and the Pacific Ocean on the west; it features the driest desert on the planet, polar ice in the south (as it claims a large portion of Antarctica), and the exotic and remote Easter Island (*Rapa Nui*). Chile's political history is as multifaceted as its diverse geography, and largely shaped by the latter. Conquistadors exercised varying levels of influence over the diverse indigenous populations of the 2,500-mile-long country. Even though it shares a legacy of Iberian colonialism with the rest of South America, in contrast to most of its neighbors, it has enjoyed a long history of almost unbroken democratic rule since its independence from Spain in 1818.

Shifting Structures of Governance

In terms of governance, Chile emerged in the 1830s as a relatively stable country. Stability was put to the test in the late 1960s and early 1970s, when severe left–right political polarization and turmoil, marked by violence, strikes, and mass demonstrations (both by government supporters and opponents), led to the September 11, 1973 coup d'état. The coup overthrew Salvador Allende, the first Marxist Socialist president to be freely elected in Latin America.

Elected in 1970, Allende's sweeping socialist reforms seeking to strengthen the Welfare State included redistribution of land and nationalization of copper mines, banks, and the health care system. Even though Allende was an educator by nature and an extraordinary orator, he was unable to articulate how his innovations differed from those of Castro in Cuba or Marx in Europe. He did not need to seize power by force but gained authority by educating people and bringing social justice, thus transforming the existing capitalist relations of class and property.

National mayhem preceded a gruesome 16-year right-wing anti-Communist military dictatorship, in the coup led by General Augusto Pinochet, notorious for human rights violations and restraints on political expression and civil liberty. The coup was suspicious in many ways. First, it was an act of perfect synchronization carried out simultaneously (by sea, air, and land) along the 4,270-km-long country by both the military forces and the police, with support from the civil population. Second, its signature was a series of violent massive arrests, torture, and slaughters in impromptu concentration camps for Allende's sympathizers. Third, as Pinochet initially qualified as an ally against communism, he received clandestine support from the U.S. government, who financed groups opposing Allende, thus assuming an active role in staging the coup. It is well known now that President Nixon and his Secretary of State Henry Kissinger exerted sustained pressure on Allende's government, causing food shortages and political instability. Recently declassified White House documents also reveal that once the dictator no longer served U.S. national interests, the Reagan administration removed American support and forced him to step down. Finally, unlike any other dictatorship in Latin America, Pinochet's rule achieved a significant level of approval in society. Interestingly, it still enjoys respect by many, probably due to its mixed origin and loyalties.

In this context, in an unusual referendum held under State of Exception measures (*Ausnahmezustand*), with the military occupying every city in the country, Chilean citizens approved the dictatorial Constitution of 1980. This feat paved the way for a free market economy that encouraged both domestic and foreign private investment, thus moving the country away from economic statism (GlobalEDGE, 2014).[1] The new national vision imposed by the dictatorship would begin to take shape through a series of decrees and laws stemming from the authoritarian constitution. Shaking off Pinochet's violent legacy has not been easy, and the new generation has only recently begun to challenge the social and economic structures established by the euphemistically called "military government."

In spite of, or maybe due to, its conundrum-like past, Chile is presently regarded internationally as one of the most stable and prosperous nations in Latin America, leading in human development, competitiveness, income per capita, globalization, its peaceful state, economic freedom, and low corruption. It also ranks high regionally in terms of democratic development. Thus, in May 2010, Chile became the first South American nation to join the Organization for Economic Co-operation and Development (OECD). It has gained global respect as a founding member of the United Nations, the Union of South American Nations, and the Community of Latin American and Caribbean States.

Different Models of Education

Just as in other areas, sharp contrasts also define Chile in educational terms. In fact, it has gone from being the country in Latin America with the best education system—before the military coup—to becoming a poor, underdeveloped country with a low-quality education until the 1990s. Chile is also notorious for having one of the most segregated educational systems in the world (OECD, 2013). When it comes to educational outcomes, the contrast is dismal. Although Chile has the second highest improvement globally in learning gains, it is among the lowest performers in terms of international measures.[2]

Chile has about 3.4 million students, 11,500 schools, and nearly 200,000 teachers.[3] In a report that estimated learning gains, Chile came equally second among 49 nations that had significantly improved their educational standing between 1995 and 2009.[4] This increase in student achievement at an annual rate of 4 percent translates into learning gains of more than two years.[5] Some view this as a sign that the aggressive economic, social, and educational reforms adopted over the last two decades are finally reaping results.

It is easy to draw that conclusion, considering that in the mid-1990s, Chile was by all standards a poor nation with a low-quality education system. At that time the country's GDP was US $6,500 per capita, over 25 percent of the population lived in extreme poverty, fewer than 50 percent of students finished high school and less than 15 percent of high-school graduates enrolled in tertiary education. What is more, Chile invested a mere $360 per pupil per year, as public spending on education accounted for only 2.4 percent of GDP. As a consequence, most schools had substandard conditions (no electricity or water in many rural schools, no textbooks or materials in classrooms) and poorly qualified teachers, as many lacked formal training or teaching credentials. Due to nonexistent performance incentives in schools, most hiring of teachers occurred via political connections. Together with rigid labor laws and unfair practices, incentives for better performance were nonexistent as high performing teachers were not promoted and lower performers were not dismissed.[6]

So, yes, Chile has indeed come a long way since then. However, the question remains about whether the social cost involved in the process was worth the improvement, or whether the country needs to focus on broader structural changes that may guarantee long-term and system-wide improvement, instead of a simple cosmetic surgery that may be hiding the real problems underneath. The truth is that the encouraging figures available for fourth-grade level performance do not translate to higher grade levels and do not necessarily mean that recent changes introduced are on the right track. Why, for example, have steady and substantial improvements to the standards of living and the quality of education been met with social unrest and heavy scrutiny of public service institutions (including the government) and national assessment systems?

Some examples of social unrest against severe segregation since 2001 include recurrent protests, sit-ins, strikes, occupations, rallies, and marches not only by university and high school students, but also by teachers and people from other sectors. At the core of the student movement is the belief that education is an unalienable right that should be guaranteed to all, regardless of their socioeconomic standing. This implies regulating the participation of the private sector in education, increasing investment to improve public education, eliminating selection and segregation, and providing wider access to better schools and universities.[7] In the current state of the education system, all of these factors directly impact the way society is organized, since children with limited resources are more prone to limited access to education, usually at the primary school in their neighborhoods. Their parents cannot afford private education, which is believed to be better.[8] Thus, these children's futures seem bleak, as they appear to be determined by their place of birth and socioeconomic status, resembling in way the Indian caste systems, as children are unlikely to move up the ladder based on education opportunities. Students have a much higher likelihood of attending better quality schools in the capital city of Santiago than in a rural school in the far south, for example. Increasing awareness of this situation has moved students, teachers, principals and people in general to demand all-encompassing reforms.

The Democratic Welfare State: 1925–1973

The first period in Chilean mass education, from 1925 to 1973, was called the democratic welfare state, inspired by the European welfare models of society. Within this model, the state had responsibility for taking care of its people by providing free education and free social services. In terms of investment, Chile placed a greater focus on building a state capable of providing citizens with opportunities for equity in the country. Although this period built upon previous laws regarding state-mandated provision of education, the Constitution of 1925 marked a change in government focus. In place until Pinochet's coup in 1973, it defined the state as an active agent in the pursuit of welfare, explicitly enshrining the right to protection of one's health and to shelter, labor, and social welfare, including education.[9]

In the educational arena, the new constitution led to the creation in 1927 of the Ministry of Education to manage education, previously operated by the

Ministry of Justice. The role of educators was professionalized, with normal schools (an older form of teachers' colleges) created to train high school graduates to become teachers and to establish teaching standards or norms. President Pedro Aguirre Cerda, elected in 1938 with the motto "to lead is to educate," viewed education as an instrument to overcome poverty and social inequity and defended compulsory, nonconfessional, tuition-free education for all.

In 1964, Eduardo Frei Montalva (from the Center Christian Democrat Party) was elected president in the midst of rising social discontent, student protests, and political unrest, all seeking structural reforms in education. Educational reform was a central axis of Frei's political campaign, with an emphasis on coverage and quality. By the time he left office, Chile had built 3,000 new schools all over the country, extended primary education from six to eight years, and consolidated secondary education (in three areas of knowledge: humanistic, scientific, and technical and professional) from six to four years.[10] By 1970, coverage was 97 percent for primary education and 50 percent for secondary education. Simultaneously, pre-school education gained importance, supported by a special law that regulated the creation of day-care centers for one- to six-year-olds.

In 1970, Salvador Allende (Socialist) took office as president of Chile. He declared 1971 as the year of democratization of education. His main goal was to connect education with the productive world, the community, and social organizations. His government explicitly proclaimed the role of education as a catalyst for social transformation through fairness and solidarity on the road to socialism. He also sought to unify the education system under the leadership of the National Council for Education (*Consejo Nacional de Educación*), Regional Councils, and Councils in every province, with representation from social organizations.

However, Allende encountered bitter resistance to the democratization law in 1973 from his political opponents and from the Catholic Church, forcing the executive branch to withdraw it. This episode is extremely important as it reveals a root cause for applying the neoliberal model to education with such attention to detail and discipline—none of the aforementioned political actors would ever risk seeing their vested interests threatened by a system of state-funded public education that retained 80 percent of total enrollment in the country.[11]

Figure 2.1 shows the peak of Chile's public provision of education, with students in 1974 receiving the highest historical percentage of primary and secondary education coverage—80 percent—while private education included around 20 percent of students in the country. In general, language schools (English, German, and French), religious congregations (mainly Catholic) and corporations (among others, the Freemasonry at a fairly low level) provided the supply of private education. However, during this period, in terms of funding, the state assumed all investment in public education. That would change after Pinochet's coup and the turn toward neoliberalism.

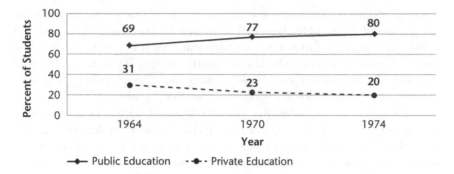

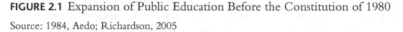

FIGURE 2.1 Expansion of Public Education Before the Constitution of 1980

Source: 1984, Aedo; Richardson, 2005

The Neoliberal Experiment: 1973–1988

Similar to many Latin American countries from the late 1960s to the early 1970s, Chile endured spiraling inflation as a product of an increase in the purchasing power of the population and a decrease in the production capacity. The decrease occurred due to either lower agricultural production or to increased replacement of national production with imported goods, also known as the import-substitution model. From an economic standpoint, inflation represented a social scourge Chile needed to correct.[12] However, the combination of structural measures implemented by various center-left governments (including Allende's), ideals such as the Welfare State, and strategies such as the import-substitution model, all fell into disrepute and were rendered unsuccessful due to the deep political and economic crisis. At the time, no one seemed to notice the real causes (increased purchasing power and decreased capacity) of the economic and subsequent social crisis.

From a political perspective, in a polarized competition with the U.S.S.R. for worldwide influence, the United States regarded a Marxist Socialist president with strong ties to the Communist Party as highly dangerous. Declassified U.S. records on Washington's covert operations in Chile between 1968 and 1975 provide evidence that the CIA actively sought to remove Allende by destabilizing the country and undermining his support.[13] The resulting unrest paved the way for General Augusto Pinochet's coup d'état in 1973, which not only installed a government perfectly aligned with U.S. geopolitical and economic vested interests in the region but also sent the message that any similar socialist initiative would likewise fail.[14]

With the advent of the military regime, privatization followed. The conditions in Chile were ripe for an open economy promising to remedy the maladies by facilitating foreign investment. In reality, economic liberalism meant that state-run companies, such as Codelco (the mining operation in charge of copper production), would keep their mines, but new mining ventures would be tendered to foreign (particularly American) and domestic (particularly from the right wing) investors. As a result, a small number of politicians and businessmen from the right began to take control of key businesses in the country. As the governing political right sold, the economic right bought, with substantial revenues for buyers.

According to Möckenberg, this circular trade approach undergirded a political strategy seeking to reinforce the power of the right even after the decline of the dictatorship.[15] In fact, many of the privatized businesses owned by the right today used to be state run in the 1980s, particularly the most strategic and profitable ones—electricity, telecommunications, petrochemical, and steel companies. This shift to private ownership included a move to monetarist policies, permitting the implementation of measures that could only succeed under a government with clear dictatorial style, a de facto civil-military dictatorship.[16] As it turned out, the more Pinochet consolidated power as a military dictator, the more Chile systematically and steadily reversed Allende's economic and education reforms.

These changes occurred on the recommendations of a group of Chilean economists, known as the "Chicago Boys," who carried out a full-fledged neoliberal experiment in Chile between the mid-1970s and the late 1980s. Called upon by the regime to end the economic depression in Chile, these graduates from Universidad Católica de Chile had all either studied or identified with Milton Friedman's neoliberal economic theories, which advocated free market policies for closely controlled economies. These policies called for widespread deregulation and privatization. Unregulated capitalism, with its laissez-faire economic liberalism strategy, sought to enhance the role of the private sector in the economy and decentralize the state by: (a) privatizing welfare and social programs, (b) extensively liberalizing the economy, (c) expanding free trade, (d) reducing government spending, and (e) deregulating the market.

After implementing these policies, Chile's economy became extremely unstable, alternately experiencing deep plunges and soaring growth, resulting in the country having the slowest growth of any Latin American country during that period, and, even worse, bringing about severe income inequality. As a consequence, most workers actually earned less (after adjusting for inflation) in 1989 than in 1973, while the incomes of the wealthy skyrocketed.

The formula followed significantly reduced state powers and transferred them to the private sector, pinpointing public spending (not unregulated capitalism!) as the culprit for the emerging crisis. According to Foxley, after the 1973 coup, the military and civilians who took the lead in the governance process focused on changing Chile's wrecked economy, which they labelled as inefficient and demagogic.[17] From 1975, the Chicago Boys found ways to reverse nationalization and promote privatization of public assets, open natural resources to unregulated private exploitation, privatize social security, facilitate foreign investment and greater openness to international trade, and significantly reduce import tariffs.[18]

After liberalizing prices (previously tightly regulated to keep inflation at bay), inflation soared. The monetarist solution to counterbalance the situation was to decrease the money supply (previously in constant expansion), thus reducing the fiscal deficit by cutting spending and increasing tax revenue. This is when clearer ideological aspects began to appear—inflation was attributed to the size of the public sector, not to the newly imposed neoliberal model.

At this point, the concept of a "subsidiary state" appeared. Its role was creating and preserving an appropriate institutional framework for the development of neoliberal practices.[19] For example, the state had to ensure the quality and integrity of money. Similarly, it had to control the functions of the military, defense, police, and legal bodies and create the necessary structures to ensure the rights of private property, and guarantee (by force, if need be) the proper functioning of markets. On the other hand, in those areas lacking markets (such as land, water, education, health care, social security, or environmental pollution), the state needed to create one. However, the state was not to venture beyond the role prescribed by the above management tasks. State intervention in markets (once created) needed to be minimal because, according to neoliberal theory, the state cannot possibly obtain the information necessary to anticipate market signals (prices) and because powerful interest groups will inevitably distort and constrain state interventions (particularly in democracies) for their own benefit.

The current Political Constitution of the Republic of Chile (approved in a controversial and tightly controlled referendum on September 11, 1980) established a subsidiary, no longer significant, role for the state. This role implies that the state must act only when private bodies cannot, and its main duty is to promote the activity of private bodies in all spheres of national life. The state and its agencies may conduct and participate in entrepreneurial or industrial activities only exceptionally and in the manner of any private participation. This neoliberal rationale underpinned the legal foundation for privatizing most of the companies that once belonged to the Chilean public.

In 1981, social security witnessed the birth of the pension fund managers (*Administradoras de Fondos de Pensiones* or AFP). Not only do these private institutions invest workers' retirement savings in the capital market but also charge steep handling fees. Employees thus become unwilling promoters of the asset concentration scheme that characterizes neoliberal theory. As for health, the market opened private insurance companies called *Instituciones de Salud Previsional* or ISAPRES. These companies work in coordination with private clinics and private hospitals. In terms of labor laws, free affiliation to a union is guaranteed, which means that every worker may choose to belong or not to belong to a union. A union may be created with only 10 percent of the workers of a company assembled to cast a vote. This leads to the proliferation of unions and therefore defeats their intrinsic purpose of uniting workers. Participation by associations of unions in a collective negotiation is nonetheless forbidden. This also holds true in the public sector. The right to hold strikes is heavily restricted, as workers who do participate in a strike for over 60 days are automatically laid off. Employers may also hire temporary workers to substitute for workers who are on strike. In this way, the previous negotiating power of workers was reduced or eliminated.

Education During the Military Regime: Neoliberalism Enters Schools

Just as in other spheres, the 1973 military coup marked the end of democratic participation by citizens in the development and implementation of public education policy. In 1981, Pinochet gradually but steadily put into place a series of neoliberal measures that completely transformed the educational system. The first step introduced seven modernizations by means of statutory decrees passed by the Military Junta. This was easily accomplished because the dictatorship replaced the legislative power when the Honorable Congress of Chile was dissolved on the day of the coup (September 11, 1973). The seven measures were as follows:

1. The principle of tuition-free education is only reserved for people in extreme poverty and is only available for primary education.
2. Decentralization of educational supply is conducted in the belief that allowing the private sector to enter the educational realm will naturally guarantee efficiency and effectiveness. This will occur because private schools will need to ensure quality, not only to attract students but also to keep them enrolled. The most tangible impact of decentralization in the early 1980s was transferring the administration rights of the once state-run technical and professional high schools to professional guilds connected to businesses.
3. Public education (both primary and secondary) was transferred to municipalities in 1986. The argument was that this would create a closer relationship between schools and families and the opportunity for families to engage in and influence their children's education. However, one result was that teachers were no longer public (civic) servants, so the general labor law covers their contracts.
4. The privatization of education provides state subsidies (equal to that given to public schools) to private citizens (including teachers) willing to create a school. The idea behind this measure was to expand educational supply and supposedly to stimulate more efficient management practices independent from the state.
5. A subsidy, or voucher, was attached to student attendance (who actually comes to school on a given day) instead of enrollment.[20] This form of subsidy had a negative effect on public schools in poorer neighborhoods because many children in socioeconomic disadvantaged situations have to miss school to help provide for the family or to take care of their younger siblings while their parents go to work.
6. Tertiary education provided by universities, professional institutions, and technical schools became viewed as a private benefit accruing only to the student attending school (not as a common good to society at large). As such, the rationale stipulated that higher education should not be subsidized at all and, therefore, tuition should be part of the equation. By doing this, tertiary

education became a new market, which theoretically would not only mean better funding for educational institutions but also improved quality, which would need to be ensured in order to attract students. This new market would also benefit students with more options to choose from and, thus, they could select the best schools. Since students would have to pay for their education, they would obviously do their best to succeed academically. This measure would be complemented with scholarships, bursaries, and loans to allow for wider coverage.[21] While charging tuition and fees for higher education did result in some choices, it also eliminated the possibility of pursuing education for many poor Chileans, thus restricting social mobility.

7.   Another complementary measure to the privatization of education was the implementation of a nationwide assessment system. In 1988, a new battery of tests known as the Quality of Education Assessment System (*Sistema de Medición de la Calidad de la Educación*, SIMCE), replaced a previous version and remains in use. This assessment system is designed to provide measures of achievement in mathematics, language (Spanish and English), and sciences, at specific levels (2nd, 4th, 6th, 8th, 10th and 11th grades) as part of the strategy to implement the subsidiary state within the neoliberal model and promote a technocratic and market-driven society. Specifically, the market-driven education system equated academic achievement with "quality", necessitating a measure of achievement to help consumers (both parents and guardians, and policymakers) to make informed decisions about schools (where to send their children, and where to allocate more resources).

In 1990, the SIMCE became the responsibility of the Ministry of Education.[22] On Pinochet's last day in office, the Military Junta passed the Bill *Ley Orgánica Constitucional de Enseñanza* (LOCE), which required that SIMCE test results be made public. SIMCE test results are aggregated by type of school (public, subsidized, private, and corporate), socioeconomic levels, and other factors, with the first public release of results occurring in 1995. As discussed below, this SIMCE serves as yet another contributing factor in consolidating privatization of education in Chile.

Detriment to the Teaching Profession

Another aspect of neoliberal education policies has been their detrimental effect on the teaching profession and their lingering consequences that continue to affect teachers. In the beginning, the governing Military Junta fired all the teachers who were "not qualified" to perform their professional duties as defined in the new context: namely, teachers loyal to the recently defeated socialist ideals. Thus, they were killed, sent to prison, exiled, or made redundant, as their educational institutions or universities were closed down or taken over by force.[23]

According to a study conducted by CENDA, teachers' salaries in Chile experienced the highest increase in real terms during the democratic period between 1960 and 1972.[24] Considering a starting point of 100 in 1971, teachers' salaries (measured by Índice de Remuneraciones Reales del Magisterio, IRM) rose from an index of 42 in 1960 to 113 in 1972.[25] Meanwhile, the general index for salaries and wages (*Índice General de Sueldos y Salarios Reales*, IGSS) went from 45.4 in 1960 to 103.7 in 1972—a 12.7 difference in favor of teachers. Between 1974 and 1975, the situation was totally reversed. A generalized drop in salaries occurred as a result of inflation brought about by the free pricing decreed by the Military Junta. For teachers' salaries, the drop was even steeper, as they were repositioned in a single scale of compensation. Using the same reference point as above (1971=100), teachers' salaries fell from 113 in 1972 to 28 in 1975. Meanwhile, the IGSS dropped from 103.7 in 1972 to 51.3 in 1975. Between 1975 and 1981, teachers' salaries did improve, though always below the general index for salaries and wages (IGSS). Between 1982 and 1990 they plummeted again, reaching in 1990 the same record low as in 1975.

During the dictatorship, teachers' unions were the first to suffer from intervention. The Single Labor Union for Education Workers (*Sindicato Único de Trabajadores de la Educación, SUTE*) was instantly dissolved and many of its members were either imprisoned or killed. In its place, the Military Junta created the National Teachers Association or *Colegio de Profesores de Chile*, which was made up of teachers who were loyal to the regime, and which became in fact a labor union that used repressive strategies. Similarly, nontertiary teacher training for primary education was eliminated when Preceptors' Normal Schools (*Escuelas Normales de Preceptores de Chile*) were shut down.[26]

Special legislation for tertiary education created a distinction between universities, professional schools (*Institutos Profesionales* or IP), and technical training centers (*Centros de Formación Técnica* or CFTs), granting different levels of degrees. Universities were given the exclusive mandate to grant higher education degrees, such as bachelor's and postgraduate degrees, while professional schools could only offer 12 undergraduate professional degrees, including education or pedagogy. Education was no longer given the status of a bachelor's degree as it did not require the completion of an undergraduate thesis. This measure was yet one more step towards the devaluation of the teaching profession that began with the steep decrease in salaries. As a consequence, enrollment in teaching programs dropped by 30 percent between 1983 and 1990.[27] As a result of protests, pedagogy programs were repositioned into higher education within the LOCE, with the general education law passed one day before the end of the military regime in March, 1990. Today, teaching degrees take at least nine semesters and require the completion of an undergraduate thesis as well as several levels of practical work, including one semester of professional pre-service practice or internship under the supervision of a mentor teacher.

Increasing Private Roles in Higher Education

Statutory Decree number 1 of 1981 mandated deep structural changes in higher education to consolidate neoliberal ideals such as structural diversity in terms of funding and educational supply. The newly created professional schools (*institutos profesionales*) offered programs, such as pedagogy and nursing, that previously were exclusively available at universities, while technical training centers (*centros de formación técnica*) offered two-year degrees to prepare technicians who would aid engineers, doctors and other professionals in different fields. Neither professional schools nor technical training centers received any state funding for many years. Students attending these institutions sustained them by means of tuition fees. Only recently have some of them begun to receive state funding once they have been accredited by quality assurance agencies.

As for universities, it was possible now to open private universities. By law, they had to be nonprofit; however, no regulation prohibited them from an association with real-estate companies, for example. Therefore, owners found a way to make money legally. Just like the other new educational institutions for higher education, these private universities received no state funding. Later, however, they began to receive indirect state funding for any enrolled student who obtained a high score in the Standardized University Admission Test (*Prueba de Selección Universitaria*, PSU).

Universities created during the democratic period, called traditional universities, belonged to the Consejo de Rectores de las Universidades Chilenas (CRUCH) and served more heterogeneous populations. Figure 2.2 shows that in 1987, CRUCH universities were no longer the majority provider of higher education. In 2010, private universities surpassed them in terms of enrollment. In 2012,

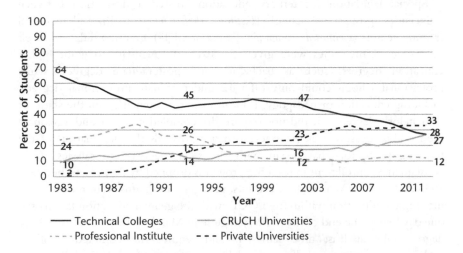

FIGURE 2.2 Enrollment in Tertiary Education, by Administrative Affiliation, 1983–2012 (%)

Source: MINEDUC, Estadísticas de la Educación, 2013

CRUCH universities accounted for only 28 percent of total enrollment in higher education, whereas private universities had reached 33 percent and professional colleges, 27 percent. Some of the latter are linked to traditional universities, thus compensating somewhat financially for the decline in university enrollment.

The 1973–1990 military regime in Chile generated a profound transformation of the educational system at all levels. This transformation was marked by clear neoliberal political and economic ideology. These radical changes were only possible as a product of the violent regime that introduced a market economy, allowing education to be permeated by private interests.[28]

The Return to Democracy: 1989–2010

The first democratic government after the military dictatorship set up two task forces, *Comisión Rettig* and *Comisión Valech*, to investigate and determine the damage to thousands of victims of torture and abuse. Both reports officially acknowledged a total of 40,018 victims, including 3,065 deceased or missing persons.[29]

A series of demonstrations and other forms of social protests in the 1980s gave early signs of social movements demanding the end of the dictatorship. Parties opposing the military regime organized under the umbrella name *Concertación*, formed a viable coalition that could succeed the regime in power. The severe political crisis that polarized the whole country even gave rise to far-left urban guerrilla organizations. In this scenario, it came as no surprise that during the national referendum in 1998 (with the intervention of the U.S. government) on whether the military leader should extend his office, 66 percent chose the "No" option. Consequently, in 1989, Pinochet transferred power to the democratically elected President Patricio Aylwin.

With the object of maintaining peace and the rule of law and order, the emerging political coalition—*la Concertación*—had no choice but to compromise and give in to the pressures of the Military Junta. They made no amendments to the 1980 Constitution regarding the three pillars of the legal document: (a) the binominal election system (that preserved the political power of the military) of the national congress; (b) the neoliberal economic model; or (c) the designated senators, appointed by the military regime. As for education, on March 10, 1990, the day before Pinochet's unseating, the general education law (LOCE) was passed. Not only did this law dictate the compulsory contents of the curriculum but also the subsidiary role of the state regarding education.

These three sets of laws converged malevolently to prevent the new government from introducing any amendments to any of their articles. For example, the binominal election system practically guaranteed an uneven number of senators in favor of the right wing, while ensuring a balanced number of representatives from the two most important political factions—the *Concertación* (center-left) and the *Alianza* (center-right)—disregarding the fact that the political parties making up the *Concertación* had a clear advantage in the number of votes in the elections. Similarly, the neoliberal economic system (still currently in place in Chile) allows the private sector to have a strong hold on the country, with little or no intervention by state-run audit offices. Last but not least, appointed senators came mostly from the ranks of the military and did not favor the policies inherited from the preceding Socialist government of Allende. Therefore, introducing changes was virtually impossible, as it was highly unlikely to gather the number of votes that the Constitution of 1980 required. People remember former President Patricio Aylwin precisely because of his saying, "justice to the extent that it's possible," referring to the straightjacket of a constitution that the democratic government inherited from the dictatorship. These constraints also impacted on the economic arena and all aspects regulated by the constitution.

The year 1990 marked the beginning of a long process toward regaining full democracy in Chile. Among the urgent measures in education, it is fair to highlight the efforts displayed to tend to the desperate needs of the public sector. The most outstanding of these was the launching of the 900 schools project, funded by Sweden and Denmark for three years. Its aim was to improve facilities, provide books, and teaching resources, and increase teacher training. This project was followed by larger-scale initiatives to widen and deepen intervention, such as the Program for Quality Improvement (*Programa de Mejoramiento de la Calidad de la Educación*) in rural and urban education at both the primary and high school levels.

Simultaneously, the education reform approved in 1996 began implementation with the introduction of full-time schooling (*Jornada Escolar Completa* or *JEC*). This measure sought to improve quality in education by increasing the number of school hours per week. Toward the same aim, the 2003 Constitutional Reform measure established increased compulsory schooling from 8 to 12 years. Universal coverage for primary and secondary levels was practically a reality by 2000. Despite the evident impact of these measures on the improvement of education quality in Chile, it was impossible to repair the structural damage involving school ownership and management, as well as mitigate the resulting inequity.

Initiatives for Funding the Educational System

Since the restoration of democracy, Chile has implemented several policies, reforms, and programs to improve quality in education. However the system has continued the fundamental changes introduced during the military regime. Three legal initiatives for funding passed during the shift to democracy are worthy of mention here. Although their original purpose was completely different, they have undoubtedly contributed to legitimizing the pernicious neoliberal model.

First, the Shared Funding bill (*Financiamiento Compartido*) was passed in 1989. This law authorizes voucher schools at all levels (including municipal high schools) to introduce a compulsory charge to parents and guardians. This funding mechanism gave a sudden push to the creation of such schools, whose numbers increased to a similar or even higher extent than in the 1980s, and whose outcomes in terms of quality have been heavily scrutinized.[30] Beside the money received directly from parents, many schools also received state funds, which contributed to the growth of semi-private schools in the country.

Second, in an effort to finance higher education, the State-Guaranteed Student Loan Program (*Crédito con Aval del Estado* or CAE) was created. This loan is available to low-income students who enroll as freshmen at accredited universities, whether public or private, including those not considered traditional universities and therefore not part of the Council for Higher Education (*Consejo de Rectores de Universidades Chilenas* or CRUCH). The interesting feature of this loan is that the state will repay a student loan in cases where the student is not able to, and now, the student will owe the money to the state. This strategy gave private universities access to direct state funding previously unavailable to them. Consequently, their likelihood of long-term sustainability greatly increased, an unthinkable possibility before this measure. Hence, enrollment in private universities soared.

Finally, the Preferential School Subsidy (*Subvención Escolar Preferencial* or SEP) Bill was passed in 2008. This law was a product of the so-called Penguin Revolution (*Revolución de los Pingüinos*) of 2007. The Advisory Council to the President (*Consejo Asesor Presidencial*) presented this law as a response to the crisis generated by high school students who were demanding higher quality in education. The law intended to address the fundamental problems of public education and increase its quality and resources to levels similar to those that private education enjoyed. The voucher system already in place at the time meant there was an unequal distribution of resources among the poorest schools, since many of their students typically have very low attendance due to child labor. These students either need to go to work to help provide for their families or stay home to take care of their younger siblings while their parents or guardians go to work. They also fall sick easily and it is harder for them to recover as they have no adult supervision during the day to take care of them, and access to public health may be slow or insufficient. As subsidy in the form of vouchers became available to both public and private schools, more private schools opened their doors to students with a high degree of vulnerability, thus levelling the playing field in a way.

An important caveat exists for the preceding discussion, however. Even if the Preferential School Subsidy (SEP) was a step in the right direction, it should not be viewed as a defining mechanism to bridge the quality gap between private and public education.[31] So-called autonomous schools (those harboring students with high levels of vulnerability and the best scores from the national assessment system or SIMCE) have demonstrated better performance as a product of SEP than schools with lower scores. On the other hand, evidence suggests that its impact on school segregation has been close to null.

Reprofessionalizing Some Aspects of Teaching

During the reinstitution of democracy and as a result of negotiations between the National Teachers Association (*Colegio de Profesores*) and former President Patricio Aylwin's government, the Statute of Teachers was enacted on June 27, 1991. This law restored work stability for teachers in municipal schools, subsidized private schools, and schools with delegated administration (these transferred to unions in the business sector). The Statute of Teachers clearly defined the concept of "education professionals" as persons who hold a professional teaching degree or the title of educator granted by normal schools for preceptors, universities, or professional institutions. Likewise, the concept includes every individual who possesses a legal license to work as a teacher and has authorization to do so.

Right-wing politicians heavily criticized this law, arguing that work stability has made it impossibile to remove teachers from their positions, resulting in low performance in the educational public sector. This kind of criticism gave rise to the enactment of a new law in 2011: the Quality and Equity in Education Law (*Ley Calidad y Equidad de la Educación*). This law gives school principals and headmasters the power to lay off up to 5 percent of their teachers every year whose work performance has been classified as "basic" or "unsatisfactory" in the latest teacher evaluation process. The law also establishes that for those schools with 20 or fewer teachers, the principal or headmaster may terminate employment of at least one ineffective teacher.

The teacher evaluation policy, in effect since 2004, resulted from another agreement between the Ministry of Education and the Chilean Association of Municipalities. Originally, leaders conceived of teacher evaluation as a formative process to strengthen professionalism among teachers by providing feedback on their classroom performance. The aforementioned process only included teachers in municipal schools. The overall results of this process are made public, which is a major consideration. The results of teacher evaluation are matched with the scores students in the public-sector obtain on the national assessment system (SIMCE), leading to the automatic conclusion that any low performance of students is a direct consequence of the poor performance of teachers in municipal schools. This causes a distorted perception that teachers in municipal schools are ineffective teachers, a perception driven by overgeneralization and incorrect attribution of causal effects.

The Continuing Tug of War: 2010–present

Chile is currently submerged by social agitation similar to that transpiring shortly prior to the return to democracy in 1990. Recent demands, however, may seem paradoxical as they seek to reclaim rights already considered inherent to the fight against the military dictatorship—equity, the decentralization of power, and quality education. These ideas are all part of the slogans that fuel the social movement even today. The contradiction lies in the reality that democratic governments have embraced democracy without making the structural changes expected by Chilean society, including more participation by the state in the economy and a more equitable distribution of resources for education. Moreover, during the course of consecutive terms in office of the *Concertación* (the coalition of center-left political parties, including the Communist Party), the neoliberal economic model has only grown stronger as politicians have designed reforms within the same framework. As a result, existing inequities have increased.

The perception of Chilean inequality is confirmed by statistics. The Gini coefficient is the most commonly accepted measure of inequality in a country, representing the dispersion of income of its residents. A Gini coefficient of zero expresses perfect equality in which everyone has the same income, whereas a Gini coefficient of one expresses maximum income inequality, where only one person has all the income. According to the OECD report released in March 2014, Chile has the highest income inequality (0.50) among both rich and poor nations within the OECD (the OECD average is 0.31).[32] The report ranks Mexico in second place (0.47), followed by Turkey (0.41), the United States (0.38)[33]. Countries with the least inequality are Iceland (0.24), Slovenia (0.25), Norway (0.25), and Denmark (0.25), all exhibiting twice as much equality levels than that of Chile, as measured by the Gini coefficient.[34] Wilkinson and Pickett have explained that countries with more income inequality perform worse in social sectors, including education.[35]

In the realm of education one example of the inability of subsequent governments to reverse the damage of the military government's legacy is the continued existence of the voucher system. In this system, the state directly funds voucher schools (both public and subsidized private schools) according to student attendance. Therefore, the parents and guardians of schoolchildren control whether to allocate state money to public or private schools. The voucher system has also allowed voucher schools to charge additional tuition in order to improve educational services. This feature of parents "topping-up" means that families can purchase incrementally better education for their children, creating many layers of inequality.

Another example of the prevalence of neoliberal strategies in education after the return to democracy is the creation of the State-Guaranteed Student Loan Program (*Crédito con Aval del Estado* or CAE) in 2005, also still in place today. Most college students who request this bank loan attend nontraditional private colleges, which charge higher tuition fees. This co-payment is also considered detrimental as it deepens social stratification and exacerbates inequality. Although today democracy is back in Chile, a laissez-faire culture persists, and many social programs remain in private hands.

Funding: The Ongoing Influence of Vouchers

Widespread reforms introduced in the 1980s during the military dictatorship stripped the state of its function as provider of education, as the Chilean

Constitution of 1980 replaced the long-lived Constitution of 1925. As part of the new rules, the state would decide whether to open, maintain, or close schools. Reforms included universalization of private providers in all areas of education: pre-school, primary, secondary, and tertiary education. Requirements for stakeholders to open a school were minimal: a high school diploma and meager facilities.

Chile is unique in the way education has been funded over the last few decades, having the same mechanisms for public and for subsidized private schools. State monies come in the form of a voucher, with the amount depending on student attendance (not enrollment). Vouchers have introduced competition among schools to capture students in order to obtain more resources. The law also allows the private sector to make donations, which are eligible for tax deduction. These donations are an extra source of revenue for private schools and for the private sector at large.

Higher education, which was once tuition-free, is now paid for by students and their families. Even state universities must self-finance about 80 percent of their total costs, mostly through tuition fees.[36] This creates the dual effect of universities competing against each other for students as well as denying higher education to poorer students that cannot afford it, thus reinforcing educational and social stratification. This is directly related to the market taking hold of Chilean higher education as a product of a number of reforms introduced during the dictatorial government of General Augusto Pinochet, perpetuated by subsequent democratic governments.

In fact, in primary, secondary, and higher education, Chile tops the list of countries with the highest level of private investment, with 23 percent in primary and secondary and 78 percent in higher education. This is almost a complete U-turn compared to the situation in 1973. Figure 2.3 shows the effect of Chile's full-fledged market approach, ranking highest on private expenditures. In this scenario, it is virtually impossible for the Chilean state to devise and implement education policies aligned with the Welfare State, despite a return to democracy.

To recap, the Constitution of 1980, instituted under Pinochet, incorporated the concept of "freedom of education," now commonly known as "school choice". That freedom of choice for parents resulted in the implementation of the law aimed at decentralizing education and allowing the private sector to participate in the provision of education services at all levels, with the subsequent results already discussed. After 32 years of applying the regulations dictated by the Military Junta, the proportion of public schools drastically dropped from 72 percent in 1980 to 46 percent by 2012. Meanwhile, the number of voucher (private) schools increased from 18 percent in 1980 to 49 percent in 2012. Figure 2.4 shows the decline of public schools and the corresponding rise of private subsidized schools, which increase inequality through the combination of state subsidies and private parent donations, which serve to reproduce social class within education.

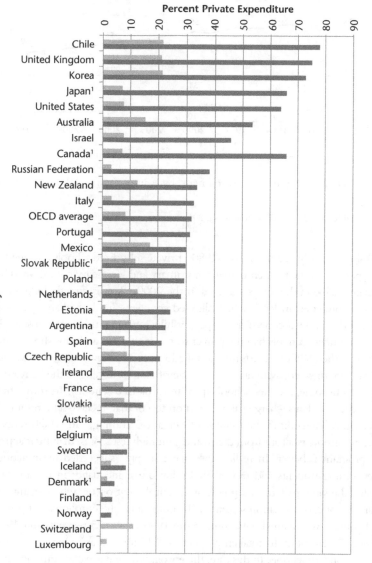

FIGURE 2.3 Share of Private Expenditure on Educational Institutions, 2010 (%)

Source: OECD. Argentina : UNESCO Institute for Statistics (World Education Indicators Programme). Tables B3.2a and B3.2b. See Annex 3 for notes (www.oecd.org/edu/eag.htm).

Legend (from chart):
- Primary, secondary and post-secondary non-tertiary education
- Tertiary education

1. Some levels of education are included with others. Refer to "x" code in Table B1.1a for details.
Countries are ranked in descending order of the share of private expenditure on educational institutions for tertiary education.

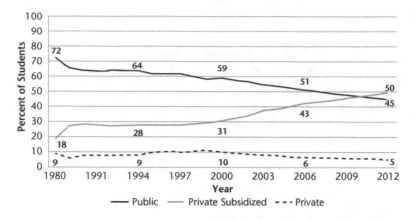

FIGURE 2.4 Total School Education Enrollment, by Administrative Affiliation, 1980–2012 (%)

Source: MINEDUC, Estadísticas de la Educación, 2013

Figure 2.4 shows clearly that in the mid-1980s, private subsidized schools managed to capture 28 percent of the total enrollment in primary and secondary education. That figure remains stable in the 1990s and rises in the 2000s. This is directly linked to a law that came into effect in 1995, which allowed voucher schools to charge parents a monthly mandatory fee, known as co-pay, while retaining the state subsidy. In addition, the voucher schools had the power to select students and thus show better performance of their school on tests measuring educational achievement. Finally, they could profit from these copayments to secure their finances, leading to the increase in applications to become voucher schools (private subsidized schools). In some, they could select their students, charge parents, and on top of that, receive state resources.

In effect, this law codifies the strategy of "cream-skimming," in which schools choose the best students, profit from them, and gain high test scores, making it appear like their program is better. In reality, they have simply "succeeded in attracting" higher-performing students and exacerbated educational inequality in the process. Additionally, the same pattern of segregation in enrollment occurs when examining primary and secondary education separately. In both cases, the enrollment of private subsidized education remained stable during the 1990's, over 25 percent after 1993, increasing to 52 percent of the total enrollment in 2012 for primary education and 50 percent for secondary schools. In this case, the enrollment of delegated administration (private) schools belonging to business corporations (professional-technical secondary education) shows a stable trend from the time they were created.

Impact of Policy on the Quality and Equity of Education

It is fair to conclude that education funding in Chile has impacted the quality and equity of the education system, especially when examining measures of student performance. Two domestic standardized tests are used nationwide to compare and contrast school performance on the one hand, and universities, on the other: namely, the SIMCE (for primary and secondary education) and the PSU (for tertiary education). Along with these measures, the PISA is used internationally to compare the achievement of education systems around the world. All of these tests have consistently provided evidence of severe inequities in the Chilean education system. Nevertheless, the way data has been collected and the results interpreted may be misleading and could drive conclusions in the wrong direction.

For example, SIMCE results for primary and secondary education generally show that, when controlling for socioeconomic factors, private schools have the best scores in both language and math, followed by private subsidized schools. Public schools display the lowest performance in both areas of knowledge at any specific time. However, when comparing learning gains over stretches of time, public schools show a more sustained upward curve than do subsidized private schools and completely private schools. This is an important finding, considering the literal competition among schools for higher performing students who end up migrating from public to subsidized schools, thus leaving lower performing students in public schools (through the "cream-skimming" effect described above). If public schools were as bad as the citizenry has been made to believe, the gap between public and subsidized schools should increase over time due to consistent migration of their better students. Yet, the gap stays constant. The logical question is whether subsidized private schools are actually better, judging by their higher scores, or if they are only better at attracting students with higher cultural capital.

Not surprisingly, results on the PSU (university entrance examination system) show similarities to those yielded by SIMCE, as it also focuses on measuring the school curriculum. Students with lower cultural capital are typically found in lower socioeconomic sectors and served by public education, and their disadvantage on tests that measure what the system perpetuates is obvious. The evolution of scores remains largely unchanged over time. Public education serving the poorest sectors of the population yields lower scores and, conversely, higher scores come from students in private schools, who have the advantage of matching their cultural capital to that demanded by the education system. None of the subsystems shows major increases on test scores over time.

Figure 2.5 shows the relationship of the socioeconomic structure of the system to the type of school. Low and middle-low income students in Chile are concentrated in public education. Middle and middle-high income students are concentrated in private voucher schools. High-level income students are exclusively located in private schools. Poor students comprise three-quarters of the population of public schools, have minor representation in privately owned subsidized schools, and are inexistent in completely private schools. Conversely, all private school students belong to the highest SES group, while three-quarters

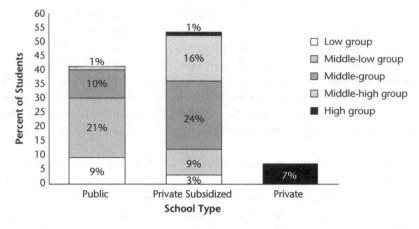

FIGURE 2.5 Distribution of Students by School Type and Socioeconomic Quintile, 2012

Source: Agencia de Calidad de la Educación (2013)

of the students in private subsidized schools are middle to upper class. This is radical stratification, a sort of apartheid in education, as Waissbluth states.[37] This serious situation decreases social mobility throughout the life cycle and serves as the main impetus for student protests and demonstrations.

When it comes to measuring the quality of education in secondary education, the instrument used for this purpose is the PISA test because of its international validity. Figure 2.6 and Figure 2.7 below show school performance by school type on the two occasions that the test analysis has considered this factor. On the reading test, scores aggregated by every school type declined in relation to the previous test three years before.

On the math test, only private schools have maintained their performance level, with a slight upward tendency, while private and public school scores dropped in the latest measurement.

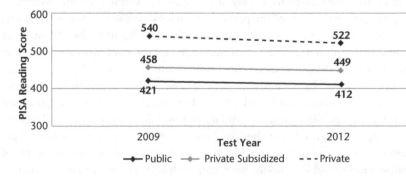

FIGURE 2.6 Chilean PISA Reading Scores by School Type, 2009 and 2012

Source: Agencia de Calidad de la Educación (2013)

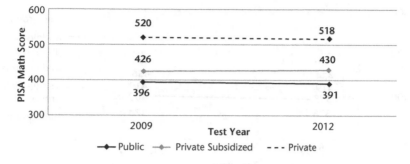

FIGURE 2.7 Chilean PISA Math Scores by School Type, 2009 and 2012

Source: Agencia de Calidad de la Educación (2013)

Based on these PISA results, the education system in Chile is apparently not working for anyone. It is also important to note the substantial raw score differences between schools, with private school students performing above the OECD average of 500, while public school students are a full standard deviation (100 points) below in reading. The performance differences on the math test for students in public and private schools are even greater, around 1.2 standard deviations.

The apparent reduction of the performance gap between public and private schools is explained by a sharper decrease in scores of private schools, not because any school type has improved. Although scores of public school students dropped less, they remained lower in 2012 than in 2009, with the gap still largely unchanged.

PISA also provides disaggregated results by socioeconomic (SES) group. As shown in Figure 2.8, all socioeconomic groups achieved lower performance on the latest reading test, except for students in the upper-middle class. All SES quintiles are below the overall PISA average.

On the math test, the sharpest drop in scores in 2012 is exhibited by the lowest SES group, while the middle-low class shows a slight improvement, as shown in Figure 2.9.

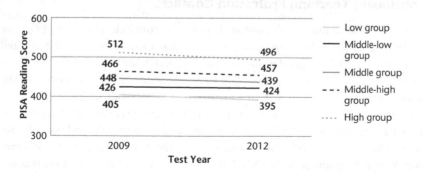

FIGURE 2.8 Chilean PISA Reading Scores by Student Socioeconomic Status, 2009 and 2012

Source: Agencia de Calidad de la Educación (2013

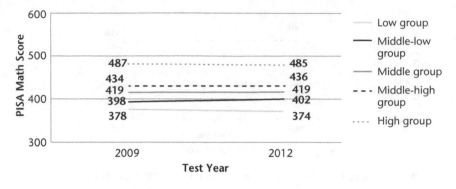
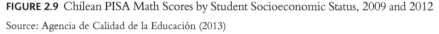

FIGURE 2.9 Chilean PISA Math Scores by Student Socioeconomic Status, 2009 and 2012
Source: Agencia de Calidad de la Educación (2013)

It is important to note that PISA does not assess how well students have mastered a school's specific curriculum but rather mathematics, reading, and science literacy. It also claims to measure education's application to real-life problems and lifelong learning. On the first application of this test in Chile, 48 percent of students were placed at proficiency levels 1 and -1. On the most recent assessment in 2012, the percentage at the lowest levels was considerably reduced, to 33 percent. Even though these data appear to be encouraging, it is important to keep in mind that this percent of students only meet the minimum level of understanding that the test measures.

Based on the data gathered from both domestic and international performance measurements, it is fair to say that student achievement in any education subsystem in Chile (public, subsidized, or private) is directly related to their socioeconomic stratification, which in turn seems to be associated with their cultural capital rather than with the quality of the school that they attend.

Continuing Teaching Profession Conflicts

From the aforementioned discussion, it is fair to conclude that since 1973 the teaching profession has systematically been degraded from a well-respected profession in Chile. This devaluation has negatively affected salaries, working conditions, and, especially, pre-service training, with a pernicious effect on the quality of education. The situation is even more serious when taking into account that, generally speaking, those who enroll in teaching programs in Chile for the most part are students who have low reading and writing skills and who do not master the disciplinary contents, as measured by the exit examination for students in teaching programs (Prueba INICIA). Just like the teacher evaluation process, the INICIA program was expected to inform pre-service training providers (universities and professional institutions) about the level of attainment of their exiting students on standards set by the Ministry of Education. Unfortunately, these results have been misused to generate rankings of teaching programs nationwide as part of a marketing strategy within the neoliberal system.

The situation described above constitutes a paradox that is hard to understand—the professional guild with the best potential to improve quality in education and with the most involvement in the generation of a number of laws to achieve this goal is precisely the one that is most criticized. What is more, teachers have been solely blamed for students' low scores on national performance assessments such as SIMCE and international tests such as PISA and TIMSS.[38]

There is currently an ongoing dispute between the National Teachers Association (*Colegio de Profesores*) and the government regarding regulation of the teaching profession, specifically the teaching career. The *Colegio de Profesores* places emphasis on the importance of taking the type of school into account when evaluating teacher performance, since working at a school with a population that is highly vulnerable is much harder than working at other types of school. The government, on the other hand, places an emphasis on individual teacher performance in terms of student learning, regardless of the type of school.

Higher Education Today

In their 2013 report "El Aseguramiento de la Calidad en la Educación Superior en Chile," the OECD indicates that in the last two decades, tertiary education in Chile has experienced an astonishing increase in student enrollment and a fast growth in the variety of institutions and programs available. However, greater coverage and diversification are only part of the reality. Chilean society continues to be very inequitable in economic and social terms. Along the same lines, the quality of the academic, technical, and professional programs offered is not uniform. The fact that Chilean students or their families must directly pay a substantial part of the cost of the programs has focused attention on education value for money and the likelihood of pursuing a professional degree that will pay back after graduation. Establishing a culture of quality in tertiary education beyond accreditation and providing precise and reliable information have become topics of interest not only for institutions, students, and employers, but also for the general public at large.[39]

Based on ownership, at present, higher education in Chile is made up of 25 CRUCH universities, 16 of which are state run (stemming from Universidad de Chile), six Catholic universities, and three private universities belonging to nonprofit corporations.[40] In terms of funding, all universities in the country rely mostly on tuition paid by degree-seeking students. For private universities this accounts for 79 percent of funding, while for CRUCH universities, it is 42.4 percent. As for funding from the state, the highest percentage goes to CRUCH-related institutions, with 20.5 percent of allocated funds, while private universities only obtain 5 percent on average.[41]

In order to make improvements that aim at correcting the shortcomings highlighted in its 2013 report, the OECD has made a series of recommendations.

They are as follows: (a) promote equity, relevance, and efficiency; (b) guarantee baseline norms; (c) encourage a culture for quality and professionalism leading to continuous improvement; (d) support active participation of stakeholders, particularly of students and businesses in order to promote effectiveness and pertinence; (e) take into account the diversity of institutions, programs, and types of higher education; (f) provide transparency and openness to inspire trust and security; and (g) be open to experiences in other countries.[42]

The fact that the OECD has a critical view of higher education in Chile and, as a consequence, has offered recommendations for solutions that are perceived as radical within the country is very interesting. This is especially true when considering that the key to public policy in higher education in Chile has been the emergence and development of student movements in over a decade, desperately begging for scholarships, lower tuition fees, more openings in programs, a level field for admissions, and quality undergraduate programs. These were in fact the aims of the 2001 student movement known as "el mochilazo" (the backpack rally), the 2006 "revolución de los pingüinos" (the Penguin Revolution), and the ongoing movement, which has been active since 2011.

The latter student movement succeeded in engaging ample social support, culminating in the election of four representatives to the National Congress of Chile from among the students who lead the movement. The current education minister has used two strategies in response to growing student pressure, including recruiting former student leaders as part of his ministry and creating an supervisor position in the Ministry of Education (*interventor de universidades en crisis*). This position oversees universities that might exhibit irregularities, such as illegal profit making, poor record keeping or even allegedly bribing certification authorities. The law ensures that any whistle blower (student, parents, and faculty members) may initiate an inquiry and request investigation.

More recently, in 2014, new clashes with the second administration of President Bachellet have been the background discussion for the new education reform that is expected to bring profit, selective enrollment, and co-payment to an end by 2017. This time, even teachers went on strike for weeks to demand that the reform include their interests. In sum, this new law will essentially: (a) prohibit profit in educational institutions using state money; (b) put an end to selection of students by academic performance or any socioeconomic factor; and (c) abolish co-pay by parents and guardians in subsidized private schools. This last measure will be implemented by increasing the public subsidy per student to schools that comply with (a) and (b). Most likely, the impact of these measures in terms of segregation and increased privatization of the educational system will prevent an increase in the number of subsidized private schools. Currently, even though for-profit education is explicitly banned by law, more over 50 percent of students in Chile currently attend publicly-subsidized high schools and universities, most of which are not only private but also for profit! In December 2015 the government will announce the specific measures that will be taken to ensure tuition-free university education and/or a scholarship system.

Final Discussion

Over the course of its republican history, Chile has progressively developed an education system in which the state acquired more and more prominence, reaching its highest level during the government of President Salvador Allende. During that period, enrollment in primary education was virtually universal, and it dramatically increased in high school and higher education due to social movements that included students.

From the late 1960s to the early 1970s, education became a measure of social equity and development of the country, as the state was expected to finance not only primary and secondary education with public money, but also the CRUCH universities. The Ministry of Education as a centralized body was in charge of the administration of general public education, and through offices in each province it was responsible for curriculum implementation, management, funding, and teacher training. Higher education was managed by the CRUCH, presided over by the Ministry of Education, and was responsible for distributing financial resources. The CRUCH was also required to ensure that admission procedures for higher education were the same throughout the country. Its relationship with the rest of the country's economic structure was weak. Graduate studies and research were dismal in relation to the needs of the country, although greatly debated at the universities. Notwithstanding, Chilean education made steady progress, seeking to meet the needs for coverage and equal opportunities for quality for all. Socially, education was highly valued and teachers were well regarded, receiving the highest salaries in the history of the country.

After the 1973 coup d'état, there was a radical change. Universities began to charge tuition in 1994 and 1995. The reasoning behind this measure was given as the need for each individual to assume part of the cost of their professional training as a sign of responsibility for their decisions and, by sharing the cost of education, to demand quality in the education offered by universities. The same argument was used in the early 1980s, when Pinochet announced decentralization, municipalization, and privatization measures together with changes in the funding of general education.

Another change from the Pinochet era was the advent of school choice. Parents and guardians had to become active participants in selecting the best schools and curriculum for their children. This neoliberal notion of choice was supposed to spur competition and increase the quality of education. Likewise, more transparency was offered, in that parents would be informed of educational outcomes by school and type of school, so that parents would make informed decisions. None of these measures really brought about better quality. They did, however, widen the gap among social classes.

Interestingly, the same argument discussed above regarding quality continues to be used by center-left governments after the return of democracy. This is still true today, when there seems to be a sharp conceptual change leading back to the historical path that considers education as a public asset.

Two lines of action continue together as the foundations of the education system in Chile: (a) the principle of equality on the part of the state to provide equivalent services; and (b) educational freedom—parents choose the school for their children. This means that resources from the state may go to the private sector, on condition that it provides the same services as public education. However, the private sector may require admission tests for selection purposes, a family background that agrees with the values of the school (for example, religion), co-payment by the parents, and it may even obtain profit. Due to the fact that private schools are not public, once resources are allocated by the state, these schools do not need to be accountable for the tax money they receive.

In contrast, public institutions must abide by the law and be accountable to the state. Therefore, they cannot select their students nor request co-payment from parents due to their socioeconomic condition. Every year, the government publicly announces the results of the national measurement system (SIMCE), showing that public schools have the lowest scores. It fails to inform the public, however, that when comparing students *within* the same socio-economic level, public education generally fares better. This may run counter to both common wisdom and the research consensus, since students in private schools do in fact obtain higher scores on tests and therefore do better academically than students in public schools. However, after accounting for the demographic differences among different school sector populations, traditional public school students perform better than their private school peers; that is, their learning gains are higher over the course of time.

Something similar happens with higher education. By definition, private universities, by law, are nonprofit institutions. However, owners of private universities that are not part of the CRUCH may create real-estate investment companies in partnership with the very owners of the private universities, and, using that partnership, divert the profits obtained by the real-estate company when renting the facilities to the university, for example. Another way of increasing profits is by selling shares of the university on the market. Finally, both private and public schools generally do not pay taxes when they are in the education business.

The mechanisms described above are the main cause of the poor and unequal status of the educational system in Chile—the Principle of the Common Good seems to have disappeared together with the state's responsibility to enforce it and ensure proper conditions for it. The Welfare State has ceased to exist and has been replaced by force and by the mechanisms of the free-market economy. Individualism based on authoritarian principles is encouraged, supported by a cultural and historical heritage of conquest, usurpation of indigenous lands, first by the authority of the King of Spain and later by the authority of the Chilean governments.

The changes brought about by neoliberalism in Chile were first observed in the educational realm. However, there is evidence they were caught up in other areas of public concern, such as health coverage and social security. Education seems to have been only the tip of the iceberg. The same resistance and scrutiny of the model in education is at play now in other areas where the state is lacking inherent responsibilities that have been transferred to the market economy. These are key topics in the ongoing public debate. Only time will tell if society at large gets involved and follows the lead of students and teachers.

Notes

1 GlobalEDGE. (n.d.). *Chile: History*. GlobalEDGE: Your source for Global Business Knowledge. Retrieved from http://globaledge.msu.edu/countries/chile/history
2 Elacqua, G. and Alves, F. (2014). "Rising Expectations in Brazil and Chile: Reforms lift student performance but middle-class families want more." *EducationNext*, 14(1). Retrieved from http://educationnext.org/rising-expectations-in-brazil-and-chile/
3 Elacqua, G. and Alves, F. (2014). "Rising Expectations in Brazil and Chile: Reforms lift student performance but middle-class families want more". *EducationNext*, 14(1). Retrieved from http://educationnext.org/rising-expectations-in-brazil-and-chile/
4 Hanushek, E. A., Peterson, P. E., and Woessmann, L. (2012). *Is the U.S. Catching Up? EducationNext*. RSS. Retrieved from http://educationnext.org/is-the-us-catching-up/
5 Elacqua, G. and Alves, F. (2014). "Rising Expectations in Brazil and Chile: Reforms lift student performance but middle-class families want more". *EducationNext*, 14(1). Retrieved from http://educationnext.org/rising-expectations-in-brazil-and-chile/
6 Elacqua, G. and Alves, F. (2014). "Rising Expectations in Brazil and Chile: Reforms lift student performance but middle-class families want more". *EducationNext*, 14(1). Retrieved from http://educationnext.org/rising-expectations-in-brazil-and-chile/
7 Smink, V. (2011). *Las razones de las protestas estudiantiles en Chile*. Retrieved from http://www.bbc.com/mundo/noticias/2011/08/110809_chile_estudiantes_2_vs.shtml
8 Sepulveda, P. (2011). Student Protests Spread Throughout Region. Retrieved from http://www.globalissues.org/news/2011/11/25/11997
9 *Constitución política de la República de Chile*. (1925). Santiago: Imprenta Universitaria.
10 Castillo, F., Cortés, L., and Fuentes, J. (1996). *Diccionario histórico y biográfico de Chile*. Santiago: Editorial Zigzag.
11 Castro, P. (1977). *La educación en Chile de Frei a Pinochet*. Salamanca: Tierra 2/3.
12 Foxley, A. (1982). *Experimentos neoliberales en América Latina*. Santiago: Corporación de Investigaciones Económicas para América Latina (CIEPLAN).
13 U.S. State Department, CIA, White House, Defense and Justice Department records retrieved from http://www2.gwu.edu/~nsarchiv/news/20001113/
14 Mönckeberg, M. O. (2001) *El Saqueo de los Grupos Económicos al Estado Chileno*. Santiago: Ediciones B.
15 Mönckeberg, M. O. (2001) *El Saqueo de los Grupos Económicos al Estado Chileno*. Santiago: Ediciones B.
16 Mönckeberg, M. O. (2001) *El Saqueo de los Grupos Económicos al Estado Chileno*. Santiago: Ediciones B.

17 Foxley, A. (1982). *Experimentos neoliberales en América Latina.* Santiago, Chile: Corporación de Investigaciones Económicas para América Latina (CIEPLAN).

18 Harvey, D. (2007). *Breve historia del neoliberalismo.* Madrid: Akal; Stallings, B. (2001). *Globalization and Liberalization: the impact on developing countries.* Retrieved from http:// archivo.cepal.org/pdfs/2001/S017565.pdf

19 Foxley, A. (1982). *Experimentos neoliberales en América Latina.* Santiago: Corporación de Investigaciones Económicas para América Latina (CIEPLAN).

20 Peña, M. (2011). *Sujeto político y vida pública: privatización de la educación en Chile y sus consecuencias en los sujetos que se educan.* Santiago: Polis, Revista de la Universidad Bolivariana, 10(30), pp. 199–215.

21 Castro, P. (1977). *La educación en Chile de Frei a Pinochet.* Salamanca: Tierra 2/3.

22 Cariola, L., and Rivero, R. (2008). *Sistemas de Evaluación como Herramientas de Políticas Revista Iberoamericana de Evaluación Educativa.* 1(1). 64–78. Retrieved from http:// www.rinace.net/riee/números/vol1-num1.html.

23 Castro, P. (1977). *La educación en Chile de Frei a Pinochet.* Salamanca: Tierra 2/3.

24 CENDA (Centro de Estudios Nacionales de Desarrollo Alternativo) (2002). *Estudio de Remuneraciones del Magisterio.* Santiago.

25 Rojas, P. (1998). *Remuneraciones de los profesores en Chile.* Centro de Estudios Públicos. Retrieved from http://www.cepchile.cl/dms/archivo_1584_733/rev71_rojas.pdf

26 Castro, P. (1977). *La educación en Chile de Frei a Pinochet.* Salamanca: Tierra 2/3.

27 Cox, C. (2012). "Política y políticas educacionales en Chile 1990–2010". *Revista Uruguaya de Ciencia Política,* 21(1), 13–43.

28 Cox, C. (2012). "Política y políticas educacionales en Chile 1990–2010". *Revista Uruguaya de Ciencia Política,* 21(1), 13–43.

29 *Informe de la Comisión Nacional de Verdad y Reconciliatción sobre Violación a los Derechos Humanos en Chile 1973–1990* (Informe Rettig). (1995). Santiago: Ministerio Secretaría General de Gobierno. Retrieved from http://www.ddhh.gov.cl/DDHH_informes _ rettig.html; *Informe de la Comisión Nacional de Prisión Política y Tortura* (Informe Valech). (2005). Santiago: Ministerio Secretaría General de Gobierno. Retrieved from http:// www.comisiontortura.cl/inicio/index.php.

30 Anand, P., Mizala, A., and Repetto, A. (2009). "Using school scholarships to estimate the effect of private education on the academic achievement of low-income students in Chile". *Economics of Education Review,* 28(3), 370–381; Benedetti, C. (2010) : *Análisis y evaluación de la gestión educacional municipal.* Memoria para optar al titulo de ingeniero civil industrial: (Guía de Tesis: Alejandra Mizala) Santiago: Universidad de Chile; Elacqua, G., Montt, P., and Santos, H. (2013). *Evidencias para eliminar—gradualmente—el Financiamiento Compartido.* Santiago: Instituto de Políticas Públicas Facultad de Economía y Empresa, Universidad Diego Portales, Mayo 2013, Número 14.

31 Valenzuela, J-P, Villarroel, G., and Villalobos, C. (2013). *Ley de Subvención Escolar Preferencial (SEP): algunos resultados preliminares de su implementación.* Pensamiento Educativo. Pensamiento Educativo. Revista de Investigación Educacional Latinoamericana 2013, 50(2), 113–131.

32 Cingano, F. (2014). *Trends in Income Inequality and its Impact on Economic Growth.* Paris: Organization for Economic Cooperation and Development; *Society at a Glance 2014 Highlights: CHILE OECD Social Indicators.* Retrieved from http://www.oecd.org/ chile/OECD-SocietyAtaGlance2014-Highlights-Chile.pdf

33 Cingano, F. (2014). *Trends in Income Inequality and its Impact on Economic Growth*. Paris, France: Organization for Economic Cooperation and Development; *Society at a Glance 2014 Highlights: CHILE OECD Social Indicators*. Retrieved from http://www.oecd. org/chile/OECD-SocietyAtaGlance2014-Highlights-Chile.pdf

34 Cingano, F. (2014). *Trends in Income Inequality and its Impact on Economic Growth*. Paris, France: Organization for Economic Cooperation and Development; *Society at a Glance 2014 Highlights: CHILE OECD Social Indicators*. Retrieved from http://www.oecd. org/chile/OECD-SocietyAtaGlance2014-Highlights-Chile.pdf

35 Wilkinson, R. and Pickett, K. (2009). *The Spirit Level: why more equal societies almost always do better*. London: Bloomsbury Press.

36 OPECH (Observatorio Chileno de Políticas Educativas). (2010). *Acceso a la Educación Superior: el mérito y la (re) producción de la desigualdad*. Santiago: Research Group CESCC–OPECH.

37 Waissbluth, M. (2013). *Cambio de rumbo*. Santiago: Random House Mondadori.

38 Waissbluth, M. (2013). *Cambio de rumbo*. Santiago: Random House Mondadori.

39 OECD (2013). *Revisión de Políticas Nacionales de Educación Revisión de Políticas Nacionales de Educación El Aseguramiento de la Calidad en la Educación Superior E*. Paris: Organization for Economic Cooperation and Development, p. 3.

40 DIVESUP/MINEDUC (2012). *Informe Nacional de Antecedentes. "El Aseguramiento de la Calidad de la Educación Superior en Chile."* Santiago, Chile: Comité de Coordinación. Sistema Nacional de Aseguramiento de la Calidad de la Educación Superior en Chile (SINAC-ES).

41 DIVESUP/MINEDUC (2012). *Informe Nacional de Antecedentes. "El Aseguramiento de la Calidad de la Educación Superior en Chile."* Santiago, Chile: Comité de Coordinación. Sistema Nacional de Aseguramiento de la Calidad de la Educación Superior en Chile (SINAC-ES).

42 OCDE (2013). *Revisión de Políticas Nacionales de Educación Revisión de Políticas Nacionales de Educación El Aseguramiento de la Calidad en la Educación Superior E*. Paris: Organization for Economic Cooperation and Development, p. 12.

3

FOUR KEYS TO CUBA'S PROVISION OF HIGH QUALITY PUBLIC EDUCATION

Martin Carnoy

The Cuban Context

Cuba is a rather low-income country even by Latin American standards. The Cuban economy is run by the state and the Cuban bureaucracy does a mediocre job of it, even taking into account the 50 plus years of a United States economic blockade. But somehow the Cuban education system is the envy of the rest of Latin America. It probably would be the envy of some U.S. states if they knew more about it. Cuban elementary pupils score much higher in math and language tests than children in other Latin American countries. The only countries that came close to Cuba on the Latin American-wide UNESCO 1997 Laboratorio Latinoamericano de Evaluación de la Calidad de la Educación (LLECE) test and the 2007 Segundo Estudio Regional Comparativo y Explicativo (SERCE) test were Uruguay (the highest-scoring Latin American country in the Program of International Student Assessment (PISA) test[1] and Costa Rica.[2] Sixth-grade students in Uruguay and Costa Rica scored about 0.6 and a full standard deviation lower in mathematics than those in Cuba, and 0.5 and 0.3 standard deviations lower in reading. We don't know whether this outstanding academic performance continues into secondary school since Cuba does not participate in either the PISA—applied to 15-year-olds in a large number of countries every three years—or the Trends in International Mathematics and Science Survey (TIMSS), applied since 1995 every four years to fourth and eighth graders, also in many countries worldwide.

What makes students in Cuba so proficient in mathematics and reading? Some of the reasons derive from socioeconomic conditions that also made Uruguayan and Costa Rican sixth graders score high on the LLECE and SERCE tests. The parents of the children in school in Cuba, Uruguay, and Costa Rica are relatively well educated, violence in the schools is relatively low (extremely low in Cuba), few children work outside the home, and income distribution is relatively equal (very equal in Cuba). But beyond these more favorable social conditions, Cuban education is a cut above the others, better than in richer Uruguay and Costa Rica. Cuban children attend schools that are intensely focused on instruction and are staffed by well-trained, regularly supervised teachers in a social environment that is dedicated to high academic achievement for all social groups. Combining high-quality teaching with high academic expectations and a tightly controlled school management hierarchy with well-defined goals is what makes the Cuban system tick. It distinguishes Cuban education from other systems in Latin America. In essence, Cuban education gives most Cuban pupils a primary education that only upper-middle-class children receive in other Latin American countries.

During the years 2003–2009, teams from Stanford University attempted to better understand Cuba's successful approach to education within a Latin American and a broader developing country context outside Latin America. Working with local researchers, we analyzed the quality of elementary school mathematics teaching in Cuba, Brazil, Chile, Panama, Costa Rica, Botswana, South Africa, and Kenya.[3] All the studies focused on classrooms. We filmed teachers, analyzed how they allocated their time, and observed student engagement and the mathematics content being taught. As in studies in developed countries, we found considerable variation from classroom to classroom in teacher mathematics knowledge and how well teachers communicated mathematics concepts to students.[4]

However, we also found major differences between countries. Part of these differences could be explained by the country's overall level of development. Students in lower-income countries are more likely to be poor, have much lower educated parents, and be less prepared to enter a school culture environment than students in higher-income countries. Students in Africa score lower than students in Latin America in part because students in Africa have fewer family academic resources. In the same way, students in Latin America score lower than students in Europe in part because Latin Americans have fewer family academic resources.

It is not only students that come to school with fewer resources in lower-income countries. Teachers in lower-income countries tend to have lower levels of education and to have had access to lower-quality education than teachers in higher-income countries. Income distribution also makes a difference. Typically, within a country, the single best correlate of higher test scores is a pupil's or student body's social class background. On average, students who come from homes and neighborhoods where families are less educated and less well off economically come to school in first grade already less well prepared academically. In countries characterized by greater inequality of incomes and wealth, the disparity between the quality of schooling for the mass of low-income students and those for high-income students tends to be greater.[5] Particularly effective teachers and schools can make a dent in poor students' academic disadvantage, but the likelihood that effective teachers teach in schools attended by poor students is low.[6] This makes it even more unlikely that schools can overcome the effect of home and community environment on achievement.[7]

Yet, even among those countries where we did our research, we also observed that some education systems seem to be characterized by higher student achievement levels than those in countries with the same or considerably higher-economic resources per capita. Cuba is one of those countries in which students achieve at a level much higher than their socioeconomic background or national income per capita would predict.[8] Even when we account for the higher level of parents' education in Cuba than elsewhere in the region, Cuban pupils' adjusted scores are still much higher than the adjusted scores of students in six other Latin American countries.[9]

Our findings are not surprising. Cuban children attend schools in a social context that supports children's health and learning. A government that guarantees employment to adults, provides reasonably good health care to all, and enforces child labor laws may not have an efficient economy, but it does assure that low-income children are well fed and do not have to work when they are not in school or instead of attending school. Strict government social controls are not good for individual *adult* liberties, but they do assure that lower-income children live in crime-free environments, are able to study in classrooms with few student-initiated disturbances, and attend schools that are more socially mixed. In an important sense, low-income children's rights are far better protected in Cuba than in other Latin American countries, whereas adult rights and, to a much lesser extent, upper-middle-class children's rights are reduced. Cuban students can learn more in these conditions than similar low-income children who have to work for wages and who sit in frequently disrupted classrooms in schools that are highly socially stratified.

Children in Cuba attend schools with generally high-quality teaching. On average, we observed that Cuban teachers seem to know more about the subject matter (mathematics) and appear to have a clearer idea of how to teach it effectively than most of their counterparts in Brazil, Chile, Panama, and even Costa Rica, which also has a long tradition of reasonably effective teaching (in Latin American terms). Children with more knowledgeable, pedagogically effective teachers are bound to learn more in school. However, it is not so obvious *why* some countries such as Cuba have teachers teaching primary school who know the subject matter well, teach a demanding curriculum, know how to deliver it effectively, and get to teach in peaceful classrooms to children who do not work outside school and face little or no violence when they are not in school, whereas in other countries conditions are considerably less favorable to student learning.

From studying Cuba's Latin American counterparts in Brazil, Chile, Costa Rica, and Panama (as well as our studies of classrooms in Africa), we learned a number of important lessons that help answer this puzzle. Cuban students' high performance is not a fluke. True, it is partially a result of the higher average education of parents and more books in the homes of most Cuban families, especially in comparison to Brazilian and Panamanian families. This is a standard (and valid) explanation for higher test scores. Yet student performance is also the result of differing sociopolitical contexts in these countries. And they are the result of just plain better preparation of teachers, a more demanding curriculum, and more instructional focus in schools, from top to bottom. This last finding is the most important because it is the most "transferable" to other countries. We must always keep in mind, however, that many of the organizational advantages in Cuba derive from the sociopolitical context in which Cuba's school system's organization developed.

The introduction to this book discusses how the different decisions that countries made decades ago have set the stage for difficulty (student protests in Chile) or success (Finland's high PISA performance). Cuba chose a similar trajectory to that of Finland by investing heavily in education as part of its socialist program. In 1961, shortly after the revolution, Cuba embarked on a yearlong campaign to eliminate illiteracy.[10] An estimated 250,000 volunteers spread across rural areas and helped over 700,000 people work on their literacy skills.[11] Cuba's literacy campaign set the stage for ongoing public investment in education, investment that has led to high achievement and a capable, professionalized teacher labor force. This chapter further explains the results of Cuba's education investment.

To keep things simple, we focus here on four lessons we draw from our studies, especially those in Latin America. There are particular factors in Cuba, such as the peculiarities of teacher recruitment in a command economy, which would be difficult to transfer to other countries, and, indeed, are eroding in Cuba under gradual marketization of the Cuban economy. It remains an open question of what will happen as Cuba is further exposed to the Global Education Reform Movement (GERM) as part of the removal of sanctions from the United States and other countries. We will discuss these factors where relevant.

Lesson #1: State-Generated Social Capital Matters

Our model for understanding why students achieve at higher or lower levels— like most—starts with the premise that a student's family life influences his or her capacity to learn. James Coleman's notion was that families influence their children's learning through human capital—the amount of education parents have—*and* social capital—the amount of effort that parents put into their children's schooling.[12] He also includes influences on family social capital from parents' interactions with neighbors and the community at large, for example, through churchgoing.

Our model takes the possible influence of social capital a step further: We extend the notion of social capital to national government policies affecting children's broader social environment—what we call *state-generated social capital*. Thus, there are national social capital or "neighborhood" effects that include state interventions in children's welfare and a national focus on education that can raise educational expectations for all children, particularly the educationally disadvantaged. Governments can therefore generate a cohesive and supportive educational environment on a regional or national scale that creates learning benefits for all students. As we have tried to show throughout this book, educational delivery based on a market model is unlikely to generate such a cohesive and supportive educational environment. Indeed, quite the opposite may be the case, mainly because markets are based on competition, not cohesiveness, and tend to create greater social segregation, hardly conducive to developing a cohesive and supportive educational environment for most children in a nation's schools.

Like other studies that focus on the social environment outside schools—whether in family or community—our study considers that the social environment is important in shaping what schools and teachers do. There is a structural aspect to social context, in the sense that social and political institutions are powerful shapers of individual behavior and the way that individuals approach institutions, including schools.

The most important indicator of state-generated social capital, as we defined it, appears to be the degree of social inequality. Cuba is a low-middle-income country when measured by the material goods Cuban families consume. The average Panamanian, Chilean, Costa Rican, and southern Brazilian is probably better off than the average Cuban in those terms. But Cubans consume more health care and education than all but higher-income groups in these other Latin American countries. Poverty exists in Cuba, but even the very poor have access to food, shelter, health care, and education. The result is that almost no third and sixth graders work outside the home in Cuba, whereas in Brazil and Panama, a number report that they do.[13] This affects performance in school. Children in all three countries reporting that they work even occasionally outside the home score much lower on the tests, especially in Brazil, where the difference is largest and statistically significant. Many more Brazilian, Chilean, and Panamanian teachers report classroom disturbances than do interviewees in Cuba. Disturbances also have a negative effect on academic performance. Cuba may be a society with little material consumption, but it is a society that stresses education and a safe and healthy environment for children in and out of school. Other Latin American countries have much more political freedom for adults but much more inequality, poverty, crime, and greater numbers of street children. Among the countries we studied, this is especially true in Brazil and Panama. It is not difficult to imagine in which of these social contexts children come to school better prepared to learn.

Cuban students reap another advantage from their society's greater income equality. Cuban salary structures are fixed by the state—not a very efficient system for much of the rest of the economy (the most skilled labor is not necessarily allocated to the most profitable industries and firms). This structure enables education, where salaries are not very different from other sectors, to attract higher-skilled labor than in the other countries we studied. Students are therefore better served in Cuba, perhaps at the cost of more efficient production in other sectors. Cuban leaders are quick to point out that this is a choice that they have made: provide high-quality public services at the cost of less consumption of material goods (and political freedom). It is questionable whether Cuban parents would make this choice.

On the other hand, the mass of lower-income Brazilian, Panamanian, and Chilean parents seem to want greater income equality and greatly improved teacher quality. They also seem to want more resources spent on their children's schooling. They are getting all this only gradually, perhaps because such changes require that more politically powerful middle- and upper-middle-class families pay higher taxes and consume fewer material goods. Yet, in Panama, Chile, and Brazil, income inequality has gradually declined in the past ten years, even though it remains very high. In Chile, legislation passed in 2008 allocated large increases in spending per student in primary schools for low-social class students, and this seems to have had a positive impact on achievement for students in high-poverty schools. However, in Costa Rica, whereas income distribution used to be more equal than in the rest of Latin America, it has grown steadily more unequal. The consequences of such growing inequality became evident in the latest UNESCO test in Latin America, the TERCE, held in 2014. Costa Rican scores declined statistically significantly from SERCE results in third-grade reading and sixth-grade reading and math, by 15–20 points, although third-grade math did increase by similar margins.[14]

Achieving greater income equality in this day and age is not easy politically, but that does not mean it is not possible. One lesson for all countries is that reducing poverty and income inequality almost certainly means improving student performance in school. There are many reasons for this. A major part of reducing poverty is reducing the correlates of poverty—ill-health of pregnant mothers' and infants' health, lack of access to clean water, insufficient nutrition, and regular health checkups and vaccinations for children, family need for children's labor, and high levels of violence in poor urban communities. These correlates of poverty are strong predictors of low capacity and motivation to perform well in school. In addition, when the social distance between low- and higher- social class students is great, low-social class students are more likely to be concentrated in low-social class schools. A society and its political system that allow such social distance to persist is less likely to invest the resources needed in the mass of schools catering to low-social class students. It is also more likely to blame parents and teachers for the low academic performance of students in these low-social class schools, rather than to assign responsibility to the society, economy, and political system that created the conditions for such low performance. This book details the results of such segregation in the U.S. chapter, in particular.

Beginning in the 1960s, a key aspect of Cuban educational reform was a large-scale effort to equalize access and quality across schools in urban and rural areas and among urban neighborhoods. By the 1980s, universal tenth-grade education had been achieved. Curriculum reforms also aimed at equalization in the standards for student performance. As a consequence, Cuban students experience considerable equity in their educational conditions.

In contrast, systems in places like Costa Rica more recently, and Chile in the 1990s and early 2000s, experienced growing income inequality along with growing disparity in the quality of schools available to more and less affluent children. One of the great ironies of this concentration of low-social class students into low-performing schools is that it contributes to students suffering academically even in high-social class schools. The mass of low-achieving students/schools sets a (low) standard for the entire system. Parents of high-social class children in their private or selective public enclaves believe that their students' *relatively* high achievement is proof that they are doing exceptionally well academically. This is not true.

On an international scale, the top 10 percent social class Brazilian and Chilean students—with all the advantages of a higher-social class upbringing and most attending elite private schools—score about the same in math and lower in reading on international tests such as the 2009 Program of International Student Assessment (PISA) as middle-class students in the United States and considerably lower in math than lower-middle-class Canadian students. The bottom line is that elite private Brazilian and Chilean schools (and Latin America's elite schools more generally) gauge their students' performance against the poorly equipped, poorly staffed schools catering to their low-social class students. This results in lower academic standards for all students, including the so-called academically elite.

Thus, at least in primary and secondary schools, healthy doses of parent choice and economic inequality—that is, market conditions in education—don't seem to produce more learning, societywide. The negative aspects of inequality and markets, especially as they play out at the bottom of the social scale, seem to offset any positive effects of parents' "freedom" to pick and choose among schools. As detailed in the Chilean chapter, one outcome of greater choice—a key economic rationale of market-based proponents—was the increase in the concentration of students by social class, leading to these negative results.[15] Conversely, Cuba's public investment strategy has provided a positive national effect, using the education mechanism of focusing on teachers, which is Lesson #2.

Lesson #2: Curriculum Matters, but its Implementation Depends on Teacher Capacity

All school systems depend for their "technology" on curricula constructed by the state and on teachers trained to deliver them. Curricula may be national, with a central government printing textbooks based on the required curriculum, or, at the other extreme, schools and teachers may pick curricula by choosing textbooks designed for publishers by educators and content experts. Cuba represents the first option. Over the years since the revolutionary government came to power, the Cuban Ministry of Education developed, with the help of eastern European models, a math and science curriculum to one central standard. The ministry also developed a national Spanish-language curriculum, a social studies curriculum that met its socialist and Cuban objectives, and so forth.

The curriculum that a national school system, a provincial system, or a municipality uses can be coherent and integrative, considered "good" by experts in the field, or can be fairly incoherent and below standard. The United States, for example, has been criticized for a math curriculum that is "a mile wide and an inch deep" because U.S. commercial textbooks, which tend to define curriculum in most states, try to cover as many subjects as possible to appeal to the largest number of states and school districts. In this way U.S. publishers sell more textbooks.

No matter how good the curriculum, however, it may be implemented very unevenly unless teachers have the content knowledge and pedagogical training to teach higher-level subject matter to their students. Because teachers in almost every country do not come from the upper stratum of college students, their level of subject matter knowledge, especially in mathematics and science, depends almost entirely on the level of high school math or science required in secondary school for college-bound students. In the United States, for example, high school students need to take much less math than an average student in, say, France, the Czech Republic, Singapore, or Korea. An applicant to a university educational faculty in Brazil and Chile knows less mathematics than an average secondary school graduate in Cuba. Thus, a primary teacher graduating from a pedagogical institute in Cuba is better prepared in math than primary teachers in other Latin American countries. Among the three countries we studied, this is particularly true in Brazil and Panama, where a high percentage of primary school teachers never took math past the eighth grade.

In reviewing the third-grade math textbooks in three of the countries we analyzed, Brazil, Cuba, and Chile, we found that all three cover similar material. The Cuban curriculum tends to teach math concepts in a more theoretical context, but two of the Brazilian textbooks cover more material—for example, fractions and certain kinds of measurements as well as division by two digits. Thus, if we had just looked at the textbooks, we might have concluded that pupils in Brazilian classrooms are getting a much greater opportunity to learn. Yet just the opposite seems to be true.

Cuban students cover fewer subjects but cover them more profoundly. This is a European-style math curriculum, deemed by math experts as more effective in teaching students mathematics. Cuban students of all social classes everywhere in Cuba are also highly likely to be exposed equally to the entire prescribed curriculum. Brazilian and Chilean students cover more topics more superficially and are likely to be exposed to the prescribed curriculum in a highly variable way.

We can draw two possible conclusions from this contrast. The first is that curriculum writers in Brazil are much less interested in modifying their textbooks to fit the capacity of Brazilian teachers to teach the material in them. There is a major disconnect between the level of mathematics prescribed by the textbooks and the level of the material we observed being taught in Brazilian third-grade math lessons. The second possible conclusion is that what teachers cover during the third-grade year in Brazil varies greatly, and the textbooks provide both lower-income and upper-middle-class schools with a curriculum they can use for their own purposes.

In Chile, the single national textbook covers similar material, but at a less advanced level than either the Cuban or the "best" two Brazilian textbooks. From extensive interviews with teachers and ministry officials in Chile about the process of the curriculum reform that began to be implemented in 1999 in the lower grades of primary schools and then moved into secondary schools by 2001, we concluded that curriculum writers must and do take into account teacher capacity in designing curricula. If they had not, Chilean reformers correctly argue, the curricula would not have been implemented or at best would have been only partially implemented.

This was the case in the United States with the "new math" curriculum—a European-style, integrated math program that few teachers were able to teach effectively because of their mediocre math preparation. Even fewer U.S. parents could understand new math, never having learned math in this way. The same may happen now with the new Common Core standards and curricula, adopted by 46 U.S. states, which is a much less radical departure than the new math but will still require major changes in teaching and will look very different to parents from what they covered when they went to school.

Most countries' educational systems are marked by a great diversity in how much of the curriculum is actually covered in schools and classrooms. Teacher surveys in Chile indicate that in schools with lower-socioeconomic students, less of the curriculum is implemented than in middle-class schools. We don't have similar studies for Brazil and Cuba, but it is evident from what we observed in classrooms in the two countries that children in Brazilian schools get a broad diversity of exposure to the contents of the recommended frameworks, perhaps an even greater variance than in Chile, whereas in Cuba, exposure is more equal.

Interestingly, students' greater access to curricular knowledge in Cuba has not been achieved through market-based reforms or high-stakes testing. Whereas Chile provides incentives through school competition and monetary rewards for higher test scores, in Cuba tests are used to inform educators but not to "drive" teachers or schools. Cuban municipalities are responsible for testing sixth- and ninth-grade pupils to provide feedback to the Ministry of Education and to the schools on how well the system is doing. However, test results are not released to the public. They are used for organizational decision-making, translating results into actions aimed at more effective education in all schools. The assumption seems to be that teachers, rather than tests, drive improvement.

The Key Role of Teaching Quality

One key to explaining the variation in applying curricula among different classrooms is the variation in teacher capacity in each country. Raising the quality of Cuban education for students from rural and working-class urban neighborhoods has dominated Cuban educational reform since the early 1960s. The main strategy for improving quality was to supply all schools with well-trained, highly motivated teachers. The effort was aided by a policy that fixed incomes so that they varied little among professions and between workers and professionals. Teaching quickly became a highly desirable profession. In a revolutionary society, education is a "frontline" activity and teaching in schools a prestigious occupation.[16]

By itself, Cuba's capacity to recruit young people into teaching is not a strategy transferable to other Latin American countries. Almost all employment in Cuba is, even today, public employment. The government sets wages at very low levels, and the state provides Cubans with basic commodities (shelter, food, and basic human services) at very low prices. Thus, markets—to the extent that they exist—are highly restricted in Cuba. A teacher gets a very low salary, but in most of Cuba, alternative employment at higher wages is practically nonexistent. Individuals are allocated to occupations based on education, taste, and proficiency. Teaching is considered a relatively prestigious profession, and wages (about 300–450 pesos per month, or U.S. $13–18) are only somewhat lower than what physicians earn and about the same as in other professions.

Until recently, this wage structure has assured the Cuban government a steady supply of potentially talented teachers, attracted to teaching mainly on the basis of wanting to work with children and adolescents in a relatively prestigious job. Good secondary school students were likely to choose pedagogical universities and teaching over education for other professional jobs because wages were approximately the same. Because Cuban education has been functioning at a reasonably high standard since the 1970s, average secondary school students have received a relatively higher level of math, science, and language training, which they have brought with them into teacher education. By training these student-teachers in government-run pedagogical institutes to teach a well-designed national curriculum, the Ministry of Education could deliver reasonably "good" teachers, trained to teach the required curriculum to every school in Cuba, even rural schools in provinces distant from the capital, Havana.

Teacher recruitment issues in a command economy differ substantially from those in market economies, where salary levels and working conditions for teachers and competing opportunities (especially for women) in the private sector are crucial variables in determining the prestige of the teaching profession. Hence, the academic qualifications of those who are likely to choose to become teachers, the quality of secondary school graduates more generally, and the quality of teacher training are variables that market economies can influence to affect the competence of future teachers.

Before turning to the lessons that Cuba can provide to other countries in teacher training, we need to point out that Cuba's long-term investment in educational quality also gives it an advantage in the quality of its teachers. Among primary teachers, the variance in teacher capacity among countries depends largely on the quality of their secondary education. A "virtuous" circle occurs when there are high-quality math and language programs in secondary school. The subject knowledge of primary teachers is higher, curricula can be more demanding, and students benefit.

The circle can also be "vicious". If secondary school math and language programs are of low quality, the average subject knowledge of primary school teachers (who take little subject matter preparation after high school) is quite low, the curriculum will necessarily be less challenging, or challenging curriculum will be only partially implemented, and students will suffer the consequences. In Cuba, the core curriculum serves as the basis for training teachers in Cuba's pedagogical universities. Further, thanks to an early establishment of relatively high standards in Cuban schools, more than a generation of teachers has passed through schools that taught them high levels of mathematics, science, and language skills, which they now can use in their classrooms to teach the prescribed Cuban curriculum at a much higher level than anywhere else in Latin America.

Lesson #3: Teacher Education Needs to Be Practice-Based and Tightly Coordinated with Existing Curricula: This Does Not Occur Spontaneously

Although the "revolutionary" aspect of teaching has faded in the past ten years as teaching salaries remain pitifully low compared to what teachers can earn in tips by working in the tourist sector, even as hotel chambermaids, and young Cubans desire more material progress than the government seems able to deliver, teachers are generally still well trained. Special teacher-training schools were created in the first years after the new government took power in 1959. These schools focused on developing teachers to work in isolated rural areas under difficult conditions. In the 1960s, upper-secondary teacher-training institutions were founded in each province to train primary school teachers, and post-secondary institutions to train secondary teachers. These institutions were controlled by the central government, and training was always closely tied to the national curriculum.

The contrast of Cuba's teacher pre-service training with pre-service training in other Latin American countries is stark. Although Cuba's future teachers get a healthy dose of the works of child-centered educational philosophers, particularly Dewey, Vygotsky, and Makarenko, their training focuses heavily on practice—in particular, teaching the Cuban national curriculum. Furthermore, they are intensively supervised during a long induction period once they start teaching. The practice of teaching the Cuban curriculum is well defined and is strictly implemented as a craft.

Cuba's teacher pre-service education is centrally controlled. Although there are teacher-education university-level institutes in each province, their curriculum is developed by the Ministry of Education and constructed around teaching the official school curricula using well-developed teaching techniques. These techniques are based on educational research and theory encouraging student engagement in active, collaborative learning contexts where deep understanding of concepts, rather than rote memorization, is the goal. Teacher educators in these institutes have generally been teachers themselves who have gone on for advanced degrees in education or specific subject matter. Prospective teachers are trained in cadres, with each cadre overseen by a mentor teacher who will follow them into and oversee their student teaching. Because training is focused on teaching the required curriculum, both content and pedagogical knowledge are taught using the curriculum students will teach.

The objectives of the two-year undergraduate training program are clear: to teach student teachers to deliver the national curriculum, to serve as a social and pedagogical guide for students, and, for primary school teachers, to nurture their young pupils in their early years.

Cuban education and the preparation of teachers starts from a developmental perspective on student learning that is expressed both in the training teachers receive and the structure of schools. Primary teachers generally stay with their pupils for the first four years and even six years of primary school, developing a long-term relationship in which teachers get to know students well. This also enhances accountability, as there can be little finger pointing at other teachers if students do not make progress. Greater responsibility is placed on both teachers and supervisors to assure that students are learning the curriculum as planned.

This approach was recently extended to lower secondary school (seventh through ninth grades), where students now have one main teacher for all subjects except English and physical education, in order to ensure stronger relationships and more guidance for students. This focus on teaching the child relies in part on teachers' preparation in child development and also on their preparation to skillfully teach the adopted curriculum. In this book, Finland and Canada are also depicted as investing heavily in the praxis of teaching and supporting teachers in a manner similar to Cuba.

We are not the first to identify poor teacher education as a major roadblock to improving student academic achievement, nor the first to suggest that the autonomy of teacher-training colleges from direct state control is the most obvious part of the problem. These are well-known issues in the United States and Latin America, both with fairly similar systems of university-based teacher education only indirectly regulated by government educational authorities.

Comparing Brazilian, Chilean, Costa Rican, and Panamanian teacher education with the Cuban system underlines two parts of the autonomy problem. The first has to do with faculty incentive systems in non-Cuban Latin American universities that stress the superiority of "theory" over teaching education students better practice; and the second has to do with the absence of any notion of "quality control" in certifying graduates of teachers' colleges or university faculties of education and in following through once a young teacher begins teaching by supervision and support in the classroom.

It is sensible to make even primary school teaching a university profession, as all but Panama in our sample of Latin American countries have done,[17] as this means that primary teachers would complete secondary school math and language requirements. But beyond that important advantage, preparing primary teachers in universities rather than in secondary-level teacher-training colleges may have disadvantages if universities preparing young people to teach in a national education system focus on "ideologies" of teaching rather than turning out highly competent instructors of well-defined curriculum frameworks.

Thus, each university should be made to focus the core of its teacher education on the notion that every teacher should be an expert at teaching to the pertinent national, state, or municipal curriculum standards. In many countries, this will require teaching education students to take more math and language courses, even if they intend to teach only at the primary level. This is the case in Brazil, Chile, Costa Rica, and particularly Panama, where many primary teachers—even the new crop graduating in the past few years—are underprepared in math and language subject knowledge. Many schools of education in those countries also underprepare secondary teachers.

Worse still, the least prepared teachers are sent to teach lower-social class students in rural areas and poor urban barrios. As an example, we interviewed students at Panama's main primary teacher-training college (Normal School) in Santiago. This is a secondary school that includes an extra year of teacher training. It caters to rather low-social class students, and most end up teaching in the local province, Veraguas, or in rural primary schools, many in hard to reach regions in the west and north of the country. According to our questionnaires and short math tests, these young future teachers were very poorly prepared in mathematics—they would be hard pressed to deliver anything more than a rudimentary level of math skills to students in already difficult social conditions, themselves little prepared to learn math skills even with a very good teacher. Further, they are unsupervised in their initial teaching and often isolated in rural schools in difficult social conditions. Not surprisingly, Panama's sixth-grade students scored near the bottom on UNESCO's 2007 SERCE test.[18]

In the short run, in the absence of the kind of instructional leadership and supervision provided by principals and vice principals in Cuban schools, we concluded that Brazil, Chile, Costa Rica, and Panama need to provide a mechanism for evaluating teaching skills on the job. Testing the teaching skills of young teachers is more complicated than testing their subject knowledge. Usually, teachers first undergo an apprenticeship as a student teacher, then go through an employment probationary period in which they are closely supervised and assisted to improve.

The problem in most countries of Latin America is that there are no clear standards of what is considered good teaching, and there is very little evaluation of teaching, even of student teachers and teachers in the first stages of their career. In most occupations, at least implicit measures of work output exist. Sales, customer satisfaction, low-error assembly, number of pieces produced per hour, creative capacity, writing ability, problem-solving skills, and caseload are all common measures of employee performance. It should also be possible to evaluate teaching quality, even in qualitative terms, if clear performance standards exist and managers are capable of applying such standards consistently.

Chile has developed a teacher evaluation system in which all public school teachers (about one-half of Chile's schools are public) present a portfolio of lessons and a sample-of-teaching videotape to a panel of peers. In theory, this could at least provide an overall assessment of the state of teaching in Chilean classrooms. If peers do their job, it could also provide feedback to teachers with particularly poor pedagogical skills. Yet besides the logistical difficulty and cost of implementing an assessment on this scale, a "one-hit" peer evaluation falls far short of the ongoing, week-after-week supervision and feedback that young Cuban teachers are subjected to in the early years of their career. We will deal further with this below, in Lesson #4.

Such shorter-run efforts to make teacher-training institutions conform to standards by measuring the quality of their output are useful but not sufficient. Governments in countries such as Brazil and Chile should also consider developing well-defined university curricula and course requirements for teacher training and adopt more stringent accreditation requirements, particularly regarding subject matter preparation and how such institutions prepare teachers to teach the national curriculum (Chile) or national frameworks (Brazil).

These suggestions fly in the face of analyses that argue for fewer teacher certification requirements. Many market advocates consider that certification requirements, required courses and degrees, and other state controls over who can teach create barriers to entry that impede many talented individuals from entering the profession, hence reducing the talent pool, especially in "shortage subjects" such as math and science. This is the strategy underpinning the deployment of programs such as Teach for America (TFA) and their expansion internationally. TFA provides college graduates with a six-week emergency course and then places them into the most challenging classrooms, replicating the Panamanian problem described above of serving the most at-risk students with the least-prepared teachers.

In one scenario, it would be possible for anyone to pass a certification test and a teaching evaluation such as those just discussed. If standards were high, this in itself would not be a bad idea. But if standards were high, few individuals would be able to walk off the street and pass the certification, especially the teaching part. It therefore makes good sense to provide for certification for walk-ons but also to assure that teacher training institutions are kept to desired standards in their teacher-education programs through a stringent accreditation process. This implies that a clear vision exists of a high-quality, successful teacher-education program. We think that there are such models—we saw one of them in Cuba, but there are others—and all of them revolve around real instruction rather than the ideology of instruction currently being taught in many Latin American universities.

Lesson #4: Instructional Leadership and Supervision Is Key to Improving Instruction: Market Incentives Are No Substitute for Good Management

The final lesson we learned from the comparison with other Latin American countries is that Cuban schools are much more likely to be organized around high-quality instruction than Brazilian, Chilean, Costa Rican, and Panamanian schools, and that this instructional focus is reflected largely in the greater emphasis that Cuban schools place on observing and improving classroom practice, particularly of young teachers.

Many teaching skills are learned on the job while teachers are teaching courses in classrooms. This process starts when a person is a student teacher, continues in the teacher's first job, and continues for a number of years. How teachers are mentored and supervised during these early experiences can make a major difference in a teacher's capacity to teach effectively. The mentoring has two major components: first, assuming that the recommended curriculum is an effective basis for teaching students academic skills, mentoring can be a crucial aid to understanding how to apply the curriculum effectively. Second, "good" teachers and knowledgeable supervisors can help new teachers become better pedagogues and classroom managers by working closely with them over several years.

Where mentoring and instructional supervision is not an integral part of educational management, new teachers have to learn by doing, with little or no feedback. Some of them become effective on their own at delivering the curriculum. They become good teachers based on natural talent, sensitivity to how well they are communicating with students, and a high level of conscientiousness in their practice. But left to learning on their own, most teachers fall into patterns that are not at all effective, and they either do not know that is the case, or do not care. A certain proportion of teachers in every system regard teaching as just another way to get a paycheck, and if they can avoid showing up for work and still get paid, they will do so. For a large-scale educational system to function well, it has to have a management system in place that develops reasonably high levels of teaching skills through experience and guarantees that teachers show up for work and provide the required opportunity to learn to all students.

Our observations in Cuba suggested that its management system is much more focused on *instruction*. Further, teachers in Cuba are accustomed to being observed in their classrooms by school administrators and "evaluated" constructively. Beginning teachers are heavily mentored to assure a "learning transition" into teaching, and greater responsibility is placed on both teachers and supervisors to assure that teachers are implementing the curriculum according to plan, and that children in the cohort (students stay with the same teacher for four years) are achieving as well as in other cohorts in the same school and in the municipality.

It seems strange that administrators in Brazilian, Chilean, Costa Rican, and Panamanian schools, who are just as aware as the Cubans that good instruction is the foundation of high-quality education, do so much less to supervise and improve teaching in their schools. School directors in all these countries play largely administrative roles, overseeing the day-to-day functioning of the schools, public relations, and, in many schools in Chile, fund-raising. Urban schools in Brazil and Chile and many in Costa Rica and Panama also have assistant directors who supervise teachers' preparation of course plans to make sure that they conform to the national frameworks, but these technical-professional administrators, as they are known, rarely go further to check how well the course plans are being implemented.

In Chile, the inspector as supervisor disappeared during the military regime and tended to be replaced by the notion that market forces—schools competing for students—would suffice to promote high-quality teaching. Chile's lack of supervision illustrates how teaching quality can suffer when subjected to competition and deregulation (as discussed in the introduction) because the system no longer provides the appropriate support and guidance for teachers at the school level. Combined with the under-preparation of teachers, this privatization model produces vastly different educational opportunities for Chilean students, mainly based on their socioeconomic status.

The second explanation for lack of supervision is that school administrators in Brazil and Chile have no clear idea of what constitutes high-quality teaching of the required curriculum, nor do they have the capacity to supervise teaching constructively. To do that, they would have needed considerable training and experience as, say, mentor teachers charged with assisting other teachers to improve.

A third explanation is that Brazil and Chile's teaching culture emphasizes teacher autonomy in the classroom. "The classroom is the teacher's sanctuary," a board member of the Chilean teachers' association (union) told us. School administrators are reluctant to observe teachers' practice with the intention of commenting on it, even constructively.

These explanations suggest why privatizing schools in Chile did not neatly lead to improved teaching, and why private school administrators are not necessarily more likely to be instructional leaders than public school administrators. We met a few instructional leaders in both Chilean public and private schools, but they seem to appear serendipitously rather than as part of a systemic effort by the ministry to develop administrators who would play such a role. Our explanations also suggest that instructional leadership from school administrators at any level is not going to develop spontaneously. Between the lack of capacity among school administrators to recognize poor teaching or know how to improve it and the cultural barriers to "interfering" in classroom teaching, school administrators in Latin America are not currently in a position to create the kind of instructional focus that exists in Cuban schools.

In the past ten years, Chile has tried to improve teacher effort, curriculum implementation, and quality of classroom practice with forms of "indirect" supervision, namely, testing student performance. Chile has used test results since

1995 to pay bonuses to teachers in schools that made the largest gains in each region on the fourth- and eighth-grade national SIMCE tests. Undoubtedly, student testing has had a positive effect on teachers' becoming aware that their students' performance on these tests is important.[19] In turn, it may have caused some teachers to improve their teaching. Yet until now, there is no evidence that such teacher incentives improve student performance and some evidence that it does not.[20]

Cuba tests students at the end of primary and lower secondary school, but this test is conducted by the municipality and seems to be used mainly as a way for the ministry to check overall performance of the system. Results are not released to the public. Thus, student testing in Cuba is fundamentally used to evaluate the system internally to the bureaucracy—a means of self-regulation to be used by the ministry for decision-making, not as a government mechanism to regulate a decentralized system (Brazil and Chile) or as a measure of output in a marketized system (Chile).

Thus, Brazil, Chile, Costa Rica, and Panama rely largely on teachers delivering the required curriculum effectively without any institutional mechanisms in place to assure that they do so or even systematically to assist them in achieving this crucial goal. There are many talented teachers in these countries, and they teach effectively, although even in those cases, they are likely to have lower standards than effective (and many ineffective) teachers in highly developed countries. Costa Rica and Panama do have inspectors. Chile has relied on competition among schools and indirect monetary incentives to induce teachers to improve learning in schools. Brazil has inspectors and is now experimenting with indirect and direct incentives. But because no sanctions are imposed on schools in either Chile or Brazil that make low or no test score gains, teachers do not have to respond to competition or incentives, and most do not change how they teach unless their students are doing much worse than others in the school. Even then, public schools are not likely to be able to fire or move their teachers.

The administrative team in a Cuban school is *required by the political system* to act as instructional leaders. This translates into a school culture of directly supervising and assisting teachers in their early years to improve their teaching. It also puts much greater direct responsibility on every primary school teacher for the learning of a cohort of children. We observed this in every school we visited—in schools catering to children of relatively highly educated parents, to schools in the more "proletarian" suburbs of Havana to rural two- or three-room schools in the provinces.

This culture of supervision and teacher responsibility is undoubtedly embedded in the hierarchical governance structure of Cuban politics and society. But it is also embedded in a strategy in which the state takes primary responsibility for assuring opportunity to learn for every child in the society. Teachers in Cuba are considered professionals and responsible for delivering the state curriculum, but their professionalism does not include autonomy at the expense of student learning.

The organization of schools in Cuba is subject to the categorical imperative of achieving the goals of the curriculum in every classroom, and school principals and vice principals share responsibility with teachers to assure that the teachers in their school are doing their job. Municipality officials, in turn, share responsibility for student performance in schools in their district. Teachers know that if they do not act responsibly to assure that the children in their charge learn the material, they will be relieved of their duties; at the same time, the teachers we talked to believed in their work and had real affection for the children they taught.

We don't want to idealize this system of supervision because it is hardly flawless. Not every teacher in Cuba is effective, and we are sure that a lot of poor teaching slips through the cracks. However, classroom teaching is, on average, more effective in Cuba than in Brazil or Chile; and from what we observed, at least part of this greater effectiveness is due to a much more pervasive system of administrative involvement in and vigilance toward the quality of instruction. Our interviews with principals, vice principals, and teachers in Cuba centered on that issue. A principal of a primary school with 400-600 pupils could name every child with learning difficulties and the steps that were being taken to help the child, including sending a teacher home to speak with the parents, checking on issues with the family, and trying to work on particular parts of the curriculum with which the child was encountering difficulties.

At the same time, most teachers in Cuba have been empowered by very good training and constructive supervision to be effective in their job— they are not only made to feel responsible for the children they teach, they are given the skills to turn those feelings of responsibility into high levels of student learning.

Conclusions from Cuba

Cuban students' higher performance is the result of a number of factors. We were able to measure the effect of some of these factors through standard production function estimates.[21] Yet these estimates could not explain a significant portion of Cubans' superior math skills, particularly those resulting from differences in the quality of teaching in classrooms and a management system that assures that a fairly demanding national curriculum is applied universally regardless of students' social class. To understand the existence and potential impact of those effects, we turned to a combination of qualitative analysis—interviews in schools, analysis of textbooks, and videotapes of third-grade math lessons in individual classrooms. The qualitative analysis suggested that Cuban children are getting a fairly demanding math curriculum delivered more effectively by better-trained, more frequently supervised and guided teachers, in schools that are, on average, more directly focused on instruction than Brazilian or Chilean schools.

In our production function estimates we included student family background variables, school resource variables, and a less-established set of variables we called "social context," or state-driven social capital. These sociopolitical context variables, mainly related to children's social condition outside primary school and the social class distribution of children among schools, are important in explaining at least part of Cuba's higher test performance. This is an interesting finding with important implications for educational policy. Countries, regions, or school districts can expect to continue to have difficulty achieving high levels of student learning in school if the children live in a sociopolitical context outside school that does not provide the safety, health, and moral support needed to function well in a classroom environment.

Similarly, unequal learning, characterized by much lower expectations and results for low-income children, is reinforced by school systems that tend to concentrate children with similar social class backgrounds in schools that are identified as low-income schools. Chilean research suggests that a higher proportion of teachers in low socioeconomic schools feel less well prepared to teach the Chilean mathematics curriculum, suggesting that the least "able" teachers eventually end up teaching in such schools. Thus, the greater the concentration of students by socioeconomic status in different schools, the more likely school resources are to be distributed more unequally, and the more likely the system will be to produce more unequal results.

In our qualitative analysis, we identified other effects of state-generated social capital that are important in explaining Cuba's higher test scores. Because of wage setting by the state, Cuban teachers are more likely to be drawn from a pool of high school graduates who performed better academically than the teacher candidate pool in Chile, Costa Rica, and, particularly, Brazil and Panama. With access to young people who have higher levels of subject matter knowledge, Cuban curriculum writers have been able to bring a reasonably demanding curriculum into all levels of schooling, especially primary school.

State-driven social capital is an important construct for understanding why children in some countries do better in school, but it is difficult to transport higher social capital from one country to another. State-generated social capital is usually the result of historical forces that are rather country specific and is both the product and shaper of specific cultural values. Nevertheless, nation-states can improve children's welfare substantially by providing free early-childhood education beginning with very young children, providing family subsidies to low-income families contingent on sending children to school and prohibiting child labor, and providing access to school-based nutrition and health care.

Many of our findings concerning Cuban school success, however, can be attributed directly to what takes place within the Cuban education system. Three of the four main lessons we learned from our study could be incorporated into other Latin American (or other) education systems, beginning with much better initial training of teachers, with more emphasis on subject matter preparation (in part to compensate for low levels of subject matter learning—especially math— in Latin American secondary schools) and learning to teach the required curriculum frameworks.

Beyond getting tighter control of teacher education in universities and teacher-training colleges, Latin American education authorities can learn a lot from the way Cuban school principals are charged with supervising new teachers and assuring a high standard of curriculum delivery in Cuban classrooms. They could also shift to a system of keeping the same cohort of pupils with one teacher from first to fourth grade. When Chilean students take their fourth-grade SIMCE test or Brazilian students, the *Prova Brasil* test, the result would be the cumulative effect of one teacher's work, increasing the responsibility of the teacher and the school (as in Cuba) to assure that each teacher is providing a high quality of instruction.

As a final thought, we would like to remind the reader of the possible conflict in democratic societies between individual freedom in most other aspects of human life and in schooling, which is hardly democratic. Few children beyond third grade would voluntarily choose to spend 30 or more hours a week for 40 weeks per year sitting in classes, but they are compelled to do so. As part of the individual freedoms guaranteed by democratic societies, parents often demand the right to choose schools for their children or to choose to send their children to work, and teachers demand many "rights," including the right to professional autonomy in their classrooms. Such autonomy is meant to protect teachers from uncalled-for interference by administrators in the way teachers conduct their teaching, and to protect teachers from ideologically based judgments of what constitutes good teaching.

The Cuban educational system is not faced with these contradictions, and because the Cuban state is genuinely interested in delivering high-quality basic academic skills, the system is able to invoke collective interests in pressuring families and teachers to conform to its standards for student learning. In doing so, the state takes ultimate responsibility for children's education, including the responsibility for assuring that parents, who, coincidentally are also state employees, do their share in guaranteeing that children reach high levels of academic performance. This is possible only in democratic societies when the public sector—the state—has the implicit confidence of civil society. Parents have to have full confidence that the state is capable of delivering high-quality services and that state employees (such as teachers) are totally committed to that task.

We did not find these conditions prevailing in the other Latin American countries—Brazil, Chile, Panama, and (less so) Costa Rica, with good reason. In Brazil, the state has historically not been committed to delivering high-quality education to most of the Brazilian population. In Chile, as in Brazil, good public education existed in the past for an upper-middle-class elite, but not for the masses. As a result, once vouchers were made available in Chile, there was a rapid flight to private education. In Panama, public education is very poor, even by Latin American standards. Even low-quality private education in Brazil, Chile, and Panama is preferable to public. Under such circumstances, the central role of the state as the guarantor of high-quality services loses its meaning, and the competitive individual, struggling to gain advantage over others, reigns supreme.

The notion of pulling together—teachers, administrators, parents, and students—to improve children's learning degenerates into placing the highest value on parents' and teachers' individual choices and individual rights, in the premise that if adults use those rights wisely, children will come out ahead.

The Cuban system has obvious severe drawbacks, especially in the lack of political freedom and limits on individual choice. The high level of self-discipline and cooperative behavior that make Cuban classrooms function so smoothly at the primary level are important for developing basic skills and proficiency in problem solving. But at higher levels of education, in middle and high school, creative rebellion and dissent—traits that flourish to the extreme in societies such as the United States—are largely suppressed in Cuba.

The path to better education in democratic societies need not be a turn to authoritarianism. The lessons we have drawn from the Cuban experience do suggest, however, that the state has to be much more of a *guarantor* of quality education for all—the state needs to take public responsibility for children's success. The state has to be an effective activist in transforming educational management toward greater control over what happens at the school. It has to take full responsibility for improving instruction, even at the cost of decreasing faculty and administrative autonomy of universities' schools of education in their initial formation of teachers, and of decreasing the autonomy of classroom teachers who do not show the creativity and competence to function at a high level when given autonomy.

The state needs to guarantee that all teachers are effective in producing student learning by regularly evaluating them, from initial certification to evaluative supervision of their work in classrooms. By setting high standards for schools and teachers and enforcing them, the state reduces the need for parents to agonize over where they should send their children to school, as almost all schools would be delivering similarly and reasonably high-quality education. This is what the public wants in a democratic state, and this is what the public should get.

Notes

1 In 2009, Uruguay had the highest math scores in the PISA in Latin America across all social classes (as measured by books in the home or mother's education). But Chile had higher reading scores (author's estimates from PISA 2009 database).

2 Laboratorio Latinoamericano de Evaluación de la Calidad de la Educación (LLECE). (1998). *Primer Estudio Internacional Comparativo sobre Lenguaje, Matemática y Factores Asociados en Tercero y Cuarto Grado.* Santiago: UNESCO; Segundo Estudio Regional Comparativo y Explicativo (SERCE). 2008. *Los aprendizajes de los estudiantes de América Latina y el Caribe.* Santiago: UNESCO.

3 Carnoy, M., Gove, A. and Marshall, J. (2007). *Cuba's Academic Advantage.* Stanford, CA: Stanford University Press; Carnoy, M., Luschei, T., Marshall, J., Naranjo, B., and Sorto, A. (2007). *Improving Panama and Costa Rica's Education Systems for the Twenty-First Century Economy and Society: A Comparative Study.* Stanford CA: Stanford University School of Education (mimeo); Carnoy, M., Chisholm, L., and Chilisa, B.

(2012). *The Low Achievement Trap*. Pretoria, S.A.: HSRC Press; Carnoy, M., Ngware, M., and Oketch, M. (2015). The Role of Classroom Resources and National Educational Context in Student Learning Gains: Comparing Botswana, South Africa, and Kenya. *Comparative Education Review*, 59(2), 199–233, May.

4 For example, see: Hill, H., Rowan, B., and Ball, D. (2005). Effects of Teachers' Mathematical Knowledge for Teaching on Student Achievement. *American Educational Research Journal*, 42(2), 371-406; Measures of Effective Teaching Final Report (Gates Foundation). (2013). *Ensuring Fair and Reliable Measures of Effective Teaching*. MET Project. Retrieved from http://www.gatesfoundation.org/media-center/press-releases/2013/01/measures-of-effective-teaching-project-releases-final-research-report.

5 Adamson, F. (2010). How Does Context Matter? Comparing Achievement Scores, Opportunities to Learn, and Teacher Preparation across Socio-Economic Quintiles in TIMSS and PISA. Unpublished doctoral dissertation. Stanford, CA, Stanford University.

6 See, for example: Carnoy, M., Ngware, M., and Oketch, M. (2015). The Role of Classroom Resources and National Educational Context in Student Learning Gains: Comparing Botswana, South Africa, and Kenya. *Comparative Education Review*, 59(2), 199–233, May; Simielli, L.(2015). Equidad Nacional no Brasil. Unpublished doctoral dissertation, Sao Paulo: Fundação_Getulio Vargas; Schmidt, W., and McKnight, C. (2012). *Inequality for All: The Challenge of Unequal Opportunity in American Schools*. New York: Teachers College Press.

7 Rothstein, R. (2004). *Class and Schools*. New York: Teachers College Press.

8 In Africa, Kenyan students achieve at much higher levels than higher-income Botswanan and South African students. Some of what we learned from the Cuban case also applies to Kenya, particularly with respect to teacher training and the level of standards in schools (see Carnoy *et al.*, 2015).

9 Carnoy, M., Gove, A., and Marshall, J. 2007. *Cuba's Academic Advantage*. Stanford, CA: Stanford University Press.

10 The film *Maestra,* directed by Catherine Murphy, documents the story of this literacy effort in 1961.

11 Bhola, H. S. (1984). *Campaigning for Literacy: Eight National Experiences of the 20th Century*. Paris: UNESCO..

12 Coleman, J. S. (1988). Social Capital in the Creation of Human Capital. *American Journal of Sociology*, 94, S95-S120.

13 Segundo Estudio Regional Comparativo y Explicativo (SERCE) (2008). *Los aprendizajes de los estudiantes de América Latina y el Caribe*. Santiago: UNESCO.

14 UNESCO (2014). *First Release of Results: TERCE*. Santiago: UNESCO.

15 When the Chilean government became democratic again in 1990, it recognized the harmful effects of growing inequality in the school system, as evidenced by the so-called Brunner Report: Comisión Nacional para la Modernización de la Educación, Comité Técnico Asesor del Diálogo Nacional sobre la Modernización de la Educación Chilena (1995). *Los Desafíos de la Educación Chilena frente al siglo XXI*. Santiago, Chile: Editorial Universitaria.

16 Gasperini, L. (2000). *The Cuban Education System: Lessons and Dilemmas*. LCSHD Paper Series 20966. Latin America and Caribbean Regional Office: The World Bank.

17 Brazil has long required fifth- to eighth-grade teachers to have a university degree, but only recently is it beginning to require lower-grade primary teachers to be university

trained. Many lower-grade teachers are only secondary-school trained, and in low-income regions, a majority still have secondary-teacher education or less.

18 Segundo Estudio Regional Comparativo y Explicativo (SERCE). (2008). *Los aprendizajes de los estudiantes de América Latina y el Caribe.* Santiago: UNESCO.

19 Mizala, A., and Romaguera, P. (2001). Regulación, incentivos y remuneraciones de los Profesores en Chile. Santiago, Chile: CRESUR.

20 Carnoy, M., Brodziak, I., Molina, A., and Socias, M. (2007). The Limits of Teacher Pay Incentive Programs Based on Inter-Cohort Comparisons: The Case of Chile's SNED. *Education Finance and Policy*, 2, summer.

21 Carnoy, M., Gove, A., and Marshall, J. (2007). *Cuba's Academic Advantage.* Stanford, CA: Stanford University Press.

4

FROM CITIZENS TO CONSUMERS

The Transformation of Democratic Ideals into School Markets in Sweden

Björn Åstrand

1948:

Democracy draws upon the voluntary collaboration of all citizens. Such collaboration depends on autonomous individuals, hence the prime role of schooling is to educate democratic humans.

The Swedish school commission[1]

2006:

To run a school and to sell refrigerators are one and the same. It's about having your ear to the market and to understand where the needs are for our customers, the pupils.

Tord Hellmark, Founder of a private Swedish school company[2]

The Turning Tide for Swedish Schools

In 2008, the *Economist* reported that "BIG-STATE, social-democratic Sweden seems an odd place to look for a free-market revolution. Yet that is what is under way in the country's schools."[3] The reporter appears stunned by the radical nature of the system: more or less anyone can start a private school, admit students, and have the state fund the school.[4] Money follows individual students in the current Swedish school model, built upon market logics since the early 1990s.[5]

This was not always the case. During the social-democratic era, Sweden realized its goal of the welfare state model and, concurrently, its educational system gained a prominent democratic reputation worldwide.[6] In addition, Swedish pupils came out on top in the predecessors to current international assessments like PISA.[7] However, current data show that, among OECD countries, Sweden has the most rapid growth of inequality, the Swedish educational system has profoundly changed into a market model, and PISA scores have plunged to an all-time low.[8] How did this all happen?

This chapter describes the evolution of the Swedish school system as the result of two significant and systemic U-turns in education policy. These shifts revolve around a continuing tension between public and private forms of education. The first important turn of the tide took place after World War II, when Sweden decided to end an educational system characterized by a mix of private and public institutions, parallel educational tracks, early selection of students, and high inequality. It replaced this unequal school model with a unified and comprehensive model geared toward democratic ambitions and equality, with substantial success through the 1980s.

The second important turn of the tide occurred around 1990, when Sweden redesigned its welfare-based school model, now 30–40 years old, according to a market-oriented model based on individual choice, private alternatives, and competition. From the 1950s to the 1990s, private alternatives maintained a significant continuity in the discourse as being educationally superior, providing value by positively influencing the public schools. By the 1990s, however, private schools had evolved beyond their role in the social-democratic model as sites of positive influence that complement public schools. Instead, in the market-based system, the mission of private schools became that of replacing regular public schools.

A shorter historical perspective considers the transformation of education into a school market model as a profound shift, challenging the norm of the welfare- based public school system. However, extending the historical perspective reveals how the turn toward democratic schooling after World War II itself represented a major reform. Zooming out to this wider view shows that societal democratization and the development of the welfare state actually pushed back the private alternatives previously in place. These private alternatives, however, regained their position rather quickly (after 30–40 years of social democracy) and today they form a significant part of the Swedish educational system.

This broader perspective suggests that Sweden did not fully implement a comprehensive and democratically oriented education system during the post-war era, but left the door open for older, less democratic, and less equity-oriented structures to survive. These structures reactivated during the political and economic circumstances of the 1990s and recaptured the education system. Figure 4.1 shows how these different perspectives alter the viewpoints of "typical" and "atypical" Swedish narratives about the welfare state's role in education. The first arrow shows a shorter perspective in which privatization appears to diverge from the social-democratic norm. However, the second arrow zooms out to show that the welfare state itself represents a fairly short-lived social experiment, bookended by educational inequities through World War II and those recommencing in the 1990s.

Comparing these timescales also reveals the differences in transition time. It took decades of democratic processes to set up the welfare state education model, but only a few years in the 1990s to rearrange and reinsert private schools and a market-based education system. It is much easier to deconstruct something than it is to build it. This difference demonstrates how difficult, yet productive and equitable, it was to organize education democratically, in contrast to the profit-motivated outcomes of inequality and lower performance that have accrued since the shift to education as a market.

The core message of the chapter is that Sweden has recently replaced the education model that promoted Sweden's social democratic approach with a market-based model. The market model includes a competition-based system in which the emphasis on freedom of school choice trumps equality in education.[9] The trajectory of this public-to-private shift mirrors the growth of inequality in schooling within Sweden and a decrease in international measures of achievement. Furthermore, this shift represents a return to the dominant paradigm of hybrid public–private schooling and inequality that existed before the relatively short-lived education success of the social-democratic welfare state.

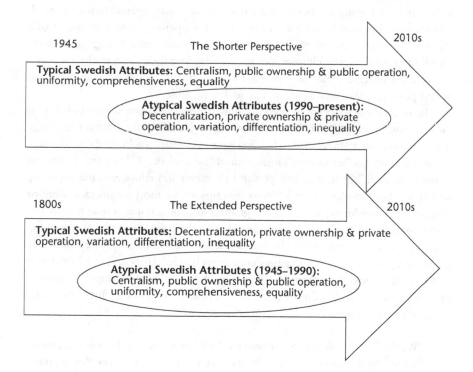

FIGURE 4.1 Alternative Historical Perspectives of Sweden's Principles

The First U-Turn: Democratically Establishing a Comprehensive Public Education System

The post–World War II years in Sweden were, in many respects, years of catching up. A democratic breakthrough had come before the war, but the post-war years witnessed the realization of the Swedish welfare state. After earlier ambitions in this direction, resources for a number of reforms became available as Swedish industry became highly profitable in war-torn Europe. Suddenly Sweden had some relative advantages and could invest in societal progress.[10] History has described the chosen model as the "welfare state," and its ambitions included the equitable provision of schooling for citizens.[11]

After World War II, Sweden designed a new comprehensive school system to prevent future totalitarian developments, with an overarching objective of education contributing to a democratic society by fostering democratically minded citizens. A key aspect of the reform argument involved the creation of a school that provided all students with a shared educational experience. Swedes saw the inclusion of classmates from all social classes as a means "to prevent human initiated catastrophes and secure a democratic society."[12]

The minister in charge of education in 1945–1946, Tage Erlander, writes in his memoirs that, during 12 years of Nazi rule in Europe, the Swedes learned the importance of having a school system that avoids strong specialization. Instead, schools must help students be aware of what is happening in society and "make them feel included in society."[13] Schools must simultaneously engage students equally to avoid shaping children's future by dividing them into tracked schools. For social democracy, the "new postwar society had to be built on universal and liberal principles that made citizens as equal as possible."[14]

The quest for democracy focused not only on the education system but also on the question of shaping individuals. According to Josef Weijne, minister in charge of education from 1946 to 1951, schooling has to do with "teaching of knowledge," but its main goal is "an in-depth formation of the student."[15] The "free formation of the individual," including their personal character and ethics, was the means by which a school could succeed "in its assignment to form democratic minded humans."[16] Accordingly, schooling also granted students an opportunity to look out "over our national borders to be familiarized with the essence of a global citizenship and what duties that carries."[17] The Swedish leaders at this time viewed democracy as resting upon integrity and independence as well as solidarity and collaboration.[18]

Olof Palme, social democratic minister in charge of education and, beginning in 1969, the Swedish prime minister, continued to advance this democratic approach to education:

> We shall abolish old class boundaries that block individual and free development. Schooling shall, to quote the Education Act, 'promote students' development into harmonious humans and to capable and responsible citizens.'[19]

Education was a key instrument for the fulfillment of a social democratic society; however, it could not be the only means. Progress had to build upon consistent policies and Palme argued that "it takes a shared and long-term commitment before schools will be able to fulfill their important role in the democratic development of societies."[20] The desired school model was one whose format, conditions, educational process and content would be available to all students regardless of where they lived and their social background. Teachers were required to take a proactive stance against "false social values" and schools were expected to promote the potential of the individual, not act as a sorting machine.[21] Schools should, according to Palme, be a "spearhead into the future" and the key "to abolishing a class-based society."[22]

One view was that Sweden previously had "in a European perspective, as late as 1950 an old-fashioned school system, not to say a backward one."[23] The problem that comprehensive school reform had to solve was the negative contribution of schooling to reproducing a class-based society. The existing parallel school system, with early tracking that determined future studies and employment, had to be changed into a unified and comprehensive model using the democratically based ideas outlined above. This new system encountered resistance in the form of arguments in favor of tracking and differentiated routes and resistance to the idea that all students could benefit from studies at higher grades (*gymnasium*, grades ten to twelve).[24] Consequently, the reformers needed to pilot their new system and anchor their claims in research.[25]

In 1950, Sweden changed to a comprehensive, mandatory, nine-year school model, shared by students from all social classes. The reform was launched with significant "political consensus after extended public inquiries."[26] The decision made it clear that Sweden was prepared to make significant public investment in education for higher quality in schools, increased equity, and equal opportunities. During the 1950s, a series of large-scale experiments was launched in which approximately one third of all districts changed to the comprehensive school model.[27]

In 1962, after these pioneering pilot projects and public inquiries, the time was ripe for a final decision in parliament about the new school model, which received parlimentary approval. National implementation followed, although Sweden did not complete the transfer to comprehensive schooling until the early 1970s.[28] Educational equity was supposed to be upheld by the national curricula and a uniform and equitable teacher education.[29] The long transition period, from the late 1940s to the early 1970s stands in contrast to the rapid shift into the school market model in the years around 1990.

By the mid-1980s, the discourse shifted and around 1990, a new set of reforms was launched. In the context of a general reform of the welfare state, the Swedish school system was also reformed. While Sweden did not have many private schools in 1990, the tradition did exist.[30] A number of school reforms related to decentralization and deregulation emerged, together with rationales of competition and freedom of school choice, to reactivate and re-establish elements of education that resulted in a school market model and a sharp increase in private schools.

Private Schools in a Unified System—a Principle Dilemma

The existing private schools were a challenge for the movement towards a unified, comprehensive school system with democratic ambitions. In the 1950s, fewer than 1 percent of students were enrolled in private schools and these schools usually received public allowances (after governmental approval).[31] Their existence was antithetical to the key ideas of the proposed reform—an acceptance of private schools "would fail the whole system."[32]

A compromise allowed the continuation of some private schools—religious, ethnic and culturally but also pedagogically oriented—as long as they were operated according to the national curricula and in line with the national objectives for schooling.[33] Regular private schools were regarded as unnecessary as they had to follow the same curricula as the public ones. The same argument was applied to existing home schooling (private individuals teaching in the home of the student).

To understand the coming reversal in the role of private schools, it is important to note that Sweden did accept private schools that focused on pedagogical experimentation and innovation.[34] The main rationale for the deliberate preservation of pedagogically motivated alternatives was due to their potential to positively influence the regular schools.[35] However, they had to follow the national curricula and not act against the ideas and objectives of the compulsory school system.[36]

The Second U-Turn: Changing from Comprehensive Schools to a Market-Based Education System

The Swedish comprehensive school reform was perceived as a leap forward and generated an international reputation—so why did Sweden change again in the 1990s?[37] Historians Österberg and Andersson note that "the welfare state was not even fully implemented when it came under increasingly strong criticism."[38] Sweden's historical narrative of the twentieth century is centered around the welfare state—as is its educational history.[39] The shift in educational policy around 1990 represents a dramatic process that "transformed the Swedish school system from being one of the most centrally planned among OECD countries into one of the most decentralized systems allowing for wide choice of school types."[40] This process led Sweden "a long way down the road of external marketization of education, and also fully embraces new public management, i.e. 'inner marketization', of education in most respects."[41] This section outlines how and why this second U-turn occurred.

Seeds of Change: The Financial Crisis and New Governmental Strategies

An economic crisis in the early 1990s was a key precursor for the transformation of the welfare state. Sweden had accumulated a national debt due to prior industrial crises and the continual growth of the public sector.[42] Increasing unemployment and budget expenditures and decreasing incomes caused a deteriorating national budget.[43] Liberalization in the financial sector caused unsustainable credit levels and for "the first time in 60 years, larger banks were threatened."[44]

The need to reform state financing became acute as the national debt expanded like an "avalanche of growth in relation to GDP".[45] Reforms addressing macro-economic imbalances were initiated, but citizens also demanded "a less complicated, more accessible, more efficient public organization."[46] The crisis reinforced ongoing processes but also became a stepping-stone for reforms that reshaped Sweden.[47]

Privatization was viewed as a possible solution, but primarily for other sectors of society than education.[48] However, together with health, the pressure for increased efficiency also appeared in education, due to its role in public consumption.[49] Reforms of education came to focus on decentralization, deregulation, and demand for increased numbers of alternative schools. The system changed from "central government grants" to one that strengthened the autonomy of municipalities "due to fewer central regulations."[50]

In 1983 the Swedish Employers Confederation collaborated with a liberal-conservative administration of a local municipality to make plans for introducing private schools using public funding.[51] The attempt was resisted with arguments stressing "that with all due respect for all professional sanitarians and trash collectors, it is a profound difference between dealing with dirty clothes and trash bags compared with caring for children."[52] Privatization was not the problem per se, but the profit motive and the initiative was perceived as "part and parcel of a neoliberal campaign against the public sector."[53] However, social democrats displayed a less hesitant attitude to private alternatives, indicating a shift in their political priorities.

Analyzing changes in media focus reveals how the framing of privatization evolved over time. In the 1950s and 1960s, the Swedish parliament perceived the value of alternative schools as their potential to contribute to novel and alternative pedagogies. However, by the 1980s, the notion of alternative pedagogy had disappeared. Instead, as shown in Figure 4.2, "freedom of school choice" surfaced as the dominant perspective from 1990–1992, followed by the concepts of independent and "free" schools from 1993 onward.[54]

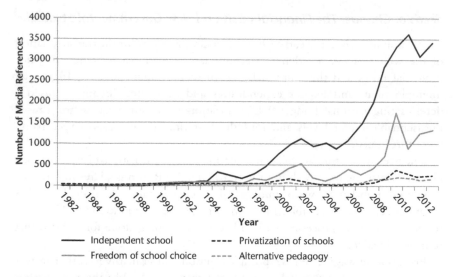

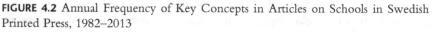

FIGURE 4.2 Annual Frequency of Key Concepts in Articles on Schools in Swedish Printed Press, 1982–2013

Source: Mediearkivet[55]

It is quite noticeable that the term "privatization of schools" disappears from the media discussion of education—as does "alternative pedagogy"—despite the push for privatization in the economy generally. This move away from the term "privatization" may indicate that the reformers advocating privatization preferred to frame the shift by using presumably less provocative terms, such as "freedom" and "independence."[56] Nevertheless, in the more exclusive political discourse in the parliament, the narrative remained focused on the market as the solution for the schools.[57]

It would be an oversimplification to say that the Swedish system changed when neoliberal ideas, from abroad, gained a foothold in the Swedish administration. Instead, the multifaceted transformation of the Swedish school system appears to have occurred along intersections of new and old traditions, born of both domestic and foreign ideas and practices. Freedom of choice and "extensive privatization schemes" came high on the agenda during the liberal-conservative administration and when the social democrats later returned to power, they had more or less "abandoned their opposition to privatization."[58] The confluence of neoliberal ideas, economic distress, and a legacy of publicly funded private schools paved the way for a strong push in the early 1980s for alternative schools using a voucher model—notably, only two decades after the introduction of the comprehensive school.

Transitioning from Public Investment to a Market-Based Model

Privatization of schools in the Swedish context is best understood both as a phenomenon related to other processes enabling the shift to privatization but also as a distinct shift in itself. Four of these "hybrid" phenomena, or factors, led to the shift toward and an increase in the use of private alternatives within the educational system: decentralization, deregulation, school choice, and school funding. Figure 4.3 shows each factor and its overall relationship to the transformation of the Swedish school system.

Factors 1 and 2: Decentralization and Deregulation—Key Elements of Transition

Social-democratic and liberal-conservative administrations moved the Swedish school system along a trajectory of increasing decentralization and deregulation from the late 1980s to the early 1990s. Politically, these activities began in the context of a social-democratic reign; however, by 1991, the new liberal-conservative government rapidly introduced school choice, providing opportunities to establish private alternative schools and make these schools eligible for public funds. This also entails a shift in priorities from an emphasis on collective values to that of individual opportunities as well as a move from a focus on citizen participation to that of consumer influence.[59]

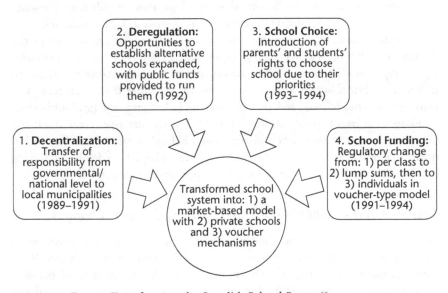

FIGURE 4.3 Factors Transforming the Swedish School System[60]

The decentralization of the governance of Swedish schools evolved into a fierce clash between politicians and teachers on whether the responsibility for education should rest centrally or locally. Initially, the social-democratic administration argued in the late 1980s for a change of the governance of schools towards a decentralized model, albeit with the responsibility for schools shared by "central and the local government."[61]

The social-democratic perspective was that the centralized model had "run out of power" and was "hampering" local development.[62] While the Swedes viewed the centralized model as essential for countering inequity and for securing the implementation of the comprehensive school reform, the preferred decentralized model displaced it to fulfill the goals of the reform. Schools were encouraged to establish their own educational profiles because the "renewal of the internal work processes in schools rests upon a local engagement."[63] Increased local responsibility was seen as the main reason, but the rationale of utilizing existing resources better was also put forward.[64]

The next step was deregulation, in which "traditional working models with centralized management of public business by directives has to be ceased" and replaced by local freedom and responsibility to achieve centrally identified objectives and opportunities for teachers to "develop schools in a more autonomous and purposeful manner."[65] Funding schemes for schools changed from per classroom allocation to the transfer of lump sums to local municipalities, restricting the role of the state to the provision of resources.[66] Equity was to be upheld by accountability, the national curriculum, the design of teacher education, regulation of teacher employment, and differentiation of resources in response to local conditions.[67]

Decentralization and deregulation is a two-sided coin. It can be part of the furthering of democracy by bringing responsibilities and rights closer to citizens. However, in the context of privatization, it may give decisions and rights to individuals—but primarily as customers/consumers, rather than as citizens. The plans for decentralization and deregulation included granting local authorities freedom to enhance quality. Instead, however, these strategies created adverse outcomes in four ways: teacher salaries lagged behind, requirements for teacher qualifications were lowered, school units were enlarged, and school districts became directed by local politicians lacking appropriate competence.[68]

Factors 3 and 4: School Choice and Funding Schemes Changes

In 1992, Sweden outlined the fundamentals for a new educational system on 15 pages, a striking difference compared to the vast documentation preceding the comprehensive school reform. The minister provided a rationale of granting opportunities for students and families to make "choices of education in accordance with their priorities."[69] To have an option, a free school choice was legitimized as an essential part of a "free society" and as something assured in international conventions. This policy was understood to vitalize schools and "increase engagement." In addition, the ministry cited the growing need for alternative pedagogical approaches because the present "uniform" system could not provide opportunities for the "variation and flexibility" necessary for the future.[70]

At the core of this transition to the market model rests the introduction of alternative, non-governmental schools that function under private management, using public money.[71] In 1992, Sweden decided that accredited private schools automatically should be eligible for public funds.[72] This was a game changer. Previously, separating private school management and public funding meant that only a few private alternatives emerged because average Swedish families could not afford fees for private schooling. In the new model of public funding, private schools had to endorse democratic principles of tolerance, equality, and openness. Hence, they had to offer space to each applicant (given size constraints) and they were not allowed to require any parental monetary contributions.[73] Concurrently, the models for the central transfer of funding changed and it became a local responsibility to decide what share of the budget should be allocated to education.[74]

Creating Competition—Breaking Up "the Public School Monopoly"

In addition to establishing legal and financial grounds for private alternatives, conditions changed for municipality schools in the form of a school market.[75] Schools were incentivized to develop profiles, "stimulating competition" to "the highest possible level," among municipality schools as well as private.[76] Cost effectiveness was also addressed but not as a main objective.

The post-war push for shared school experiences as a public responsibility suddenly transformed into an undesired school monopoly.[77] School choice in the educational sector became key for "breaking up the public school monopoly."[78] The framing quickly became an issue of *how* to break up the monopoly rather than a question of *why*. In light of the comprehensive school reform and the abolishment of parallel tracks, this was a profound change into a variety of alternatives and different educational routes.[79]

With this new policy added to the prior emphasis on decentralization and deregulation, the educational landscape changed in its constitutive elements. Competition replaced collaboration as the model for advancement and the previous idea that students from all backgrounds should come together in schooling faded away, as did the idea that centralization supports quality and equity in education.[80] From 2006, under a liberal-conservative administration, another wave of school reforms were launched that added an expanded testing and grading system to the earlier reforms and introduction of the market model.[81]

The Current Situation: Market-Based Swedish Schools

The systemic change has occurred on a number of levels that, taken together, have produced a significant impact not only on teachers' daily work and how they perceive their professions but also on the potential societal role of schooling. The current model rests upon fundamentally different ideas than those that underpinned the introduction of the comprehensive school. It now mixes marketization (and with an associated focus on competition) with a highly decentralized and deregulated system .[82] This section focuses on the key features of the current situation.

The School Market and the Growth of Private Schools

As described above, in the early 1960s only a handful of private schools existed.[83] During the comprehensive school reform, the number fell even further, although the 1970s saw a slight increase.[84] However, after reforms in the late 1980s and early 1990s granting private schools access to public funding, a systemic shift came about.[85] In 1996, just a few years after the full implementation of the different reforms, the number of private schools increased, as did the proportion of students in them, mainly located in or around larger cities (60 percent).[86]

With these changes, compared to the situation prior to 1990, the Swedish school system is another landscape today. The shift is visible in both the character and number of schools. By 2010, more than 15 percent of the primary and lower secondary schools (grades one to nine) were private, along with close to 50 percent of the schools at upper secondary level (grades ten to twelve).[87] This change has also occurred at the preschool level (nearly 20 percent of the preschools were private in 2012).[88] In 2014, reports show that approximately a quarter of the Swedish school system (K–12) nowadays is private, however unevenly distributed.[89] The highest proportion is in the larger cities (25 percent), followed by the suburbs, with a lower socioeconomic status (15 percent) and is marginally present in rural areas (5 percent).[90]

Private Schooling, a Profitable Business—But for Whom?

While advocates for the school market model declared it a means for increased educational quality, it has also promoted the growth of education companies that own a large number of schools.[91] These school companies represent a new phenomenon in Swedish education and they employ business strategies, including economies of scale, profit motivations, and rapid expansion and contraction. The spread of private for-profit schools organized in companies is largest in upper secondary schools and "five out of eight of the largest school companies, with 100,000 students, were owned by buy-out companies."[92] In 2014, the Swedish school company *Academedia* made a US $53 million surplus (EBIT) on its schools, half of which ended up as owners' profit.[93]

The history of the school company Fourfront is illustrative of the expansion/contraction dynamic. In 2006, it received a famous industrialist prize, *The Gazell*, due to the growth rate of the company. Soon after, the owner sold the company to JB Education, a company at the time already owned by venture capitalists Axcel, which was, in fact, a buy-out enterprise. JB Education had a growth rate of 1,000 percent in four years prior to its collapse in 2013 due to bankruptcy. As a consequence, the schools were either sold or closed.[94] Sweden had previously experienced school closures due to local demographic changes and political decisions. However, companies running schools going into liquidation was something new for Swedes that adversely affected the lives of children enrolled in disappearing schools.

In the early 1990s, market proponents provided an important argument for the potential of private schools to positively influence other schools. The initial phase included many of those pedagogically alternative schools. However, that trend has shifted and over 85 percent of current private comprehensive schools have a general pedagogical profile instead of a specialized or alternative one (roughly 10 percent have a religious profile and 5 percent have alternative profiles).[95] This change in pedagogical focus has occurred alongside a shift towards the for-profit model. The proportion of preschools run as a parents' cooperative has fallen from just below 40 percent to slightly above 20 percent while company and for-profit-based private schools have increased to above 55 percent.[96] Overall, private schools organized as for-profit companies in Sweden now account for nearly 70 percent of all private schools.

Businesslike Ownership—and a Businesslike School Discourse

The overarching themes in public discourse outside schools in the 1990s were about independence for schools and freedom of choice for parents and pupils. Additionally, the transformation of the school system also infused new understandings of what happens inside schools and with their administration. With school owners increasingly anchored in the financial sector and traditionally working with a wide range of companies, new understandings of schooling have come about that compete with the democratic vision set up during comprehensive school reform.

According to an article in the *Economist,* one large chain of schools, Kunskapsskolan, mirrors the IKEA concept in getting "its customers to do much of the work themselves." According to the article, the representative of a particular school chain (which does not mind being compared with McDonalds) states: "If we are religious about anything, it is standardization." Consequently, students mainly work independently on web-based assignments, meeting with tutors only 15 minutes per week. They follow a standardized syllabus, are constantly monitored, and their performance is available to parents on a weekly basis.[97]

Fifteen years after the turn of the tide around 1990, a founder of a successful school company commented that to "run a school and to sell refrigerators are one and the same. It's about having your ear to the market and to understand where the needs are for our customers, the pupils."[98] This comment indicates, to some extent, the kind of understanding and rationales that came into education with the advent of business-oriented actors.

A Swedish private school can today be organized in different administrative, legal, and jurisdictional forms as a stock company, a private company/enterprise, a cooperative, a faith-based organization, foundation, etc.[99] These schools are granted the same economic conditions as the municipality schools.[100] Private schools have the right to make a profit and, over time, the proportion of for-profit schools has come to dominate the non-profit and pedagogically motivated schools (once the original argument for preserving and extending private schools).

One important requirement for receiving public funding is that the recipient cannot extract additional funding from parents or other parties. Nor are they allowed to charge application fees or for queuing for admittance; nor can schools charge for teaching materials or for lunch.[101] These private schools can rent, purchase, or in other ways establish appropriate locations for their activities (schooling, administration, etc.) Municipality schools do not own the buildings they utilize, usually they are provided by the municipality. This prohibition against the practice of "topping up" preserves some semblance of financial equity, especially when compared with situations in the United States where parents or foundations routinely provide additional funding to already enriched student populations.

Equality in School Investments?

What about equality in a school market? The OECD has reported significant growth in inequalities in Swedish society and raises concerns about equality in Swedish schools.[102] This section maps whether the new market system allocates an equal amount of resources to students in different schools. While this initially seems like an easy issue to sort out, in reality, the distinction between equal and equitable usually applies. Should the metric be equality— schools receiving the same amount of financial support—or equity—schools receiving an appropriate amount of financial resources to provide equal educational opportunities for all students?

The Swedish voucher-like system distributes funds equally, in that municipality schools and private schools (in the same municipality) receive equal funds for running their schools. Each municipality is independent, has different levels of municipality taxation, and allocates funds locally for compulsory schooling in relation to prerequisites, conditions, and ideological preferences. The fundamental ideal behind decentralized resource allocation was its advantage in being local (with local conditions considered).[103] However, the result is that Sweden now has significant variations in school expenditure. Furthermore, when The Swedish Agency for Public Management surveyed the field, they found a link between the financial outlook of municipalities and their investment in upper secondary education. These findings indicate that municipalities not only allocate different amounts of resources for education but do so on grounds other than educational equity.[104]

The ten municipalities with the highest investment per student had expenditures between US $11,850 and US $13,850. At the other end of the spectrum, the lowest ten municipalities had expenditures between US $8,150 and US $8,350, or around one-third lower than the highest-spending municipalities.[105] Municipalities do distribute resources following a compensatory strategy and the state also includes similar mechanisms to mitigate funding disparities.[106] However, the national contribution by the National Agency for Education and The Swedish School Inspectorate is marginal, insufficient, and not primarily targeted at students' explicit needs.[107] Furthermore, individual municipalities are free to invest at a higher level and more wealthy municipalities are not restricted in this sense.[108] Therefore, some municipalities obviously invest at higher levels, producing large variations in resource allocations to schools of approximately up to 70 percent of total funding (not including buildings).[109]

While school expenditures vary *between* municipalities, the level of investment *within* the municipality is the same for publicly operated schools as well as for private schools. Private schools are free to make profit and, because teachers represent the main cost in schooling, large differences in student–teacher ratios can occur. This also happens with other personnel, for example student counselors. The average number of students per counselor in municipality schools is double the number in private schools.[110] The current market-based model of schooling in Sweden features large variations in educational investment and an unequal resource distribution, with those variations only marginally connected to student needs.[111]

Finally, the other side of the school provision coin is school choice. Sweden's market model implies a parent's theoretical ability to choose *any* school. However, regulatory and practical constraints mean that school choice does not apply to everyone in the same way. Sweden requires a municipality to provide mandatory schooling for all pupils close enough so that they do not have to sleep away from home.[112] While parents may request a particular school, municipalities can then prioritize applicants living within a defined proximity to the school.[113] In this case, municipalities ultimately control enrollment.

Private schools for grades K–9 have a first come-first served policy, with an additional prioritization for siblings.[114] Municipality schools must provide transportation for pupils based on established student criteria (age and distance) for both types of schools.[115] In practice, this means that if parents chose a private school far from home, parents will also have to take responsibility for transportation.[116] So, parental choice also includes considerations of a family's socioeconomic status and their ability to afford transportation and other incidentals to attend different private schools. Therefore, as is common in many "choice" schemes, the devil in the details is that full choice does not actually exist and some families have more options than others.

Qualified Teachers: Where Do They Go?

The decentralization of responsibility to the local level for teaching staffing coincided with the disappearance of stricter regulations for teacher qualifications.[117] In private alternative schools, fewer teachers hold required degrees. The share of staff in preschools with required teacher degrees was simliar in 1999 (50 percent), but in 2012, only 40 percent of teachers in private alternatives had degrees, while the percentage in municipality preschools actually increased slightly.[118] For grades one to nine, the proportion of teachers with required education was significantly higher in municipality schools (86 percent) in 2012–2013 than those in private schools (70 percent).[119] For upper secondary schools, this difference is also visible (79 percent in municipality schools, 62 percent in private schools).[120]

Examining qualifications more closely, the figures for teachers that teach classes they are qualified to teach have decreased. As an example, in lower secondary schools, the highest rates of qualified teachers teaching in their content specialty are those in French, German, and history (with average rates of 75 percent) compared to physics, social studies, and geography, which are down to 50–60 percent.[121] Sweden also has large regional differences in subject-area teachers as students in the northern part have qualified math teachers above a rate of 75 percent, compared with those in the southern part that are down to 50–60 percent.[122]

As mentioned above, private schools are mainly located in cities and less so in rural areas. Sixty-five percent of all students in private schools are living either in or near to the three larger cities.[123] Traditionally, staffing rural schools with qualified teachers has been difficult. However, schools located in the larger cities now have lower levels of teachers with required educational degrees than the national average.[124] The low levels of qualified teachers in private schools and the concentration of private schools in urban areas most likely explains why urban schools in general have lower levels of qualified teachers.[125] In addition, an OECD study found that in Sweden, "teachers with more experience are half as likely to work in schools with larger proportions of students from socioeconomically disadvantaged homes."[126]

Recent OECD reports on Swedish schools raise concerns about equality within Swedish schools.[127] The importance of "fairness in resource allocation" is stressed and that how "resources are allocated is just as important as the amount of resources available to be allocated."[128] In Sweden, the OECD found teachers to be "less equitably distributed among schools," noting that teacher shortages impact more on socioeconomically disadvantaged schools and are amplified by an unequal distribution of resources.[129]

Teacher shortages have recurred in Sweden, as in other countries, the consequences seemingly aggravated in a decentralized school market model. It is hard to say whether lower salaries in private schools explain the deviance toward underprepared teachers and a smaller labor force, although some evidence indicates this possibility.[130] Due to the severe shortage, a new certification system will not solve the problem of an unequal distribution of teachers.

Smaller Schools, Larger Classes: Private School Approaches to Student–Teacher Ratios

In addition to teacher shortages and less-prepared teachers, private schools are likely to have larger class sizes, even though private schools are smaller on average than public schools.[131] In private preschools, the total enrollments are significantly smaller than in public schools (for children aged one to three).[132] Private schools for first to ninth graders enrolled significantly fewer students (less than 50) compared to between 100–200 for municipality schools. This difference is also visible in upper secondary education (grades ten to twelve) as roughly half of the schools are private, but only a quarter of the student population attends these schools.[133]

Class sizes appear to follow the opposite pattern, with private schools having larger classes. The deregulation in the early 1990s abolished national regulations regarding class sizes and no such regulation exists today.[134] Consequently, no national statistics are available on class sizes, but data on student–teacher ratios exists.[135] Figures indicate that private schools have a higher number of students per teacher, and likely larger classes. Private preschools have a higher number of students per teacher (>12), with fewer than ten students per teacher in municipality schools. Upper secondary schools have 14.3 students per teacher in private schools, compared with 11.6 in municipality schools.[136] Theses differences in student–teacher ratios vary greatly by location, another feature of decentralizing the system.[137]

Private schools tend to have fewer teachers per student cohort than municipalities, but large differences also exist between particular types of private schools. Schools run by for-profit companies have a significantly lower number of teachers per student (and likely larger class sizes) compared with schools run by non-profit companies. In fact, some non-profits exceed municipality-run schools in having fewer students per teacher.[138] In addition, for-profit schools seem to make profit by selecting students by means of a cream-skimming strategy (in principle not allowed). Getting the best students in the same classroom makes it possible to combine larger classes with high student performance, notwithstanding the massive equity ramifications.[139] Private secondary schools seem to reclassify programs into different types eligible for the highest reimbursement without an appropriate change in teaching.[140]

Historically, Sweden has seen an increase in the number of students per teacher since 1990. The main increase occurred prior to 2000, with a slow improvement toward small classes since then. However, the situation today remains less beneficial to students compared with the figures in 1990, before decentralization and deregulation.[141] Despite several governmental interventions to improve the situation, the change from earmarked-funding schemes to general models has instead coincided with fewer teachers entering the profession per student cohort. The improvement since 2000 also came with a significant downturn in the proportion of qualified teachers.[142] Previously, cities had a lower number of students per teacher compared with rural districts. However, urban districts, with the highest proportions of private schools, now have a lower rate of qualified teachers.[143]

Changes in How Teachers Work

The introduction of school choice has the potential to change the rationale of the profession in several respects—and that is also the core idea when it comes to increases in quality and student learning. But are there negative consequences as well? A school market system changes a teacher's daily work: "a market-influenced pedagogical identity" is now palpable in school districts with high levels of competition between schools.[144] Administration and tasks other than teaching now occupy a significantly larger part of teacher time than before, a change reinforced by the market model.[145]

The market model also causes an extended workload that intensifies teachers' work.[146] A teacher's role now includes marketing as a way of promoting the particular schools (businesses) who employ teachers in order to attract new students.[147] Teachers can also have increased meetings with parents (customers), and to quote a poignant teacher comment: "If you lose students, someone else will get your job."[148] Teachers report that they become distracted from their key obligation of teaching. Schools themselves tend to develop an entrepreneurial approach, increasingly becoming businesslike arenas and less educational sites. As a result, teachers become less autonomous in their professional role and more dependent on principals. Marketization affects teacher identity because "most teachers' professional lives are influenced" due to the fact that their employment is at risk.[149]

The capacity for teachers to ensure quality and to function as whistleblowers when quality is poor differs between municipal and private schools. Teachers (and others) in municipality schools have a constitutional right to serve as whistleblowers, either publicly or anonymously.[150] However, due to business legislation, this right does not apply to private schools, stifling discourse about what education methods work or do not. Therefore, the comments above in which teachers exhibit concern over their employment are also likely to mask broader teacher views about quality because they do not feel fully free to speak out.[151] Finally, accountability to the public, by schools, relies upon a high degree of transparency, yet for-profit companies are not subjected to the same legislation regarding transparency as municipality schools.

One indication of the influence of the market model on teachers' professional autonomy is grade inflation. A striking fact is that, during the period when Swedish students' performance in international tests has *decreased*, grades for the same students have *increased*.[152] The National Agency for Education noted in 2012 clear "indication[s] of grade inflation in both primary and secondary schools," while also emphasizing the complexity of such an analysis.[153] For example, in 2012–2013, private schools had significantly higher average grades for lower secondary students.[154]

Studies have also indicated a higher divergence between grades and performance in upper secondary schools due to both the large share of private schools and the use of secondary school grades for admittance to higher education.[155] The issue at stake is whether these students' grades really represent their performance. Studies indicate low levels of trust in the current Swedish praxis as well as large differences in grading, leading some to argue that "solid evidence" links grade inflation to school market competition.[156]

Finally, the OECD-study on teaching and learning (TALIS 2013) seems to indicate that the transformation described here in terms of market influences on teaching has led to a changed understanding among Swedish teachers of how society values their profession. The TALIS asked teachers to respond to the statement "I think that the teaching profession is valued in society"; and Swedish teachers "strongly disagreed" at a rate higher than in any other country surveyed.[157] In addition, Swedish teachers reported the lowest "on the job satisfaction" in the study (a tendency also observed in PIRLS 2011 and TIMSS 2011).[158] These results show that the shift to markets has negatively impacted on teachers—from the number of available teachers to their level of certification, and finally, to their daily work and their overall job satisfaction.

What does the current situation for schooling in Sweden signify? An educational system can be viewed from different perspectives and education as such has wider and narrower purposes. This section has provided a description of the current situation in the Swedish school system, a description that raises concerns. This section concludes with a brief glance at what the Swedish PISA scores indicate about the potential for learning in the market-based Swedish school model, both from a domestic perspective and when compared to other OECD countries.

Studies have indicated that Swedish students were among the top performers in reading, math, and science prior to the mid-1990s. However, PISA results indicate that Swedish students' knowledge in reading, math, and science has dropped to below average over a period of two decades, that top-performers have declined rapidly, and that the proportion of students that do not reach the baseline of performance has increased.[159]

In PISA 2012, in "all subject areas, Sweden is the country whose performance has declined the most."[160] In a report to the Swedish government, the OECD highlighted a decline in all "three core subjects measured in PISA," a "significant" increase in the proportion of students that do not "reach baseline of performance in mathematics" and the fact that the "share of top performers in mathematics roughly halved over the past decade."[161] In addition, the European Commission addressed the weak educational performance in Sweden in June of 2014.[162] According to PISA 2012, 18 OECD countries, among them Finland, Denmark and Norway, perform significantly better than Sweden in all three subject areas, 25 countries perform significantly better than Sweden in mathematics and science, and 19 perform significantly better in reading literacy.[163]

A Minor Change *in* the System—or a Profound Turnaround *of* the System?

Sweden purposefully designed its modern school system in the post-war years. The key message was short and sharp: "the prime role of schooling is to educate democratic humans."[164] Consequently, the school model emerging from that historical context—nine years of compulsory and comprehensive schooling—came to harbor fundamental democratic ambitions and hopes. After 1990, the educational U-turn changed the comprehensive model into a school market model, with competition and options for profit. Lurking behind these two models are critical questions about how Swedish society views its trajectory in education, as democratic citizens or consumers.

A key question is to what degree the Swedish experiment with an educational sector designed as a school market in a voucher-like system with school choices has served Sweden and its citizen well. Some argue in the affirmative. Economists A. Böhlmark and M. Lindahl (2012) content that their findings confirm that competition promotes quality. They related a number of factors comparing municipalities with different shares of private schools and concluded:

> We find that an increase in the share of independent-school students improves the average educational performance both at the end of compulsory school and in the long run in terms of high school grades, university attendance and years of schooling.[165]

However, their results received methodological criticism because they did not fully control for conditions like grade inflation and sample bias due to socioeconomic factors that differ between private schools and municipality schools, as outlined above.[166] Economists like Vlachos also point out methodological difficulties leading to interpretations based on evidence that is, at best, inconclusive. Our point here, though, is that, on one level, schooling definitely concerns the personal qualifications on which Böhlmark and Lindahl focus; however, their economics vantage point does not account for key concerns about the socialization and democratization of students, as well as the impact of having private schools function as businesses inside a comprehensive school system.[167]

Others point to failure of the school market model. In March 2013, an article by a top analyst at the National Agency for Education argued that Swedish schools have moved in the wrong direction and had during the last decade become less and less equal.[168] He later left the agency and published a deeply critical book, *The child experiment—Swedish schools in a free fall.*[169] In his perspective, the main problem relates to the extensive decentralization and deregulation in the late 1980s and early 1990s that served as the prelude to increased educational inequality. Finally, one cannot avoid an impression of a certain naivety in Swedish policymaking during the market U-turn. The market model took a few years before expanding and turning into a mainly for-profit-oriented business. A clearer set of regulations could have preserved and supported the "influencing" strategy of private school alternatives, possibly with positive influences on the Swedish schools.

Some international analysts agree that the market model has not worked well. Although the Swedish educational system was put forward as an example to follow in the United Kingdom in 2008, the evidence did not support this perspective.[170] Susanne Wiborg of the Institute of Education at London University published in 2010 the report *Swedish Free Schools—Do they work?*. She finds substantial differences between the assumingly identical British and Swedish "free schools" and concludes that the Swedish experiment has not promoted "significant learning gains overall." Despite the rather limited length of the experiment, a central consequence appears to be increased inequality. She also stressed that the Swedish experiment is conducted in a society with a historical heritage of equality that may have countered consequences of this type.[171]

The introduction of free school choice came with aspirations of increased educational quality, and accessibility. International surveys of student performance instead indicate increased educational inequality, with growing variations in performance between both students and schools during the period.[172] Whether there is a causal link between these phenomena and how it might appear is under debate. What we know is, despite the requirement in the Education Act to compensate disadvantaged students, studies do not indicate these have had the intended effect of making a substantial impact in promoting equality. Instead, inequality has increased (as confirmed by OECD) in both education and in society writ large.[173]

The acceptance of some private schools in the comprehensive school system, the *influencing* idea, paved the way for and contrasts distinctively with the current *replacement* model and the increased differences now found in Sweden's school system, a system that nowadays has returned to the democratically problematic tracked school system in existence before the 1950s, a system that the comprehensive school reform had intended to abolish.

The bankruptcy of the private school group, JB Education, in 2013 may have been an eye-opener for the public. It caused a public debate on issues like profit and whether business-minded approaches have anything to offer regarding the upbringing and education of children. The fact that venture capitalists, buy-out companies, and other for-profit businesses had grown into prominent actors among the private schools appears to not have been widely known, or embraced for that reason.

The perceived problems with Swedish schools and the societal debate on for-profit companies in the welfare sector resulted in a parliamentary investigation. In spring 2013, however, it concluded that private schools "are here to stay" and proposed no ban on for-profit companies.[174] Despite this statement, as Sweden came closer to election in fall 2014, the debate on private schools intensified. The minister of education stressed that the downturn in international student performance surveys had no causal relation to the growth of private schools and the marketized school model, defending the system with a plea to "not jeopardize the unique right to choose a school." [175]

A majority of Swedish political parties seem to have a general consensus on this lack of causality. However, citizens appear to have a more divided approach to for-profit schools that seems to indicate that this is an unresolved issue in contemporary Swedish society. [176] The most recent political developments in Sweden signal a hesitant and divided approach to the school market model. The problems stemming from the market model appear to be recognized now, but due to the lack of sufficient political consensus on elaborating other models, the future of education in Sweden is still being envisioned in a number of separate initiatives but within a school market paradigm. Both the liberal-conservative administration and the current government have launched initiatives for a general improvement of education and for revision of the school market model.

Governmental initiatives now focus on remedies for some of the acknowledged problems with the school market model through the following actions, proposals, and inquiries:

- securing deliberate increases in educational investments in areas with greater needs; increasing transparency (requiring openness also in private schools and comparability between all schools);
- assuring that school owners are in the business for educational purposes (by introducing requirements on long-term engagement on owners and by restricting the profit potential for private schools);
- arranging a shared admittance system that can counter some segregation effects;
- providing local municipalities with a mandate to veto private school establishments (if understood to jeopardize a municipality's local educational provision); and,
- introducing financial arrangements that secure the financial grounds for students finalizing their studies in cases where school companies liquidate. [177]

However, such initiatives represent a kind of amendment strategy that limits and/ or reduces negative aspects of the current system instead of proposing other models or addressing the overarching question of what the future might require of an educational model.

Taken together, Swedish policymakers display a dual approach that clearly signals an awareness of problems but less readiness to challenge the model as such. However, a governmental school commission has been appointed to come up with proposals for increased learning and equality in Swedish schools. As mentioned above, in the years after World War II, Swedes identified a profound need to revise their outdated educational system and, in that crucial situation, a school commission was appointed for elaborating the future of education in Sweden. The fact that a second school commission now is at work may indicate governmental insights into the problems of a school market from the perspective of an historical engagement for educational equity and for advancement of learning. However, with the political situation in a moment of minority rule, the general political tensions regarding freedom of school choice, and the limited time frame for the commission restricts the space and opportunity for profound change. Despite the problem of the Swedish school market model, no third educational U-turn has appeared on the horizon; instead, there are signs of a sobering reflection. The question is whether this reflection will be followed by serious change, similar to the profound post-war process that once transformed a school system, and that contributed to citizenship and democracy.

Education and Democratic Ambitions

For a long time Sweden perceived education as a means to the development and establishment of democracy. The decentralization movement can also be understood from that perspective, motivated by placing responsibility within the realm of municipalities and local school directions and with a reduction of a stiff and far away bureaucracy. This approach was supposed to support democracy in its essence.[178] But when school choice launched and a school market was established, the rationale shifted to a consumer narrative, focused on individuals and their need for freedom. Education became about progress by competition, a profoundly different way forward than the democratic aspirations outlined only decades earlier, in the shadow of World War II and in the light of developing a democratic society and a welfare society.[179]

The Swedish school system of the 2010s differs profoundly from the version implemented in decades before the 1990s and the grand narratives have changed. Sweden has revised its educational model for the sake of better preparation for the future. Previously, Sweden deliberately chose to avoid market forces in education and instead utilized centralism for securing equity and democratic schooling. Alternative schools were accepted despite a focus on a comprehensive school model, albeit on the margin and mainly due to their potential to influence municipality schools with alternative pedagogy. In the 1990s, the emergence of market forces meant that private schools were replacing municipality schools rather than acting as influencing alternatives.[180]

As a result, the market model and its emphasis on individual choice rather than collective responsibility has tended to create a similar kind of educational differentiation that the previous U-turn to the comprehensive school attempted to resolve. A predecessor to today's international student performance surveys concluded in the late 1970s:

> the comprehensive system, by its openness, lack of selective examinations during primary and lower secondary stages, and its high retention rate, is a more effective strategy for taking care of all the talent of a nation during mandatory schooling … A system with early separation of students who are

rated to have academic potential is destined to produce good *end products*. But this advantage is bought at the price of excluding a sizeable number of students from lower social strata from further education and of limiting the opportunities of the great majority of students to get access to quality education.[181]

Has the current market model served Sweden well? The outcome of current international surveys of student performance does not indicate high quality. Furthermore, in a context of rapidly increased segregation, the questions that Sweden must address seem similar to those in 1945: is the current educational model the best one for the development of a desirable and shared society? Does it provide the best opportunities for every individual to realize their full potential? Will there be another turn of the tide into a model that better serves all students and democracy? Sweden can hope that it remains too early to recall Sheldon Rothblatt's comment on another but related educational matter: "some beautiful thoughts are only alive as thoughts. Their reality is gone, and we hear only the ghost of lost traditions whimpering upon the grave thereof."[182]

Notes

1   SOU 1948:27, p. 3 (my translation).
2   Engzell–Larsson (2013), p. 97 (my translation).
3   *Economist,* June 12, 2008.
4   On the terminology for non-governmental schools and the implication of labeling them, see endnotes 36, 56 and 71.
5   The current Swedish school model has features that resemble both the voucher system and charter system. Some scholars have chosen to describe the model as a voucher system (cf. Böhlmark, A. and Lindahl, M. 2012). That terminology is relevant due to similarities. However, as there are significant deviations as well, in search for a more nuanced terminology, we prefer to choose to label the Swedish school model a market-based model with voucher-like features.
6   Esping-Andersen 1990, p. 12.
7   International Association for the Evaluation of Educational Achievement (IEA) (Husén 1979; Husén 1972, pp. 122ff).
    Swedish students were among the top performers in reading comprehension (1970s) and studies indicated that mathematical competence rose from the 1970s to the mid-1990s. In TIMSS 1995 (Science) Swedish students were among the top performers. Skolverket 2013b, pp. 10–16; cf. Skolverket 2009.
8   Sweden is still regarded as among the most equal OECD countries (OECD 2011). In PISA 2012, in "all subject areas, Sweden is the country whose performance has declined the most." (Skolverket 2013b, p. 8; cf. Gustafsson 2011). In a special report the OECD highlights a decline in all "three core subjects measured in PISA", a "significant" increase in the proportion of students that do not "reach baseline of performance in mathematics" and the fact that the "share of top performers on mathematics roughly halved over the past decade." (OECD 2014a, p. 2; cf. European Commission on weak Swedish educational performance (COM 2014, 428)).

9 Cf. Myrdal and Myrdal 1941, pp. 89–132.

10 Cf. Hirdman *et. al.* 2012: "Of course the fortune was in play. Sweden, with its location in the far north, with three countries as shields, was spared during the war. The industry, undamaged throughout the war, could in postwar years produce and export to a Europe that experienced shortage of almost everything." (p. 618).

11 Cf. Esping-Andersen 1990.

12 Weijne 1950, governmental proposition, no. 70, p. 44.

13 Erlander 1973, pp. 237–239.

14 Berggren 2010, pp. 209ff; cf. "Educational policy was central in the social democratic politics on equality as it has to do with class, *bildung*, human dignity and freedom of thought on another level than railroads and highways" (p. 376) and SOU 1948: 27, p. 1.

15 Weijne 1950, p. 12.

16 Ibid. p. 13.

17 Ibid.

18 This perspective was no less strong in the parliamentary debate of 1962: the purpose of schooling is "for students to learn to take responsibility, for studies, actions and destiny, but also to take responsibility for others, for ones neighbor and fellow humans." (Arvidsson 1962, p. 75) It was argued that there was "a straight line" from the committees from 1946 up to 1962, demanding "a nine-year comprehensive school with explicit democratic purposes." (Edenman 1962, p. 43) The approach differed partly however; in 1950 the role of the schools for democracy was stressed but in 1962 the tone of the argument was that as society has become democratic, schools have to "adapt" and to "harmonize with society in general" (ibid. p. 45).

19 Palme (1967), p. 41. (my translation).

20 Ibid.

21 Cf. Edenman's introductory presentation on May 22 (Edenman 1962, p. 43). Spring, p.viii.

22 Nilsson 1989, p. 357; cf. Norberg 2003, p. 3.

23 Marklund 1980, p. 8; cf. Erlander 1973, p. 234.

24 Husén 1988, ch 7; cf. Marklund 1980, passim.

25 Cf. Husén 1988, Marklund 1982.

26 Österberg and Andersson 2013, pp. 287ff.

27 These experiments were combined with extensive follow-ups and a number of research reports were published. Cf. Husén 1988.

28 Richardsson 2010, pp. 115ff; cf. Hartman 2005, p. 50.

29 Cf. Österberg and Andersson 2013, p. 291. Legislation and curricula use the Swedish term *likvärdig* that has been translated both as equity and equivalence. Carlbaum clarifies, this as: "Equivalence is usually used for a certain level of parity in standards, that education has the same quality and worth, regardless of provider and location. Equity, on the other hand, …[is] to be used when it refers to reaching a certain level of equality in outcomes and results but at the same time taking into consideration differences, diversity and increased freedom of choice." (Carlbaum 2014, p. 12). The idea that teacher education is a governmental tool for equity was already present in the 1940s (SOU 1948:27) but also later, as for example in the parliamentary inquiry that proposed teacher education reform in late the 1990s (SOU 1999:63, pp. 108ff).

30 Winberg 2011; cf. Husén 1979, pp. 83ff; Lundgren 2010, pp. 87ff.

31 SOU 1961:30, pp. 534ff and Government proposal 1962:54, pp. 350ff.

32 Ohlsson 1962, p. 40; cf. Government proposal 1962:54, p. 367.

33 Gov prop. 1962:54, pp. 353ff.

34 SOU 1961:30, p. 541, 558; Government proposal 1962: p. 366f.

35 Government proposal. 1962:54, p. 366ff.

36 Government proposal 1962:54, p. 365. To be noted is the use of the phrase "experiment and independent schools" (p. 367). This appears to be the first use of the word *friskola* (free school), today's common term, usually perceived as a short form of *fristående skola* which in the beginning of the 1980s replaced the phrase *enskild skola* (detached school, meaning detached from the public system).

37 Nilsson 1987; Nilsson 1989 (cf/ Husén 1988, pp. 218ff; Husén 1989).

38 Österberg and Andersson 2013, p. 487.

39 Neave 1985 p. 322.

40 Baggesen Klitgaard 2007, p. 182. Lundahl, L. *et al.*

41 Ibid.

42 Schön 2000, pp. 468–517.

43 Schön, 2000 p. 507.

44 Hadenius 2000, p. 206; cf. Schön 2000, pp. 503ff. The Swedish currency, *kronan,* came under speculation from international actors as it was defined in relation to the European ECU. Finland, Great Britain, and Italy had previously abandoned the fixed exchange rate towards ECU (Hadenius 2000, p. 208; Schön 2000, p. 506). The Swedish central bank raised the interest an astonishing 500 per cent before Sweden had let the currency flow freely for the first time since 1933. *Kronan* lost a quarter of its value (Gustafsson and Svensson 1999, p. 52).

45 Schön 2000, p. 507.

46 Gustafsson and Svensson 1999, p. 52.

47 Due to political inclinations, descriptions vary of course. Cf. Magnusson 2006; Santesson 2012.

48 For example, at that time parliament voted to sell off more than 30 state companies that employed more than 100,000 persons (Hadenius 2000, p. 205).

49 Schön 2000, pp. 501ff.

50 Foss Hansen 2011, p. 124; cf. Forsell and Ivarsson Westerberg 2014, p. 19.

51 Via a subsidiary consulting company. Küng 1984, p. 7ff. A governmental investigation into the consequences of decentralization claims that in the early 1980s development was affected by the fact that: "Consultants and 'advocates for reform' oscillated between the municipalities and arguing for the introduction of purchase–provider model…", SOU 2014:5, p. 53.

52 Andersson 1984, p. 36; Österberg and Andersson 2013, pp. 46, 488ff.

53 Andersson 1984, pp. 37–40. It shoud be noted that the Conservative Party presented proposals to every parliamentary session during the 1980s on increased freedom of school choice. Cf. Skolverket, *Val av skola. Reformen: historik, sammanhang och intentioner. Ett tioårigt perspektiv,* p. 3.

54 This frequency tracking of concepts comes with methodological problems as well as interpretative ones.

55 As data was accessed in the beginning of December 2013, information is partially incomplete for 2013.

56 Cf. "Somewhere down the road, they took on the term 'free school,' a concept with Danish roots, and that was congenial as they then got rid of the dusty and contested term 'private school,' a term aligned with values that never would be widely endorsed in Sweden." Engzell-Larsson 2013, p. 106 (my translation).

57 Forssell 2011, pp. 206–215.

58 Foss Hansen 2011, p. 124. The National Agency for Education summarized the social democratic government's endorsement of the reform: "The current government's overarching goal is to create the most possible freedom for students and parents" in their choice of site for schooling (Skolverket, *Val av skola. Reformen: historik, sammanhang och intentioner. Ett tioårigt perspektiv*, p.15). Minister of finance, K-O. Feldt, took a positive stance to privatization in education. In the period after the assassination of Palme in 1986, and the following regrouping of the social democratic politicians, policy becomes less hesitant about the introduction of private alternatives.

59 Cf. Englund 1993; SOU 2014:5, p. 18.

60 These elements were proposed in the following governmental proposals: 1988/89:4; 1988/89:150; 1989/90:41; 1990/91:18; 1991/92:95; 1992/93:230.

61 A part of the process was the "ending the state regulation of teaching positions." Ringarp 2012: 329. (Cf. Ringarp 2011, passim, and pp. 70ff.). Despite teacher strikes, the responsibility for schools was transferred to local municipalities. Government proposal 1989/90:41; cf. p. 14 and Riksdagens protocoll. 1989/90:42, band A5, s84; Österberg and Andersson 2013, p. 47). There was nothing about privatization or marketization of education in this decision, not even the existing alternative schools were addressed (Government proposal 1989/90:41, p. 12); Government proposal 1988/89:4, p. 1.

62 Government proposal 1988/89:150, p. 33. Cf. Finance minister K-O. Feldts comments in the parliamentary debate on April 25, 1989.

63 Government proposal 1988/89:4, p. 4.

64 Government proposal 1990/91:18, p. 17.

65 Government proposal 1990/91:18, p. 17, 22.

66 Government proposal 1990/91:18, p. 53.

67 Government proposal 1990/91:18, p. 28, 62.

68 Österberg and Andersson, p. 290ff.

69 Government proposal 1991/92:95, p. 8.

70 Ibid. p. 9.

71 Understanding of "private" and "public" generally is a broad topic as is the discourse on privatization in education and definitions of private schools and privatization. Cf. Millares 2012, Alexiadou 2013 and Campbell *et al.* 2009, pp. 9ff. This study follows the notion of privatization that points to the "establishment of schools operated by non-governmental authorities, whether for-profit or non-profit." (Zajda 2006, p. 8.).

72 Government proposal 1991/92:95. p. 6, 14 (cf. Education Act, 9 ch. 4a§). Later these rules came to include upper secondary schools (Government proposal 1992/93:230).

73 Government proposal 1991/92:95, pp. 11–15. It became an obligation for municipalities to transfer funds to schools relative to the number of students, whether private or public. All schools nowadays follow this same regulation. Neave, however, argues that "private schools" have to refer to schools that are privately owned, managed, and funded.

74 Skolverket 2013, p. 6.
75 It may be more correct to call the Swedish school market a "quasi" market. Cf. Norén 2003, pp. 30ff; Rönnberg 2011 and Alexiadou 2013. (Cf. Government proposal 1991/92:95, p. 9f.).
76 Skolverket 2013a, pp. 7–9.
77 Conservatives claimed a move away from collectivism and a break-up of monopolies would be desirable. Cf. Österberg and Andersson 2013, p. 379.
78 Government proposal 1992/93:230, p. 26f. N.B.: parents "obligation to pursue active school choices."
79 Ibid.
80 N.B.: School choice among municipality schools had been introduced in some municipalities prior to these reforms. Government proposal 1992/93:230, p. 93.
81 A summary of the policy changes from 2006 to 2013 is found in SOU 2013:30, pp. 12ff. Cf Läroplan för grundskolan (curriculum for the compulsory school) 11, p. 8.
82 Cf. Lundahl, L. *et al.* N.B.: Recent policy indicates a reactivation of central authorities.
83 SOU 1961:30: pp. 534ff; Government proposal 1962:54, pp. 350ff. Cf. Ambler 1994, p. 356.
84 Mainly pedagogically motivated. Ekvall 1978, p. 106.
85 Administrative methods for reimbursement between school districts foreshadowed the new voucher type model since it calculated and transferred funds per individual student. Cf. Ekvall 1978 pp. 115ff.
86 Skolverket 1996.
87 *Ekonomifakta* 2014. Cf. Friskolorna i siffror 2014; SOU 2013:56, p. 76.
88 Skolverket 2014a, p. 17, cf. pp. 10, 28, 84.
89 SOU 2013:56, p. 77.
90 Skolverket 2014a , pp. 29, 82.
91 Cf. SOU 2013:56, ch. 4.3; Engzell-Larsson 2013; *Aftonbladet,* May 18 2011, "Stop the fortune hunters".
92 There may be some terminological issues here. "Venture capital" appears not to be fully appropriate. According to Engzell-Larsson 2013, "buy-out companies" is a more correct term to use in these cases (pp. 10ff, 102–105). Cf. SOU 2013:56, Ch. 4.3 indicates that the object of these companies is "to increase value", under a "limited period of time." (p. 100).
93 *Dagens Nyheter,* February 11, 2015, "Lönsamt – men lågt intresse för nya friskolor." (a profitable business but interest in establishing new schools slowing).
94 Engzell-Larsson 2013, p. 98.
95 Skolverket 2014a, p. 33.
96 Skolverket 2014a, p.11.
97 This company has established schools abroad (Österberg and Andersson 2013, p. 292). Alexiadou 2013, notes that Sweden distinguished itself by having an "increasingly confident for-profit, free-school sector" that also went international. For the founders' view on this, cf. Emilsson 2014). N.B.: education is regulated as a service internationally by World Trade Organization agreements like the General Agreement on Trade in Service (GATS). Cf. Siqueria 2005; Zajda 2006).
98 Engzell-Larsson 2013, pp. 97ff. A study by The Confederation of Swedish Enterprise (Svenskt Näringsliv) confirms the existence of this type of business model: "customers

are viewed as important resources within the system in which value is created and service is provided" and that "focus shifts from properties in the products, services, or resources to the customers' situation, needs and result for the customer; for example learning in schools." Edvardsson 2011, p. 68 (my translation).

99 According to legislation (SKOLFS 2011:154) seven types of ownership are accepted: joint stock company, trading company/limited partnership company, sole proprietorship, cooperative, nonprofit association, registered faith-based organization and foundation.

100 An independent school is reimbursed in accordance with the costs applied to municipality schools. According to the Education Act 2010:800, 10 ch. 38–9§, the school shall be provided with resources for: teaching, learning devices, health service, food, administration, taxes and housing. Cf. SOU 2013:56, p. 58.

101 According to the Education Act (2010:800, 10 ch. 10–11§§), compulsory schooling shall be free of charge. Minor charges, for example for an outdoor activity of "insignificant value" are permitted (Skolverket 2012a; cf. Skolinspektionen 2011a).

102 OECD 2011; OECD 2014a.

103 SOU 2014:5, p. 273.

104 Statskontoret 2013, p. 81.

105 Costs for buildings are not included. SOU 2014:5, p. 266. (These figures are from 2010 and the currency rate of September 15, 2010 is applied). For upper secondary schools, there is a national regulation of the funding, i.e. a fixed price list (Skolverket 2014e).

106 Cf. Statskontoret 2013, pp. 28 ff.

107 Skolverket 2013a, pp. 28ff, 46ff.

108 Cf. Statskontoret 2013, p. 65.

109 Statskontoret 2013, p. 48.

110 Skolverket 2014a, p. 94.

111 Statskontoret 2013, p. 88 calculates that 10 percent of the variation is due to students' needs.

112 Education Act SFS 2010:800, 10 ch. 29§. Exemptions are possible under certain conditions.

113 Education Act SFS 2010:800, 10 ch. 30§.

114 An independent school can only apply admittance rules that are accepted by the Swedish Schools Inspectorate. Cf. Education Act (2010:800, 10 ch. 35–36§).

115 Within the municipality in which the student is registered.

116 Education Act SFS 2010:800, 10 ch. 40§.

117 SOU 2014:5, p. 17.

118 Skolverket 2014a, p. 17. For the preschool class, in 2012–13 the proportion of qualified teachers was "significantly lower" in private schools (p. 24).

119 Skolverket 2014a, p. 53.

120 Skolverket 2014a, p. 93; Skolverket 2014c, p. 29.

121 Skolverket 2014c, p. 15.

122 Skolverket 2014c, p. 17.

123 Skolverket 2014a, p. 33.

124 SOU 2014:5, p. 270; cf. Skolverket 2014a, p. 93.

125 In the Swedish context, urban or inner city schools usually equates to schools with higher proportions of students with stronger socio-economic backgrounds, the opposite counts for suburban and rural.

126 OECD 2014b, p. 42.

127 OECD 2011; OECD 2014a, OECD 2015.

128 OECD 2014a, p. 3.

129 OECD 2014a, pp. 6ff.

130 According to *Fakta om Friskolor* (p. 5) entrance salaries are slightly higher in private schools, but for experienced teachers they seem to be approximately 10 percent lower than in municipality schools. Cf. *Lärarnas Tidning,* February 15, 2013.

131 SOU 2013:56, p. 76.

132 Skolverket 2014b, p. 15.

133 Cf. Skolverket 2014a, p.30, 82; SOU 2013:56, p. 76. A recent change of legal definition of a "school unit" makes figures nowadays less comparable over time.

134 Cf. Government proposal 1990/91:18.

135 The Swedish National Agency for Education in 2014 published tentative information on aggregate levels, but unfortunately without distinction as to whether schools are public or private (http://www.skolverket.se/statistik-och-utvardering/nyhetsarkiv/2.8084/19-elever-per-klass-i-grundskolan-1.219495; personal communication with Christina Sandström at the agency (January 9, 2015)).

136 Skolverket 2014a, pp. 17, 24, 93.

137 Statskontoret 2013 (pp. 52ff) indicates that the ratio can differ from 6.1 up to 11.9 teachers per 100 students.

138 For-profit-run schools have 6.8 to 7.5 teachers per 100 students (lower rates in the largest schools) compared to 8.0 to 9.6 among non-profits (municipality schools range from 7.9 to 8.1) (Svensson 2010, p. 26).

139 Svensson and Wingborg 2015.

140 School authorities label this "program camouflage" and comment that it's not illegal, but not intended. *Dagens Nyheter,* March 29, 2015 (Friskolor tjänar miljoner på kryphål i lagen).

141 SOU 2014:5, p. 263. In 1990 there were 9.1 teachers per 100 students in grades 1–9. In 2000 it was down to 7.6 and in 2011 not higher than 8.3.

142 SOU 2014:5, p. 265. Since 1991 there has been a downturn from close to 95 percent to just slightly above 80 percent.

143 SOU 2014:5, pp. 268ff.

144 Lundahl, L. *et al.* (2005) p. 151.

145 Forsell and Ivarsson Westerberg 2014, pp. 154–158.

146 Lundahl, L. *et al.* (2013) summarize studies on school market affects on schools and teachers' work.

147 Lundström and Holm 2011. A study initiated by an association close to the business sector focused on the general consequences of competition in the Swedish welfare model (Hartman 2011). The study found a lack of evidence on advantages and progress through competition; nor had there been any significant cost reductions. Instead, there were indications of a lower level of education and formal training among staff, together with a lower density of staff etc. (Cf. Österberg and Andersson 2013, p. 479) The findings caused an intense debate that was fueled by an internal attempt to withhold the report. Cf. articles by Hanspers, Mörk and Vlachos (in Hartman 2011) that point toward insufficient evidence on progress but it is well known that private schooling has resulted in a change in teachers' roles: since these

schools have a higher number of students per teacher, they are incentivized toward economic efficiency via standardization.

148 Lundström and Holm 2011, p. 196.
149 Lundström and Holm 2011, p. 197. Cf. Fredriksson 2010, pp. 254ff.
150 These two rights (*meddelarfrihet* and *offentlighetsprincipen*) are regulated in the Constitution of Sweden (in: Tryckfrihetsförordningen 1949:105, 1 kap 1§ and 2 kap 1§). Only rarely can access be refused, as the main rule is that all documents are public. In addition, it is illegal for an employer to search for the identity of an anonymous whistleblower.
151 This issue has been subject to a governmental investigation (SOU 2013: 79).
152 Cf. Skolverket 2009b.
153 Skolverket 2012c, p. 9.
154 Skolverket 2014a, p. 41.
155 Cf. Lundahl, L. *et al.* 2013, p. 60 and their referenced studies.
156 Cf. Gustafsson et al. 2014, pp. 96, 103.
157 OECD 2014b, p. 187.
158 Skolverket 2014b, p. 79.
159 Skolverket 2013b, pp. 10–16. Cf. Skolverket 2009.
160 Skolverket 2013b, p. 8; cf. Gustafsson 2011.
161 OECD 2014a, p. 2. Cf. OECD 2015.
162 European Commission, COM 2014, p. 428.
163 Skolverket 2013a, p. 8. *PISA 2012. 15-åringars kunskaper i matematik, läsförståelse och naturvetenskap*. Skolverkets internationella studier, rapport nr 398, Stockholm.
164 SOU 1948:27, p. 3.
165 Böhlmark and Lindahl 2012 p. 42.
166 Cf. Syll 2013 and Bunar 2010.
167 Cf. Biesta (2010), p. 20.
168 Kornhall, 2012.
169 Kornhall, 2013 (my translation).
170 Cf. *Independent, December* 3, 2008. After the latest Swedish PISA scores were released, opposing politicians countered his argument with the Swedish example. *Dagens Nyheter*, December 4, 2013.
171 Wiborg 2010, p. 19.
172 Skolverket 2012a; OECD 2014a (cf. 2009a, 2009b). Educational inequality is, however, still comparatively low. Skolverket 2013b partly describes a positive turn.
173 OECD 2014a; OECD 2011.
174 SOU 2013:56. Cf. the English summary on pp. 21ff and also Engzell-Larsson 2013, pp. 104ff.
175 Björklund 2014; Emilsson 2014. On Emilsson's role, see Engzell-Larsson 2013, pp. 88, 105ff. On *Kunskapsskolan,* see SOU 2013:56, pp. 100ff and 180ff. Österberg and Andersson 2013, p. 292.
176 A Swedish institute (SOM-institutet) surveyed opinions on proposals to ban opportunities to profit in the welfare sector. On average, more than 50 percent favor such a regulation. (Nilsson 2012). According to *Dagens Nyheter* April 24 2014, new data from the same institute suggested that 70 percent of Swedes oppose for-profit companies in the welfare sector.

177 Cf. investigations: U 2015:01 (on upper secondary education), U 2015:02 (on national tests), U 2014:14 (on school costs), U 2014:12 (on transparency/the principle of public access to official records in private schools), U 2014:05 (on primary and lower secondary education) and Fi 2015:01 (on public financing of privately run welfare services) and related governmental directives.
178 Cf. Englund 1993.
179 Cf. Englund 2013, p. 38.
180 N.B.: On strategies to overcome resistance to radical change, political scientist P. Santesson points to strategies that achieve change by establishing a parallel system that co-exists with what the reformers aspire to change. Santesson 2012, p. 53. (Cf. "A form of disguise appears as a hallmark for the more difficult reform decisions.", ibid. p. 157). Cf. *Valfrihet i skolan,* p. 11. Neave 1985 draws attention to the fact that Germany, at the time, distinguished between non-state/non-governmental *substitute* schools and non-state/non-governmental *supplementary* schools and "financial assistance to the non-state sector is tied to the contribution it may make to the overall diversity and provision of the Land's educational resources". (p. 331) *Supplementary* schools represent a more traditional type of private school and in general were not eligible for public funding. A non-state school exists because the government did not have to run a school in that particular locality. It could receive subsidies as it was perceived to contribute as a *substitute* school. The German distinction differs significantly from the view detailed here but deals with similar issues regarding the function of non-governmental schools (cf. Campbell *et al.* 2009).
181 Husén 1979, p. 100.
182 Rothblatt 2003, p. 1.

References

Aftonbladet, May 18th 2011, Stoppa lycksökarna.
Alexiadou, N. (2013), Privatising public education across Europe – Shifting boundaries and the politics of (re)claiming schools, *Education Inquiry*, Vol. 4, No. 3, September 2013.
Ambler, J. S. (1994), Who Benefits from Educational Choice? Some Evidence from Europe, in Cohn, E. (1997). (ed), *Market Approaches to Education, Vouchers and School Choice*, Oxford: Elsevier Science, Pergamon.
Andersson, S. (1984), Det är skillnad på sophämtning och barnomsorg, in Küng, A. *Låt Pysslingen leva*, Stockholm: Timbro Förlag.
Arvidsson, S. (1962), anförande, i Riksdagens protokoll, År 1962, Andra kammaren, Fjärdebandet, nr 22, 22 maj.
Baggesen Klitgaard, M. (2007), Why are they doing it? Social democracy and market-oriented welfare state reforms. *West European Politics*, 30:1.
Berggren, H. (2010), *Underbara dagar framför oss. En biografi över Olof Palme*, Stockholm: Norstedts.
Biesta, Gert, J. J., (2010), *Good Education in an Age of Measurement: Ethics, Politics and Democracy*. Boulder: Paradigm Publishers.
Björklund, J. (2014), Skyll inte Pisa på det fria skolvalet, Svenska Dagbladet.
Böhlmark, A. and Lindahl, M. (2012), *Independent schools and long-run educational outcomes – evidence from Sweden's large scale voucher reform*, Institute for Evaluation of Labour Market and Educational Policy (IFAU), working paper 2012:19.

Bunar, N. (2010), Choosing for quality or inequality: current perspectives on the implementation of school choice policy in Sweden, *Journal of Education* Policy, vol. 25, no. 1, January.

Campbell, C., Proctor, H., and Sherington, G. (2009), *School Choice: How Parents Negotiate the New School Market in Australia*, Crows Nest: Allen & Unwin.

Carlbaum, S. (2014), Equivalence and performance gaps in Swedish school inspection: context and politics of blame, *Discourse: Studies in the Cultural Politics of Education*, July.

Dagens Nyheter, December 4, 2013, Brittisk debatt om svenska friskolor.

Dagens Nyheter, April 24, 2014, SOM: Sju av tio vill stoppa vinst i välfärden.

Dagens Nyheter, February 11, 2015, "Lönsamt – men lågt intresse för nya friskolor."

Economist, June 12, 2008, "The Swedish model".

Edenman (1962), anförande, i Riksdagens protokoll, År 1962, Andra kammaren, *Fjärdebandet*, nr 22, 22 maj.

Edvardsson, B. (2011), Kommentarer till de fyra fallstudierna med utgångspunkt i Tjänstelogiken, in Morin, A. (2011) (ed), *Vitsen med vinsten. Fyra exempel på företag inom vård och skola som genom hög effektivitet ger uthållig vinst.* Stockholm: Hjalmarson and Högberg Bokförlag, p. 68.

Ekonomifakta (2014), Web info, accessed September 15, 2014, at http://www.ekonomifakta. se/sv/Fakta/Valfarden-i-privat-regi/Skolan-i-privat-regi/Antal-friskolor-i-Sverige/

Ekvall, E. (1978), *De enskilda skolornas ställning inom utbildningsväsendet. Kartläggnings- och diskussionspromemoria.* Ds U 1978:6, Stockholm: Utbildningsdepartementet.

Emilsson, P. (2014), *Äventyra inte den unika rätten att själv få välja skola*, Dagens Nyheter, DN-debatt, 140622.

Englund, T. (1993), *Utbildning som "public good" eller "private good"? Svensk skola i omvandling*, Uppsala: Uppsala universitet.

Englund, T. (2013), Aktuella perspektiv på skolans medborgerliga skapande, in, Hartsmar, N. and Liljerfors Person, B. (2013), *Medborgerlig bildning. Demokrati och inkludering i ett hållbart samhälle*, Lund: Studentlitteratur.

Engzell-Larsson, L. (2013), *Finansfurstarna – berättelsen om de svenska riskkapitalisterna*, Stockholm: Weyler Bokförlag.

Erlander, T. (1973), *1940–1949*, Stockholm: Tidens Förlag.

Esping-Andersen, G. (1990), *The Three Worlds of Welfare Capitalism*, Princeton: Princeton University Press.

European Commission (2014), COM(2014) 428 final, Recommendation for a council recommendation on Sweden's 2014 national reform programme and delivering a Council opinion on Sweden's 2014 convergence programme, Brussels, 2.6.2014.

Forssell, A. (2011), *Skolan som politiskt narrativ. En studie av den skolpolitiska debatten i Sveriges riksdag 1991–2002*, Stockholm: Stockholms universitets förlag.

Forsell, A. and Ivarsson Westerberg, A. (2014), *Adminstrationssamhället*, Lund: Studentlitteratur.

Foss Hansen, NPM in Scandinavia, in Christensen, T. and Laegreid, P. (eds), (2011), *The Asgate Research Companion to New Public Management*, Burlington: Ashgate Publishing Company.

Fredriksson, A. (2010), *Marknaden och lärarna. Hur organisering av skolan påverkar lärares offentliga tjänstemannaskap*, Göteborg: Göteborgs universitet.

Friskolorna i siffror 2014, web info, accessed March 7, 2014, at http://www.friskola.se/ Om_friskolor_Friskolorna_i_siffror_DXNI-25907_.aspx

Gustafsson, J-E. (2011), Försämrade resultat och minskad likvärdighet, in Isaksson, C. (2011), *Kommunaliseringen av skolan, vem vann – egentligen?* Stockholm: Ekerlids Förlag.

Gustafsson, J-E., Cliffordson, C., and Ericson, G. (2014), Likvärdig kunskapsbedömning i och av den svenska skolan – problem och möjligheter, Stockholm: SNS Förlag.

Gustafsson, L. and Svensson, A. (1999), *Public Sector Reform in Sweden*, Malmö: Liber Ekonomi.

Hadenius, S. (2000), *Svensk politik under 1900-talet. Konflikt och samförstånd*. Stockholm: Hjalmarson and Högberg Bokförlag.

Hartman, L. (2011), (ed), *Konkurrensens konsekvenser. Vad händer med svensk välfärd?* Stockholm: SNS Förlag.

Hartman, S, (2005), *Det pedagogiska kulturarvet: Traditioner och idéer i svensk undervisningshistoria*, Stockholm: Natur and Kultur.

Hirdman, Y., Lundberg, U., and Björkman, J. (2012), *Norstedts Sveriges historia 1920-1965*, Stockholm: Norstedts.

Husén, T. (1972), *Skolans kris och andra uppsatser om utbildning*, Stockholm: Almqvist and Wiksell Förlag AB.

Husén, T. (1979), *The School in Question: A Comparative Study of the School and its Future in Western Societies*, Oxford: Oxford University Press.

Husén, T. (1988) *Skolreformerna och forskningen, psykologisk pedagogik under pionjäråren*, Stockholm: Verbum Gothia.

Husén, T. (1989), The Swedish School reform – exemplary both ways. *Comparative Education*, Vol. 24, No. 3.

Independent, December 3, 2008, Michael Gove: We need a Swedish education system.

Kornhall, P. (2012), Principen om en bra skola för alla gäller inte längre, *Dagens Nyheter*, DN-debatt, 120317.

Kornhall, P. (2013), *Barnexperimentet – svensk skola i fritt fall*, Stockholm: Leopard Förlag.

Küng, A. (1984), *Låt Pysslingen leva*, Stockholm: Timbro Förlag.

Lärarnas Tidning, (2013), *Lärare i friskolor har lägre löner*, February 15.

Lundahl, L. (2005), Swedish, European, global, *World Yearbook of Education 2005*, London: Routledge.

Lundahl, L. *et al.* (2013), Educational marketization the Swedish way, *Education Inquiry*, Vol. 4, No. 3, September.

Lundahl, L. *et al.* (2014), *Gymnasiet som marknad*, Umeå: Borea Bokförlag

Lundgren, U. P. (2010), En gemensam skola – utbildning blir en nödvändighet för alla, in Lundgren, U.P., Säljö, R., and Liberg, C. (eds), *Lärande, Skola, Bildning: Grundbok för lärare*. Stockholm: Natur and Kultur.

Lundström, U. and Holm, A-S. (2011), Market Competition in Upper Secondary Education: perceived effects on teachers' work, *Policy Futures in Education*, Vol. 9, No. 2.

Magnusson, L. (2006), *Håller den svenska modellen? Arbete och välfärd i en globaliserad värld*, Stockholm: Norstedts Akademiska Förlag.

Marklund, S. (1980), *Skolsverige 1950–75, 1. 1950 års reformbeslut*. Stockholm: Liber.

Marklund, S. (1982), *Skolsverige 1950–75, 2. Försöksverksamheten*, Stockholm: Liber.

Millares, M. (2012), Om offentligt och privat: I valet mellan välfärdsstat och välfärdssamhälle, *Statsvetenskaplig tidskrift*, Årgång 114, 2012/4.

Myrdal, A. and Myrdal, G. (1941) *Kontakt med Amerika*, Stockholm: Bonniers.

Neave, G. (1985), The non-state sector in education in Europe: a conceptual and historical analysis, *European Journal of Education*, Vol. 20, No. 4.

Nilsson, I. (1987), *En spjutspets mot framtiden – en analys av de svenska enhets- och grundskolereformerna i utländsk vetenskaplig litteratur 1950–1980*, Lunds universitet.

Nilsson, I. (1989), 'A Spearhead into the Future' – Swedish comprehensive school reforms in foreign scholarly literature 1950–80. *Comparative Education*, Vol. 25, No. 3.

Nilsson, L. (2012), Välfärdspolitik och välfärdsopinion 1986–2012. Vinster i välfärden? available at: http://www.som.gu.se/digitalAssets/1447/1447207_vinster-i-v--lf--rden.pdf).

Norberg, H. (2003). *Skolmisslyckande – hur gick det sen? Expertgruppen för studier i offentlig ekonomi (ESO)*, Stockholm: Finansdepartementet.

Norén, L. (2003), *Valfrihet till varje pris: om design av kundvalsmarknader inom skola och omsorg.* Göteborg: BAS.

OECD (2011), *Divided We Stand. Why Inequality Keeps Rising*, available at: http://dx.doi.org/10.1787/9789264119536-en

OECD (2014a) *Resources, Policies and Practices in Sweden's Schooling System: An in-depth analysis of PISA 2012 results.*

OECD (2014b), *TALIS 2013: Results: An International Perspective on Teaching and Learning*, available at: http://dx.doi.org/10.1787/9789264196261-en

OECD (2015), *Improving Schools in Sweden: An OECD Perspective.*

Olsson, G. (1962), anförande, i Riksdagens protokoll, År 1962, Andra kammaren, *Fjärdebandet*, nr 22, 22 maj.

Österberg, K. and Andersson, J. (2013), *Sveriges historia 1965–2012*, Stockholm: Norstedts.

Palme, O. (1967), Education and democracy, in *Skola i demokrati, TCOs utbildningsdagar 1967*, TCO.

Richardsson, G. (2010), *Svensk utbildningshistoria. Skola och samhälle förr och nu.* Lund: Studentlitteratur.

Riksdagens protokoll, 1989/90:42, band A5.

Ringarp, J. (2011), *Professionens problematik. Lärarkårens kommunalisering och välfärdsstatens förvandling.* Stockholm: Makadam Förlag.

Ringarp, J. (2012), The problem of the welfare profession: an example – the municipalisation of the teaching profession, *Policy Futures in Education*, Vol. 10, No. 3.

Rönnberg, L. (2011), Exploring the intersection of marketisation and central state control through Swedish national school inspection, *Education Inquiry*, Vol. 2, No. 4, December

Rothblatt, S. (2003), *The Living Arts: Comparative and Historical Reflections on Liberal Education*, Washington, D.C.: Association of American Colleges and Universities.

Santesson, P. (2012), *Reformpolitikens strategier*, Ratios samhällsvetenskapliga serie, Stockholm: Bokförlaget Atlantis.

Schön, L. (2000), *En modern svensk ekonomisk historia. Tillväxt och omvandling under två sekel*, Stockholm: SNS Förlag.

Siqueria, A. C. (2005), The regulation of education through the WTO/GATS, *Journal for Critical Educational Policy Studies*, Vol. 3, No. 1, March.

Skolinspektionen (2011a), *Avgifter i skolan*, Informationsblad, Skolinspektionen, 2011-12-07.

Skolinspektionen (2011b), *Kommunernas tillsyn av enskild verksamhet*, Dnr 2010:43.

Skolverket (1996) press release 1996-05-29 (refering to *Skolan i siffror 1996*, del 2).

Skolverket 2008, *Privat och offentligt*, Stockholm

Skolverket (2009a), *Skolverkets bild av utvecklingen av kunskapsresultaten i grundskolan och av elevers studiemiljö*, Redovisning av uppdrag att utarbeta ett sammanfattande underlag avseende utvecklingen av kunskapsresultaten i grundskolan, PM 2009-01-29, Dnr 2008:3010.

Skolverket (2009b), *Vad påverkar resultaten i svensk skola? Kunskapsöversikt om betydelsen av olika faktorer.* Stockholm.

Skolverket (2011), *Certification of teachers and preschool teachers.*

Skolverket (2012a), *Likvärdig utbildning i svensk skola? En kvantitativ analys av likvärdighet över tid*, Rapport 374.

Skolverket (2012b), *Mer om … avgifter i skolan*, Juridisk vägledning, febr 2012.

Skolverket (2012c), *Betygsinflation − betygen och den faktiska kunskapsutvecklingen*, PM 2012-03-29, Dnr 2012:387.

Skolverket (2013a), *Kommunernas resursfördelning till grundskolor*, Rapport 391.

Skolverket (2013b), *PISA 2012, 15-åringars kunskaper i matematik, läsförståelse och naturvetenskap*, Stockholm: Skolverket.

Skolverket (2014a), *Beskrivande data 2013. Förskola, skola och vuxenutbildning*, Rapport 399, Stockholm: Skolverket.

Skolverket (2014b), *TALIS 2013, En studie av undervisnings- och lärmiljöer i årskurs 7-9*, Internationella studier, Rapport 408, Stockholm: Skolverket.

Skolverket (2014c), *Redovisning av uppdrag om hur stor del av undervisningen som bedrivs av behöriga lärare*, Dnr 2014:00624.

Skolverket (2014d), *Privata aktörer inom förskola och skola. En nationell kartläggning av enskilda huvudmän och ägare*. Stockholm: Skolverket.

Skolverket (2014e), Riksprislista för ersättning till fristående skolor 2014, web info, accessed July 15th 2015.

Skolverket, *Val av skola. Reformen: historik, sammanhang och intentioner. Ett tioårigt perspektiv* (without date and publishing information).

SOU 1948:27, *1946 års Skolkommissions betänkande med förslag till riktlinjer för det svenska skolväsendets utveckling*, Stockholm.

SOU 1961:30, *Grundskolan*, Betänkande avgivet av 1957 års skolberedning.

SOU 1999:63, *Att lära och leda. En lärarutbildning för samverkan och utveckling.*

SOU 2013: 30, *Det tar tid - om effekter av skolpolitiska reformer*, Delbetänkande av Utredningen om förbättrade resultat i grundskolan, Stockholm.

SOU 2013:79, *Stärkt meddelarskydd för privatanställda i offentligt finansierad verksamhet*, Betänkande av Utredningen om meddelarskydd för privatanställda i offentligt finansierad verksamhet, Stockholm.

SOU 2013:56, *Friskolorna i samhället*, Betänkande av Friskolekommittén, Stockholm.

SOU 2014:5, *Staten får inte abdikera − om kommunaliseringen av den svenska skolan*, Betänkande av Utredningen om skolans kommunalisering, Statens offentliga utredningar 2014:5.

Spring, J. (1989), *The Sorting Machine Revisited National Educational Policy Since 1945*, New York: Longman.

Statskontoret (2013), *Resurserna i skolan*, Utredningen om utvärdering av effekterna av kommunaliseringen av skolväsendet (U 2012:09), Rapport 2013:10, Stockholm.

Svensson, S. (2010), *Perspektiv på skolan − Om det fria skolvalets effekter på skolans likvärdighet*, Stockholm: Lärarförbundet.

Svensson, S. and Wingborg, M. (2015), *Färre lärare ger vinsten*, Katalys, Rapport nr 13.

Syll, L. P. (2013), *Svenska Dagbladet ljuger om friskolorna*, blog post available at http://larspsyll.wordpress.com/2013/03/31/svenska-dagbladet-ljuger-om-friskolorna/

Valfrihet i skolan, Ds. 1992:115. Stockholm: Utbildningsdepartementet.

Vlachos, J. (2011), Friskolor i förändring, in Hartman, L. (2011), (ed), *Konkurrensens konsekvenser. Vad händer med svensk välfärd?* Stockholm: SNS Förlag.

Weijne, J. (1950), Särskilda utskottet 1950, Utlåtande i anledning av Kungl. Maj:ts proposition angående riktlinjer för det svenska skolväsendets utveckling jämte i ämnet väckta motioner, Särskilda utskottets utlåtande nr. 1.

Wiborg, S. (2010), *Swedish Free Schools − Do They Work?*, LLAKES Research Paper 18, Centre for Learning and Life Chances in Knowledge Economies and Societies, available at: http://www.llakes.org/wp-content/uploads/2010/09/Wiborg-online.pdf

Winberg, O. (2011), Privatundervisning, in, Larsson, E. and Westberg, J. (eds), *Utbildningshistoria – en introduktion*, Lund: Studentlitteratur.

Zajda, J. (2006) (ed), *Decentralisation and Privatisation in Education: The Role of the State*, Dordrecht: Springer.

Legislation and Governmental Propositions (Bills)

1949:105, Tryckfrihetsförordningen 1 kap 1§ and 2 kap 1§

1950:70, Kungl. Maj:ts proposition till riksdagen angående riktlinjer för det svenska skolväsendets utveckling: given Stockholms slott den 3 februari 1950, No. 70, bihang till Riksdagens protokoll vid 1950 års riksdag, första samlingen, sjätte bandet.

1962:54, Kungl. Maj:ts proposition till riskdagen angående reformering av den obligatoriska skolan m.m.; given Stockholms slott den 23 februari 1962.

1988/89:4, Om skolans utveckling och styrning.

1988/89:150, Förslag till slutlig reglering av statsbudgeten för budgetåret 1989/90, m.m.

1989/90:41, Om kommunalt huvudmannaskap för lärare, skolledare, biträdande skolledare och syofunktionärer.

1990/91:18, Om ansvaret för skolan.

1991/92:95, Om valfrihet och fristående skolor.

1992/93:230, Valfrihet i skolan.

SFS 1949:105 Freedom of the Press Act.

SFS 2010:800, Education Act.

SKOLFS 2011:154, Ordinance on accreditation as independent school responsible person/owner.

5

THE FINNISH PARADOX

Equitable Public Education Within a Competitive Market Economy

Pasi Sahlberg

Against all expectations, Finland topped the world in the Program for International Student Assessment (PISA) in 2001. Before then, Finnish education was known for its strong focus on early literacy—Finland's 10-year-olds were the best readers in the world in their age group.[1] In domains like math and science, Finnish performance was near the international average in the first and second rounds of IEA (International Association for the Evaluation of Educational Outcomes) mathematics and science studies in the 1970s and 1980s. Because of this mediocre status internationally, information about Finland rarely appeared in any educational journals or books. Even the Finns themselves didn't pay too much attention to research or write about their own education system. The rest of the world was much more appealing to many educators and policymakers.

Those interested in finding out what made Finland's schools so successful soon realized that this Nordic country's top performance was only part of the eventual surprise. The emerging image of the Finnish education system didn't quite fit with anything that other countries had been doing with their education policies and reforms. Finland didn't seem to believe that standardization of teaching and learning was a smart way to improve the quality of schools. It didn't follow most other countries that developed national testing and examination systems for closer monitoring of students', teachers' and schools' performance. Furthermore, the Finns were not convinced of the necessity for private providers to own and run schools in order to have diversity, innovation, and choice in education. Most importantly, Finland seems to remain immune to many aspects of market-based education policies, including charter schools, free schools, or privately governed schools.

For some, education in Finland is a utopia, a dreamland where teaching is the most desired profession, authorities trust schools, and political parties agree on the direction of educational reforms. Then there are those such as Fareed Zakaria on CNN who view Finland as the education world's ultimate slacker. Children don't start school until they are seven years old. They have less homework than others. And Finland has only one external standardized test, administered in the final year of upper-secondary school.

This chapter describes how market forces and globalization have shaped the Finnish education system. Unlike much of the rest of the world, Finland has managed parental choice of schools, keeps tight control of who can own or run a school, does not allow individuals, foundations, or corporations to donate private money to schools, and has kept competition between schools at the level of friendly rivalry. What follows first is a brief illustration of social, economic, and political contexts in Finland, then a description of the Global Education Reform Movement and how Finland's education system operates in contrast to it. Finally, the chapter outlines the main education policies, reforms, and practices in Finland; how these public investment strategies differ from those of privatization of education; and how Finland's consistently high performance on international tests has silenced the critics of its approach to education.

Social, Economic, and Political Context

Finland, together with its western neighbor Sweden, is the northernmost member of the European Union. In order to understand education or any other aspect of Finland requires studying how social, cultural, political, and economic aspects have been interconnected to one another and to education. In 1968, Finland chose its place is the western world through membership in the Organization for Economic Cooperation and Development (OECD), followed by joining the European Union in 1995, and in 2002 adopting the euro as its currency, the only Nordic country to do so. Finland's social values are closely linked to those in the other Nordic countries—democracy, equality, social justice, and peace—and its economy depends on exports to the rest of Europe and to the Russian Federation.

Response to Economic Crises

The serious economic recession of the early 1990s caused some major shifts in Finland, leading to exceptional economic growth (until the global financial crisis in 2008). In the first half of the 1990s, the country suffered a severe economic decline characterized by a major banking crisis. The unemployment rate exploded from 4 percent to 18 percent and public debt soared to over 60 percent of GDP, putting Finland close to international lending limits.[2] For the Finnish economy to recover, the country had to diversify its export structures, encourage business innovation, and also open its traditionally publicly provided services for citizens to private operators. Private healthcare services became available for those who preferred (and could afford) more personalized and speedy health or dental services. The national postal service, the railway system, and many government-owned properties were partly or completely privatized. However, the education system remained untouched by private markets partly because it is protected by constitutional law. Fee-based educational services were only possible in early childhood where parents have to co-pay, based on their wealth, to top up the publicly paid cost of these services. The development of Finland's economy in general and the education sector in particular has had common features, including the emergence of new knowledge-based industries and the necessity to enhance productivity in Finland's relatively large public sector.

As a result of these recession-driven bold changes in economic and education policies in the 1990s, Finland has ever since been ranked as one of the most competitive market economies in the world. In the early years of the third millennium, the World Economic Forum (WEF) ranked the Finnish economy as the most competitive in the world. Transparency International (TI), that estimates the level of good governance, found Finland one of the least corrupt countries in the world. The Organisation for Economic Cooperation and Development (OECD) with its new school education quality yardstick called PISA placed the Finnish education system ahead of all others among the most developed nations. The country boasts a very high level of human capital, widespread use of information and communication technologies, and education and research institutions redesigned to foster innovation and cutting-edge research and development. Indeed, Finland also ranks at the top in the advancement of global information and communication technologies as well as in innovation (by WEF), prosperity (by Legatum Institute in London), and sustainable economic competitiveness (by WEF). Another important indication that Finnish society and its democratic system function well is Finland's steady top position as one of the most gender-equal countries in the world (by OECD and WEF).

Interest in The Finnish Education Model

Before Finland's success on PISA, there was very little interest outside Finland in the Finnish education system. Since then, however, Finland's education system has drawn a stream of international dignitaries, scholars, and other "educational pilgrims" for a firsthand look. They have found a few important ingredients: namely, stakeholder consideration; long-term integrated planning; flexibility; and investment in public institutions. Finland's economic and educational achievements show that a relatively small, peripheral country can transform its economy and education system into a society that is a showcase for innovation.

Beginning in the 1970s, Finland launched reforms to equalize educational opportunity by eliminating the practice of separating students into very different tracks based on their test scores by eliminating the examinations previously used to enforce this tracked approach. This shift occurred gradually starting in 1972 and was completed in 1978, resulting in a common curriculum throughout the entire system through to the end of high school. These changes were intended to equalize access to good education, raise educational outcomes, and provide more open access to secondary and later to higher education.[3] During this time, social supports for children and families were also enacted, including health and dental care provided in schools, preventive special education services, and transportation to schools.

By the late 1970s, Finland began an additional focus on investment in teachers, improving and extending teacher education. Policymakers concluded that if they invested in very skillful teachers, all schools would be better prepared to teach more diverse groups of children and find ways to help most pupils to succeed in school. These investments included expectations that teachers would move from a three-year teacher training program to five-year academic programs of study. Teaching higher-order skills like problem-solving and critical thinking became essential elements in research-based masters degree programs in Finnish universities offering teacher training degrees.

Finland's focus on equity through eliminating tracking in the 1970s, increased investments in teachers (described below), and allowing autonomous decision-making by skilled educators set the stage for education during Finland's post-recession growth period.

All Stakeholders Considered

There are some interesting parallels between education and economic policies in Finland during the 1990s growth period. First, both education and economic development were based on a long-term vision of future prospects and needs of all stakeholders in the society.[4] This vision sprang from a broad consensus between government, the private sector, labor unions, and educators. Its sustainability was supported by specific institutions, such as the Committee of the Future, the Parliamentary Education Committee, and several think tanks created jointly by industrial employers, public-sector administration, and labor unions.

Five-Year Plans

Second, both education and economic development have been guided by integrated policies. Education policy has been articulated through five-year development plans that cover all the education and research sectors.[5] These plans formed a bridge between the political mandates of outgoing and newly elected governments; hence, they became key instruments in creating sustainable political leadership in education. Economic development policies and strategies have integrated science and technology with both industry and education sectors.

Flexible and Decentralized

Third, both education and economic sectors have adopted flexible and decentralized models of accountability. In education development, this means that Finland never followed global reform trends by introducing strong measurement and testing structures for schools and teachers. In Finnish schools, accountability is spread throughout the system and is based on development-oriented sample-based external assessments and in-school self-evaluations. Assessment mechanisms are flexible—often they are created by the teachers who administer them—and no high-stakes standardized tests are used except for the Matriculation Examination at the end of upper-secondary school. Similarly, economic development has included internal, collective accountability, management, and leadership.

In the context of this book, it is important to differentiate between the Finnish version of decentralization and the decentralization encouraged by GERM proponents. Finland invests heavily in the preparation and professionalization of its teachers. This investment in turn promotes trust from the public and the government that teachers are capably instructing students. The privatization version of decentralization gives private operators control over decisions too, but privatization allows and actually encourages inexperienced teachers to enter the classroom (because they are cheaper). The privatization approach then attempts to determine if teachers can do their job using high-stakes, often multiple-choice, exams. In the case of Finland, the country knows its teachers are good because it invests in them throughout their careers, while producing the additional outcome that Finnish students perform exceptionally well on international assessments like PISA.

Reliance on Public Institutions

Fourth, both education and economic development have relied heavily on trust in public institutions that often are the leading partners in planning and setting policy. The high caliber of public institutions, deep cultural respect for the law, and practically nonexistent corruption has promoted the creation of consensus-building mechanisms. These crucial features bring the public and private sectors together to develop sound education and economic strategies. Policy development and reform principles have traditionally built upon the expertise of local players, whose experience, opinions, and abilities allow them to indicate the best ways forward.

For the purposes of this book it is interesting to see if Finland's education system has adopted any of the market-based models that have become increasingly common in other social services sectors in Finland, especially in health care. Some Finnish scholars have argued that Finland has been actively following the OECD's policy recommendations and that the ideologies of New Public Management in the 1990s found a fertile soil in Finland.[6] New terminology entered into Finnish public-sector policies at that time: results-based management models, performance bonuses to effective employers, public accountability and efficiency all became buzz words in public institutions' strategies and operational manuals.

At that same time, schools in Finland were in the midst of radical transformation from earlier top-down management to locally led, autonomous units under local governance. Educators in Finland were very skeptical about accepting that management models from the free market world would work in this new educational landscape. Education was characterized more by humanistic values, teacher professionalism, and educational leadership, all of which became pointers of success in this new era of educational management. Finland also examined from a distance the early signals from neighboring Sweden, which had introduced a voucher system allowing parents, interest groups, and also private companies to establish schools. As with earlier education and social reforms, the Finns wanted to see whether their western friends succeeded with their school reform before deciding whether to follow them or try to find another way.

Finland had one advantage over many other countries at that time: the new Finnish curriculum system that was introduced in the mid-1990s gave significantly more freedom to the municipalities who owned most of the schools. More significantly, this new era brought autonomy to schools, giving them the opportunity to design their own curricula and devise learning environments to serve all students better than before. Flexibility soon became the new norm in the Finnish education system. Finnish schools no longer needed to ask for permission to deviate from general regulations if they wanted to profile their teaching in a new way. In many cases schools designed their curricula and set the values, purposes, and visions based on the needs and expectations of their local community. Parents rarely felt that their neighborhood school was not good enough for their children and there was practically no need for any alternative schools or programs. Similarly, the private sector underwent deregulations and more flexible standards were introduced to foster networking between firms, universities, and public research and development institutions.

The recent political and economic history of Finland is characterized by close coordination and communication between the government, employers, and workers. This tripartite principle traditionally also has linked education to the interests of employers and labor confederations. From policy decisions to the implementation of reforms and supporting change in schools and classrooms, these three parties have been working in close cooperation to secure good and meaningful education for all citizens since the 1960s. Today, the Confederation of Finnish Industries continues to play an active role in providing resources to school–industry partnerships, taking part in the national policy dialog and guiding its members in putting jointly made decisions into practice.

All these developments in the Finnish education system since the 1990s raise the question of why privatization of education never became part of Finnish education policy as it did in many other countries through vouchers, charter schools, and expanding private schools. Overall, the main principles of Finnish education policy have not varied much since the early 1970s, when the equity-based education policy became a leading development principle. Although Finland has a multi-party system and coalition governments that typically consist of three to six political parties, education has rarely been a bone of contention in a new government's programs. The main disputes that have arisen over the years are all related to schedule and choice, such as the time allotted to different subjects taught in school, or the extent to which pupils and parents should have the freedom to choose their study programs and the obligatory role of certain subjects in the curriculum, namely Swedish language and religious education. But Finland has had a wide consensus on increasing technology, environmental sciences, and entrepreneurship education in schools—all of which seem to contribute positively to economic development and growth. At the same time Finnish school policies have remained immune to the Global Education Reform Movement, or GERM, that has been increasingly common around the world.

Global Education Reform Movement

The idea of the Global Education Reform Movement, or GERM, evolved from the international exchange of education policies and "best practices" between education systems. GERM is not a formal global policy program but an unofficial educational agenda that relies on a certain set of assumptions that are used as education reform principles to improve quality and overall performance in education.[7] As discussed in the introduction, the seeds of GERM were planted in the 1980s and it has gained strength from globalization and economic liberalization around the world. GERM has become accepted as "a new educational orthodoxy" among international development agencies, consulting firms, and private philanthropists. As a consequence it has shaped many recent education reforms throughout the world, including those in the United States, Australia, England, many parts of Latin America, some Scandinavian countries, and an increasing number of countries in the developing world.

Increasing Competition Over Enrollment

Since the 1980s, at least five common features of education policies and reform principles have been employed globally in attempts to improve the quality of education, especially in terms of raising student achievement. The first is increasing *competition over enrollment* among schools. Almost all education systems have introduced alternative forms of schooling to offer parents more *choice* regarding their children's schooling.[8] The voucher system in Chile in the 1980s, Free Schools in Sweden in the 1990s, Charter Schools in the United States in the 2000s, and secondary Academies in England in the 2010s are examples of faith in private markets and competition as an engine of betterment of education.

At the same time, the proportion of more advantaged students studying in private schools or independent schools has grown.[9] In Australia, for example, nearly every third primary and secondary school student studies in non-governmental schools that are often private schools.[10] Ranking schools based on their performance on national standardized assessments have further increased competition between schools. OECD data show that according to school principals across OECD countries, more than three-quarters of the students assessed by PISA attend schools that compete with at least one other school for enrollment.[11] Finally, students—especially in many Asian countries—experience stronger pressure to perform better against their peers due to tough competition for entry into the best high schools and universities.[12]

Standardization in Education

The second is *standardization* in education. Outcomes-based education reform became popular in the 1980s, followed by standards-based education policies in the 1990s, initially within Anglo-Saxon countries. These reforms, quite correctly, shifted the focus of attention to educational outcomes—that is, to student learning and school performance. Consequently, a widely accepted and generally unquestioned belief among policymakers and education reformers is that setting clear and sufficiently high performance standards for schools, teachers, and students will necessarily improve the quality of desired outcomes. The enforcement of external standardized testing and school evaluation systems to judge how these standards have been attained emerged originally from these standards-driven education policies. Standardization draws on the assumption that all students should be educated to the same, ambitious learning targets. This notion, in turn, has led to the prevalence of prescribed curricula and homogenization of curriculum policies worldwide. The National Curriculum in England in the 1990s, the New National Education Standards in Germany in the 2010s, and the Common Core State Standards in the United States are examples of attempts to bring coherence and quality to teaching and learning in all schools.

Focus on Literacy and Numeracy

The third common feature of the global education reform movement is *focus on core subjects* in the curriculum, such as literacy and numeracy. Basic student knowledge and skills in reading, writing, mathematics, and natural sciences are elevated as prime targets and indices of education reforms. Due to the acceptance of international student assessments such as OECD's PISA and IEA's TIMSS and PIRLS as metrics of educational performance, these core subjects have now come to dominate what pupils study, teachers teach, schools emphasize, and national education policies prioritize in most parts of the world. According to the OECD and research in a number of countries, national education policies are increasingly being influenced by the international student assessments, especially PISA.[13] It seems like there is more competition now also between countries in terms of who will reach the top rankings in the international student assessments.

Literacy and numeracy strategies that increased instruction time for so-called core subjects in England and Ontario are concrete programmatic examples of the Global Education Reform Movement. In the United States, the No Child Left Behind legislation led most school districts to steal teaching time from other subjects—especially from social studies, arts, and music—and playtime from children by abolishing recess in many schools so students would be better prepared for state tests that measured student performance in literacy and mathematics.[14] Many privately operated schools in the United States, England, and in the Middle East have seen a business opportunity in providing academically rigorous and behaviorally disciplined schools. At the same time, however, to be successful in life and employment requires young people who are curious, who know how to work with other people, who can solve difficult problems, and who master leadership.

Test-based Accountability

The fourth characteristic is *test-based accountability*—holding teachers and schools accountable for students' achievement through external standardized tests. School performance—especially raising students' test scores—is intimately tied to the processes of evaluating, inspecting, and rewarding or punishing schools and teachers. Performance-based pay, data walls in teachers' lounges, and school rankings in newspapers are examples of new accountability mechanisms that often draw their data primarily from external standardized student tests and teacher evaluations. The problem with test-based accountability is not that students, teachers, and schools are held accountable, but rather the way accountability mechanisms affect teachers' work and students' studying in school. Whenever school accountability relies on poor-quality and low-cost standardized tests, as is the case in many places, accountability becomes what is left when responsibility is subtracted.

School Choice

The fifth globally observable trend in educational reform is increased *school choice*. Parental choice is an idea that became commonly known as a consequence of Milton Friedman's economic theories in the 1950s. Friedman and many of his disciples and advisees—including president Ronald Reagan—state that parents must be given the freedom to choose their children's education and thereby to encourage healthy competition among schools so that they better serve families' diverse needs. Typically, school choice manifests itself through the emergence of private schools where parents pay tuition for their children's education. Today, there are scores of various types of alternative schools other than fee-based private schools to expand choice in education markets. Charter schools in the United States, Free schools in Sweden, upper-secondary school academies in England, and religious schools in the Netherlands are examples of mechanisms to advance parental choice. School choice ideology maintains that parents should be able to use the public funds set aside for their children's education to choose the schools—public or private—that work best for them.

None of the elements of GERM shown in Table 5.1 have been adopted in Finland in the ways that they have been within the education policies of many other nations. This, of course, does not imply that there is no educational standardization, learning of basic skills, or accountability in Finnish schools. Nor does it suggest that there is a black-and-white distinction between each of these elements in Finland and other countries. But, perhaps, it does imply that a good education system can be created using alternative policies that are the opposite of those commonly found and promoted in global education policy markets.

The GERM has often strengthened the tendency to increase privatization of public education. The most notable impact is through a focus on school choice and competition that in most cases is facilitated by inviting private providers to run schools alongside public schools. Business-like consequential accountability has, in many places, led to closing down schools or handing them over to private operators as a consequence of poorer than expected test scores in standardized tests. New forms of student assessments and testing that have been aligned to national standards are often disappointing and even bring new problems to schools. However, because the standardization agenda promises significant gains in efficiency and quality of education, it has been widely accepted as a basic ideology of change, both politically and professionally.

TABLE 5.1 Global Education Reform Movement and the Finnish Model of Educational Change

Global Education Reform Movement (GERM)	The Finnish Model
Competition between schools The basic assumption is that competition works as a market mechanism that will eventually enhance quality, productivity, and efficiency of service. When public schools compete over enrollment with charter schools, free schools, independent schools, and private schools, they will eventually improve teaching and learning.	*Collaboration among schools* The basic assumption is that educating people is a collaborative process and that cooperation, networking, and sharing ideas among schools will eventually raise the quality of education. When schools collaborate, they help one another and help teachers create a culture of cooperation in their classrooms.
Standardized learning Setting clear, high, and centrally prescribed performance targets for all schools, teachers, and students to improve the quality and equity of outcomes. This leads to standardized teaching through externally designed curricula to ensure coherence and common criteria for measurement and data.	*Personalized learning* Setting a clear but flexible national framework for school-based curriculum planning. Encouraging school-based and individual solutions to national goals in order to find the best ways to create personalized learning opportunities for all. Using individualized learning plans for those who have special educational needs.

TABLE 5.1 *Continued*

Global Education Reform Movement (GERM)	The Finnish Model
Focus on literacy and numeracy Basic knowledge and skills in reading, writing, mathematics, and the natural sciences serve as prime targets of education reform. Normally instruction time for these subjects is increased at the expense of other subjects (such as arts and music).	*Focus on whole child development* Teaching and learning focus on developing the whole child, giving equal value to all aspects of the growth of an individual's personality, moral character, creativity, knowledge, ethics, and skills. Instruction time and resources are evenly distributed to different areas in the curriculum.
Test-based accountability School performance and raising student achievement are closely tied to processes of promotion, inspection, and ultimately rewarding schools and teachers. Teachers' pay and the school budget are determined by students' test scores. Sanctions often include terminating employment or closing down the school. Census-based student assessment and data are used to inform policymaking.	*Trust-based responsibility* Gradually building a culture of responsibility and trust within the education system that values teacher and principal professionalism in judging what is best for students. Targeting resources and support to schools and students who are at risk of failing or being left behind. Sample-based student assessments and thematic research are used to inform policymaking.
School choice Basic premise is that parents must be given the freedom to choose their children's education, while encouraging healthy competition among schools to better serve families' needs. Ideally, parents should be able to use the public funds set aside for their children's education to choose the schools—public or private—that work best for them.	*Equity of outcomes* Basic premise is that all children should have equal prospects for educational success in school. Because school learning is strongly influenced by children's family background and associated factors, equity of outcomes requires that schools are funded according to their real needs to cope with these inequalities. School choice often leads to segregation that increases inequity of outcomes.

Public Investment in Teachers

One major difference between the Finnish model and the GERM is Finland's focus on investing in a highly professionalized teacher labor force. Among young Finns, in opinion polls of high school graduates in 2004[15] teaching was rated the most admired profession and primary school teacher education has also recently been regarded as an attractive option.[16] Becoming a primary school teacher in Finland is a very competitive process. Only Finland's best and most committed are able to fulfill those professional dreams. Every spring, thousands of high school graduates submit their applications to the departments of teacher education in Finnish universities. Usually it is not enough to complete high school and pass a rigorous matriculation examination. Successful candidates must have excellent interpersonal skills and a deep personal commitment to teach and work in schools for life. Annually only about one in every ten applicants will be accepted to study to become a primary school teacher; among all categories of teacher education, about 5,000 teachers are selected from about 20,000 applicants.

Wages are not the main reason young people become teachers in Finland. Teachers earn very close to the national average salary level, typically equivalent to what mid-career, middle school teachers earn annually in the OECD nations—about US$42,600.[17] More important than salaries are such factors as high social prestige, professional autonomy in schools, and the ethos of teaching as a service to society and the public good. Thus, young Finns see teaching as a career on a par with other professions where people work independently and rely on scientific knowledge and skills that they gained through university studies.

All teachers in Finnish primary, junior high, and high schools must hold a master's degree; preschool and kindergarten teachers must hold a bachelor's degree. There are no alternative ways to receive a teacher's diploma in Finland; the university degree constitutes a license to teach. Primary school teachers major in education, while upper-grade teachers concentrate their studies in a particular subject, e.g., mathematics, as well as didactics, consisting of pedagogical content knowledge specific to that subject.

Teacher education is based on a combination of research, practice, and reflection, meaning that it must be supported by scientific knowledge and focus on thinking processes and cognitive skills used in conducting research. In addition to studying educational theory, content, and subject-specific pedagogy, each student completes a master's thesis on a topic relevant to educational practice. Successful completion of a master's degree in teaching (including a bachelor's degree) generally takes five to seven and a half years, depending on the field of study.[18]

In Finland, as in other high-performing nations, schools provide time for regular collaboration among teachers on issues of instruction. Teachers in Finnish schools normally meet at least one afternoon each week to jointly plan and develop curriculum, and schools in the same municipality are encouraged to work together to share materials. Time is also provided for professional development within the teachers' working schedule.[19]

The focus on instruction and the development of professional practice in Finland's approach to organizing the education system has led, according to some reports, to an increased prevalence of effective teaching methods in schools. A Finnish official noted this about teaching in Finland:

> Empowerment of the teaching profession produces good results. Professional teachers should have space for innovation, because they should try to find new ways to improve learning. Teachers should not be seen as technicians whose work is to implement strictly dictated syllabi, but rather as professionals who know how to improve learning for all. All this creates

a big challenge ... that certainly calls for changes in teacher education programs. Teachers are ranked highest in importance, because educational systems work through them.[20]

This primary focus on teachers to create equity in Finland's education system has worked well, but has also required a strong set of principles in place regarding the organization, governance, and funding of schools.

Governance and Funding of Finnish schools

While maintaining its focus on equity, the Finnish education system has evolved since the 1970s. However, these changes remain rooted in public investment and collaboration instead of privatization and competition and serve as an international example for improving education by investing in teachers and local capacity. Until 1990, education management was centralized, with strong roles given to the two National Boards for general and vocational education, and to the Ministry of Education and Culture. The 1990s saw a transformation of public administration and a new structural and legal framework of education administration that shifted much of the authority to the municipalities and to schools.

A new central agency, the National Board of Education, replaced the two National Boards and now takes care of curriculum development and evaluation of education, providing professional support services to schools and teachers. The Ministry of Education and Culture is in charge of policy, the legislative framework, and financing of education. At the same time, regional administration lost much of its authority and, as a result, provinces have only a limited role in current education management, with more responsibility moving to the local municipal level.

Key Role of Local Authorities

One key to understanding education in Finland is the role of local municipal authorities and school principals in planning, implementing, and evaluating education. Finnish municipalities vary in size, averaging about 12,000 inhabitants. Most are tiny hamlets and cannot organize all municipal services for their citizens by themselves, so many join together to form federations. Finland had 455 municipalities in 1995, a figure reduced to 317 by 2015, further pressured by Finland's aging population and the exodus of people from rural municipalities. At the same time as the consolidation of municipalities, regulatory and fiscal reform in the 1990s have made them fairly autonomous in arranging their public services, including education.

Although there is notable variation in the ways local education management is arranged in Finland, in most cases it is the municipality or the federation of municipal education institutions that oversees education sector development. Municipalities now receive a lump sum subsidy from central government to provide all required public services to citizens as stipulated in laws and related government programs. This light structure of education management across many municipalities means that local leadership and management become key players in developing and maintaining the quality of education. Since education funds no longer are centrally earmarked, local political bodies and authorities make all operational decisions concerning schools independently from the government. Local political councils also now make the final decisions on how much they allocate to education and other public services in their yearly budgets. This organizational approach turns the management and leadership skills of local officials and school principals into the most important component of providing good education.

The role of school principals also has dramatically changed since the 1990s. Principals are not only the educational leaders of their schools but managers who are responsible for financing, personnel, and the overall performance of their schools. However, school leadership in Finland has kept its strong focus on pedagogical leadership regardless of the increasing amount of time required for managerial duties. Previously, a school principal was an experienced, senior teacher who was promoted for good service to education. Today's school principal must be a qualified leader (and teacher) who understands education development and has solid management skills to lead a school. Selection of new school principals is often based on procedures that assess candidates' personality and leadership skills using interviews and psychological tests to confirm the suitability of the candidate. The top requirement for the position of principal is their credentials within education, including teacher education, teaching experience, and leadership in school.

School Funding

Finland's Constitution stipulates that everyone has the right to formal education free of charge. All schools in Finland are therefore publicly funded, including about 75 "independent" schools that operate under specific licenses issued and funded by the government. These independent schools include religious schools, Rudolf Steiner schools, various language schools (e.g. English School, Deutsche Schule, Finnish-Russian School, and Finnish-French School), and teacher training schools attached to the universities that offer teacher education degrees. All these schools operate within normal public school networks. Importantly, privately governed educational institutions are prohibited from collecting student fees for tuition, ensuring that education resources are not unfairly distributed, creating inequities in access and quality. The state subsidy system underwent a complete overhaul in the early 1990s to calculate funding on a per-person basis, described below. The timing of the funding reform was fortunate because it fell during the recession and encouraged vocational upper-secondary schools to increase the number of students and to fill classes with motivated students. Thus, the vocational education system was able to accommodate increasing numbers of students without having to increase total expenditure.

It is noteworthy that vocational upper-secondary education has become a popular and also competitive educational choice for Finnish students when they decide how to continue their studies after completing compulsory education at age 16. Before the 1990s, these vocational schools were often second or last choices for youth who failed to find a place in general upper-secondary schools. Today, the majority of students in Finnish vocational upper-secondary schools attend because they've made that decision. Municipalities (or sometimes clusters of local governments) that provide all pre-university education in Finland must guarantee a study place to all 16-year-olds, ideally based on students' own preference. Educational programs in upper-secondary schools must be organized in a way that allows students to move between the two upper-secondary sectors. Equity in upper-secondary education is achieved through systematic career guidance, equal access to good schools, and inclusive education with support to those students who have special educational needs. Technically, some vocational education institutions in Finland are owned by private entities that operate under the ownership and management of municipalities or clusters of municipalities.

Municipalities and the state jointly fund the compulsory nine-year basic education in Finland. State subsidies to municipal education systems are calculated using a formula adjusted by local circumstances, such as population density, Finnish-Swedish speakers, number of islands (there are almost 80,000 islands in Finnish archipelagos in the Baltic Sea), the number of students in special education, and the number of 13–15-year-olds. The result is an estimate of municipal education expenditure based on the average spending of all municipalities. From this gross amount, a deduction is made based on the municipality's population and a per-inhabitant sum. As a consequence of the per-capita system, state money follows the pupils (not the schools) at a state-defined unit price. Some voucher proponents in the GERM model advocate money following the students, but the Finnish plan differs because it uses an equity-based formula to distribute resources, and private subsidies are not allowed to destabilize resource allocation.

The main principles of the state subsidy system are trust in the capability of municipalities and guaranteed free movement of students around the country. In reforming the state subsidy systems, part of the funding authority was transferred from the sector ministries to the Ministry of Internal Affairs, which is responsible for municipal administration. The Ministry of Internal Affairs grants general subsidies to the municipalities to level the playing field between areas with widely varying tax bases and other wealth. The formula-based budgeting reduces subsidies to municipalities with high local income and increases subsidies for poor ones.

This financing procedure has increased efficiency in the education system when schools get monetary incentives based on how many students graduate, not just based on enrollment. At the very least, it encourages local governments and upper-secondary school principals to design services and support mechanisms in their schools that help as many students as possible to finish school successfully. The local governments receive the per-student state subsidy as a gross amount, without the deduction for the municipal share of funding. These subsidies are not earmarked, leaving it up to the owner of the educational institutions to allocate the budget to the different schools and programs as appropriate. Independent schools receive their income directly from the state budget that is normally based on per-pupil expenditure deducted by a small coefficient that means that these schools must provide educational services cheaper (per student) than other schools.

More recently, policymakers have examined ways to link education funding to schools' performance. From 2002 to 2005, a small portion of vocational-education money was distributed to schools that had shown improvement on such indicators as the employability of their graduates, placement of graduates in the next level of education, dropout rate, proportion of qualified teachers and investment in staff training. This result-based funding is still limited—just 2 percent of total education spending. But it nevertheless has created a potentially powerful way to focus on—and achieve—the government's goals for improving education. This system was made permanent in 2006 and is about to be extended to other upper–secondary schools in coming years.

Nationally, Finland does not outspend other industrialized countries, allocating about the average of its national wealth that is spent in OECD countries overall, some 6.5 percent of GDP in 2012 (OECD, 2014). Just about 2.5 percent of all education (including higher education) expenditure is from the private pockets of families (e.g. textbooks at upper-secondary level), although none is allowed from private corporations or foundations.

UnFinnished Business: School Markets and Privatization

Finland's educational saga is not only about how it has managed to achieve internationally high student learning and systemwide equity but also how the Finnish education system has remained uninfected by the Global Education Reform Movement (GERM). It would be a mistake to think that the evolution of Finland's current education system has always been smooth and without criticism. There are moments in its history that could have evolved in the direction of more market-based education policies and the gradual privatization of public education would have become a real alternative.

New Comprehensive School Structure

In the 1970s, when the new comprehensive school structures and philosopies were implemented, many of the previously privately owned or governed grammar schools were amalgamated into the public school network. This new system insisted that all children should go to similar schools with equal educational expectations for all children, who were taught in socially mixed classrooms. Although this bold educational reform had enough political support, some thought that this restructuring was not only a bad idea but also unrealistic in terms of expecting that all children can learn to the same objectives.

The campaign against Finland's new comprehensive school was particularly harsh from certain politicians and part of the business community. Finnish business leaders closely followed the way this new school system was implemented. When most of the private schools lost their identity and became part of the public school systems in the municipalities, all school fees that parents had had to pay were also abolished. The Finnish Business and Policy Forum, a policy and pro-market think tank, gave funding to a foundation that opposed this ongoing school reform and wanted to see private schools as alternatives to these new schools. The Parliament's conservative right accused new school advocates of being socialist, warning that the equity- and equality-based school model would jeopardize the steady economic progress and prosperity of Finnish society in the 1970s and 1980s. The other side—especially the Social Democrats—defended the reforms by saying they would secure a good education for every child in Finland and thereby raise the wellbeing and prosperity of all Finnish society.

The debate also included the ability of the new comprehensive school to keep up with the international race for a knowledgeable and skilled labor force. These critics feared that the new school, when restricting ability tracking and streaming, would not allow the most able and talented students to progress as far as they should in school. Moreover, according to some critics, the emphasis on social equality had led to a suppression of individuality. As a solution, special schools for the gifted and talented, including private schools, were proposed. The prime minister raised these concerns at the Finnish School Principals' Annual Meeting in November 1987 in the following way:

> When believing that anyone can learn everything, the goals of the comprehensive school are set too high. When trying to educate the whole population to the unattainable comprehensive school level, the financial and mental resources of a small nation are being wasted on a hopeless task. These same educational resources would be badly needed to educate those who have proven to be talented in different areas to international high standards. Only that way can we maintain Finland's position in the hard international competition in science and the economy.[21]

Inspired by this perception of the top political leadership, Finnish business leaders launched a survey in 1988 to find out the actual state of Finland's new schools. The grim conclusion was that the schools kill talent. In other words, the system doesn't allow more able and gifted pupils to progress to their full potential because it insists on social equality by employing a unified curriculum in all schools and classrooms. These conclusions coincided with the deregulation of the economy.

The education system had to support the transition of Finnish society into a more liberal and competitive market economy. There were those—like the prime minister—who argued that the economic transformation from the post-industrial to the knowledge economy requires that able and talented students be offered opportunities to progress freely and not to wait for the mediocre students, especially in mathematics and science.

The campaign to reform the Finnish education system according to the models of the emerging New Public Management movement continued into the 1990s. Some Finns saw suitable alternatives in other countries as ways to diversify Finnish publicly governed education, including the Education Reform Act of 1988 in the United Kingdom (with the first national curriculum and common attainment targets for all), the outcome-based education policies of New Zealand, the standards-based model of the United States, and especially liberal voucher legislation with Free Schools in Sweden. They cited more parental choice, increasing competition between schools over student enrollment, and earlier specialization by schools for gifted children as a means to improve education. National assessments and regular testing of student achievement were also suggested as the necessary way to strengthen local level accountability as well as to catch up to other education systems that appeared to be increasing the gap between them and Finland in education.

Criticism continued and sharpened until the end of the 1990s, although research findings did not support the contention that students were learning less than before in the new comprehensive school.[22] Shifting the responsibility of curriculum planning, school improvement, and student assessment to municipalities and schools in the mid-1990s had strengthened support from teachers and principals to develop the Finnish school system without using models of marketplace management.

The critical voices were suddenly muted in early December 2001 when news of the first PISA study[23] was published in the global media: Finland had outperformed all other OECD countries in reading, mathematics, and science when measured for students at the end of lower-secondary school (15-year-olds). Indeed, the Finnish comprehensive school got the best possible international validation. Paradoxically, OECD's PISA study saved Finnish schools from what have later proved to be toxic influences of the Global Education Reform Movement (GERM). Privatization of the Finnish school system hasn't been seriously debated in Finland since.

The Finnish comprehensive school quickly became an internationally recognized success story. The Finns themselves became confident that earlier investments in equality of opportunity and educational equity were the best ways to make the entire school system work well. Thousands of foreign visitors came to look at the Finnish miracle, but they often failed to see how Finnish society as a whole was tuned to care for and support children and youth. Glory brought by PISA was unexpected and often uncomfortable to many teachers and students because they didn't see anything special in what they did on a daily basis in their schools. The international spotlight has made many Finnish policy-makers and politicians careful about making any major changes in education.

At the same time Finnish society was changing with the surrounding world— a new generation of children enrolled in schools with new attitudes, expectations, and habits often shaped by a faster pace of life, new global communication, and dominance of entertainment and technology in their free time. As a result—at least to some extent—students' (particularly boys') reading and mathematics achievement started to slip. Many external observers wondered whether Finnish decision-makers would respond to this by following the example of many other countries where competition, standardization, testing, accountability, and privatization have been used as a cure for lower-than-expected performance. It is interesting that despite the very difficult economic situation with shrinking public spending and thereby reduced funds available to schools, all politicians remain reluctant to allow privatization to enter into the world of public education.

Why the Finnish School System Remains Immune to GERM: Intention, Perseverance, and Good Luck

So, why was the Finnish school system not infected by GERM—that often manifests itself through various forms of privatization—as has happened in most other developed nations? Here, as in many other situations in life, the answer is a complex cocktail of intention, hard work, and good luck. The Finns have been blessed by each of these ingredients ever since they decided to leave an inequitable old school system behind and build a better one that would provide opportunities for all children to find their talents and fulfill their dreams through learning. There are three primary reasons for Finnish schools' persistence in staying the course of equity.

First, intention: Since the 1970s Finnish educators have had an insight that teaching is a high profession akin to medicine, law, and architecture and it therefore requires similar rigorous academic preparation of all teachers. Finnish teachers are not only well prepared to teach children in classrooms but they are also capable of engaging actively in following and further developing their profession. Research-based teacher education in Finland provides all teachers with a critical eye to understand and comment on the trends and ideas related to the teaching profession. Arguably, Finnish teachers and school principals are well prepared to identify good education policies from bad ones. Finnish educators are also a closely organized professional community, just like other academic professionals in Finland, and they are together strong enough to prevent their profession from absorbing toxic ideas, including stopping the GERM.

Second, perseverance: The decision to move educational authority from central administration to the municipalities and schools took place at the time of economic recession and hardship. New autonomy was particularly welcome in many schools that had been asking for more flexibility and trust from the authorities to do what they thought was good for children. Without working extra hours and without additional compensation, hundreds of schools in Finland took this opportunity to organize their schools as they saw best. Teacher professionalism was turned into collective professionalism in these schools where educators work together to make the best out of their work. Finnish teachers became more autonomous from central administration but more dependent on one another. This new emerging culture in schools brought strong educational and learner-centered values to schools. In most cases, it was the culture of the school and the sense of autonomy among teachers that was resistant to the externally imposed market-based policies.

Third, good luck: It is ironic that Finland, one of the most outspoken skeptics regarding new international student assessment, PISA, became its first hero. When the first PISA data were released in December 2001, it was more of a domestic win for those who believed in Finland's new comprehensive school than an international championship for Finland. The first three PISA cycles confirmed the success of the controversial reform of the 1970s and silenced most of the doubts and suggestions to radically alter the Finnish way of schooling. Without the international success that PISA gave to the Finns, their school system would probably look quite different—with selective schools, national standardized assessments, central control, and private-sector involvement.

Notes

1 Sahlberg, P. (2015). *Finnish lessons 2.0: What can the world learn from educational change in Finland?* New York: Teachers College Press.

2 Halme, K., Lindy, I., Piirainen, K., Salminen, V., and White, J. (2014). *Finland as a knowledge economy 2.0: Lessons on policies and governance.* Washington, D.C.: World Bank.

3 Eckstein, M. A. and Noah, H. J. (1993). *Secondary school examinations: International perspectives on policies and practice.* New Haven: Yale University Press. p. 84.

4 Sahlberg, P. (2015). *Finnish lessons 2.0: What can the world learn from educational change in Finland?* New York: Teachers College Press.

5 Ministry of Education and Culture (2012). *Education and research 2011–2016: A development plan.* Helsinki.

6 Rinne, R. and Ozga, J. (2013). The OECD and the Global Re-Regulation of Teachers' Work. Knowledge-Based Regulation Tools and Teachers in Finland and England. In T. Seddon and J. Levin (Eds.) *World yearbook of education: Educators, professionalism and politics. Global transitions, national spaces and professional projects.* New York: Routledge, pp. 97–116.

7 Hargreaves, A. and Shirley, D. (2012). *The global fourth way: The quest for educational excellence.* Thousand Oaks, CA: Corwin; Sahlberg, P. (2015). *Finnish lessons 2.0: What can the world learn from educational change in Finland?* New York: Teachers College Press.

8 OECD (2013). *PISA 2012 results: What makes schools successful? Resources, policies and practices* (Vol. 4). Paris.

9 OECD (2013). *PISA 2012 results: What makes schools successful? Resources, policies and practices* (Vol. 4). Paris.

10 Jensen, B., Weidmann, B. and Farmer, J. (2013). *The myth of markets in school education.* Melbourne: Grattan Institute.

11 OECD (2013). *PISA 2012 results: What makes schools successful? Resources, policies and practices* (Vol. 4). Paris.

12 Zhao, Y. (2014). *Who's afraid of the big bad dragon: Why China has the best (and worst) education system in the world.* San Francisco, CA: Jossey Bass.

13 Breakspear, S. (2015). Measuring How the World Learns: An examination of the OECD's PISA and its uses in National Policy Evaluation. Unpublished Ph.D. dissertation. University of Cambridge, UK.

14 Robert Wood Johnson Foundation (2010). *The state of play. Gallup survey of principals on school recess.* Princeton, NJ.

15 Helsingin Sanomat (2004). *Ykkössuosikki: Opettajan ammatti* [Top favorite: Teaching profession], February 11, 2004.

16 Taajamo, M., Puhakka, P. and Välijärvi, J. (2015). *Opetuksen ja oppimisen kansainvälinen tutkimus TALIS 2013.* Tarkastelun kohteena alakoulun ja toisen asteen oppilaitosten opettajat ja rehtorit. Helsinki: Ministry of Education and Culture.

17 OECD (2014). *Education at a glance. Education indicators.* Paris.

18 Ministry of Education (2007). *Opettajankoulutus 2020* [Teacher education 2020]. Committee Report 2007:44. Helsinki.

19 OECD (2004). *Learning for tomorrow's world: First results from PISA 2003.* Paris.

20 Taajamo, M., Puhakka, P. and Välijärvi, J. 2015. *Opetuksen ja oppimisen kansainvälinen tutkimus TALIS 2013.* Tarkastelun kohteena alakoulun ja toisen asteen oppilaitosten opettajat ja rehtorit. Helsinki.

21 Aho, E., Pitkänen, K. and Sahlberg, P. (2006). *Policy development and reform principles of basic and secondary education in Finland since 1968.* Washington, D.C.: World Bank.

22 Linnakylä, P. and Saari, H. (1993). *Oppiiko oppilas peruskoulussa? Peruskoulu arviointi 90-tutkimuksen tuloksia* [Do pupils learn in Peruskoulu? Findings of the Peruskoulu 90 research]. Jyväskylä, Finland: Jyväskylän yliopiston kasvatustieteiden tutkimuslaitos.

23 OECD (2001). *Knowledge and skills for life: First results from PISA 2000.* Paris.

6

THE CRITICAL CHOICE IN AMERICAN EDUCATION

Privatization or Public Investment?

Frank Adamson and Linda Darling-Hammond

The United States is at a crossroads in its education system. Policymakers have spent decades debating how best to improve school quality and bridge large gaps in student achievement. While race and class disparities in children's outcomes are not in dispute, the solutions remain highly contested, with two distinctive approaches increasingly in play: market-based systems that privatize school management, and capacity-building approaches that deepen public investments. Properly evaluating these solution pathways requires understanding their logic, applications, and results.

Supporters of market-based approaches have advocated for choice in education. For some, the main idea is that competition will force schools to provide a good product or they will go out of business, while providing families with a choice of schools through vehicles like vouchers and charters. For others, the goal is to create opportunities for innovation and diverse options that can enable students to find the optimum fit for their interests. Research has shown mixed results, with some charter and voucher schools outperforming public schools but most performing at or below public school levels.[1]

Other reforms have focused on investing in professional learning and equalizing funding and curriculum opportunities as strategies for closing the achievement gap. Some of these efforts, when properly focused and implemented, have resulted in substantial gains, especially for historically underserved students.[2]

This chapter examines the evolution of these perspectives in both policy and practice. We summarize research on the outcomes of various approaches, and we examine specific cases of education privatization: the nation's first significant voucher program, followed by the widespread introduction of charters, in Milwaukee, Wisconsin, and the largest current initiative—the systemwide charter expansion currently occurring in New Orleans, Louisiana. We compare the approaches and outcomes used in these two cities with those used in the state of Massachusetts, which has had among the steepest improvements in achievement. The state now ranks first among U.S. states on most achievement indicators and among the top-ranking countries on international assessments such as PISA, when different jurisdictions are compared.

Competing Economic Paradigms

The United States has always experienced competing impulses—a press for equity in tension with forces favoring a concentration of wealth and power. The press for equity in social sectors, including education, has occurred in cycles in U.S. history, often following eras where inequality has become extreme. Emancipation and Reconstruction occurred in the 1860s as slavery was ended. Groups unified in the battle for women's suffrage and civil rights in the 1890s. In the 1930s, the Great Depression followed on the heels of an economic crisis caused by a concentration of wealth and precipitated Roosevelt's New Deal. The 1960s and 1970s saw civil rights protests resulting from a recognition of inequalities that ultimately triggered desegregation and school finance reforms to increase educational equity.

Over the past 30 years, since the 1980s, the conservative approach has dominated, leading to greatly increased inequality in both income and in education outcomes.[3] This inequality has occurred alongside, and in some ways as a result of, the general adoption of a neoliberal political and economic approach.

Liberal and Keynesian Economics—A 20th-Century Tension

The United States has employed two main economic theories in the past two centuries: liberalism (including its reincarnation with a twist, neoliberalism) and Keynesianism.[4] The 1800s saw the use of a *liberal*, laissez-faire system. The fundamental tenet of this market-based system, articulated by Adam Smith, involves the removal of government from the "free" market. Smith claimed that a "free" market functioned as an "invisible hand" that organizes consumption and production, always eventually returning the supply and demand curves to equilibrium.[5]

However, the Great Depression demonstrated the failure of liberal, free-market economics and heralded the emergence of a new paradigm designed by John Maynard Keynes. Keynesian economics, or controlled capitalism, posited a role for the government in increasing investment in public sectors, controlling the money supply, and regulating the markets and banks to prevent runaway inflation and crippling deflation. The adoption of a Keynesian approach from the 1930s onward, combined with the growth of infrastructure aided by World War II (and a host of other factors), saw stable, positive, fairly equally distributed growth in the American economy for more than a half-century.

Civil Rights Achievements

This positive economic trajectory saw corresponding advances in the social sectors. The civil rights movement won expanded rights for African Americans, including the right to vote and the desegregation of schools.[6] This period saw "intense anti-bias activity" spearheaded by the Equal Employment Opportunities Commission and backed by federal courts favoring "active equal employment and affirmative action programs."[7]

The Great Society era, under Presidents Kennedy and Johnson in the 1960s, began to tackle long-standing educational inequalities in the United States. This inequality has been both a result of racial discrimination through historically sanctioned and unequally funded dual systems of schools as well as a result of state school finance systems based largely on local property taxes that produce unequal revenues for schools. Even after the Supreme Court outlawed de jure segregation in the *Brown v. Board of Education* decision in 1954, the disparities in funding for more and less advantaged students across public school systems were enormous, with some districts spending more than ten times as much as others.

Federal investments in education made a large dent in this inequality, specifically with the 1965 Elementary and Secondary Act and other legislation supporting desegregation, education for handicapped children, teacher education, and more equitable distribution of teachers, curriculum reforms, and higher education access. Anti-poverty and employment initiatives also created substantial improvements in the lives of low-income children and their families. Perhaps not surprisingly, the largest reductions in the achievement gap between black and white students occurred during the 1960s and 1970s when these investments reduced inequality and expanded educational opportunity.[8] This era also saw near-elimination of the gap between minorities and whites enrolling in higher education, with the expansion of financial aid in concert with affirmative action.

Most of the federal investments that produced these advances were reduced or eliminated during the Reagan administration, when market-based ideologies were rekindled and government services dramatically curtailed.

Free-Markets, Supply Side Economics, and Neoliberalism

The stage for these changes was set by economic anxieties that emerged at the end of the 1970s, when President Carter pointed to what he termed an emerging energy crisis, rooted in dependency on foreign oil. Carter introduced the notion of personal belt-tightening to reduce energy use and to support a stronger economy. On a practical level, the combined expense of expanding social services, military expenditures (especially from the Vietnam War), and the 1973 oil crisis all strained the economic system. A new phenomenon of higher interest rates combined with higher unemployment and lower growth developed, termed stagflation.

The malaise of stagflation opened the door for the main proponent of "free-market" economics, Milton Friedman, to influence policy. Leader of the economics department at the University of Chicago, Friedman proposed a "monetarist" policy that ensured a stable supply of money. Instead of Keynes' focus on government spending,[9] Friedman argued that the state's primary role was to ensure the operation of the free market and that "monetary policies should take precedence over fiscal policy (taxation and redistribution policies) devised by 'big government.'"[10] Friedman was also a key proponent of the voucher system as a means of privatizing education in the name of school choice and competition—an idea that he brought to Chile during the 1970s and propounded in the United States during the 1980s.

After a contested presidential victory in 1980, Ronald Reagan began an economic approach called "supply-side" economics. This economic system repackages the strategies of liberal economics with a "twist." Instead of deregulation of companies, allowing them to compete on the "free" market and meet consumer demand, supply-side economics claims that increases in the supply of goods will increase consumer demand all by itself. Increased supply then leads to increased demand, which ultimately leads to more profits in the business sector and, allegedly, reinvestment in production and wages.

The combination in the 1980s of the liberal tenets of Friedman's "free-markets" with the new "supply-side" economics of Reagan led to what is generally called "neoliberal economics." During a short period in the 1980s, neoliberal strategies coincided with a brief economic recovery, but that recovery also produced record budget deficits and a savings and loan crisis. Over the longer run, these strategies have corresponded with a flat-lining in middle-class wages, decreases in social and educational equity, and increased income and wealth inequality.

The latter has never been more extreme than it is today. A recent analysis by economists Emmanuel Saez and Gabriel Zucman shows that, since 1980, not only has income inequality grown but wealth inequality has grown even more dramatically.[11] The top 1 percent of families controlled less than 10 percent of national income in the late 1970s, which rose to more than 20 percent by the end of 2012. Even more alarming, the share of household wealth owned by the top *one-tenth* of 1 percent of the U.S. population has increased from 7 to 22 percent. The top 0.1 percent includes 160,000 families with total net assets greater than those of 145 million families at the bottom of the income distribution. Figure 6.1 shows that the situation is nearly comparable to the disparities at the end of the 1920s, just before the market crash that led to the Great Depression.

As Saez and Zucman show, the most equitable distribution of wealth over the last century occurred at the end of the 1970s, followed by a steep and nearly continuous rise in the share of national wealth controlled by the richest individuals since the early 1980s. This trend in the economy, supported by tax cuts for the wealthy as well as government bailouts of corporations and banks that supported

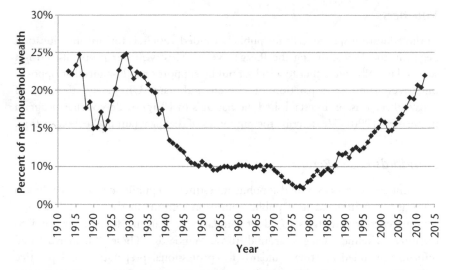

FIGURE 6.1 Share of Total U.S. Wealth Owned by the Top 0.1 percent of Families, 1913–2012

Source: Emmanuel Saez and Gabriel Zucman (2014).[12]

outsized executive compensation, has been accompanied by other public policies that have encouraged the privatization of services including education.

Neoliberalism and Education

The neoliberal support of private interests over public governance combined with inequality of opportunity have translated into the education sphere in several ways:

- Support for public funding of private choices through vouchers and, later, charter schools, sometimes allowed to be selective in which students they choose and keep;
- Resistance to equalizing funding of public schools that would provide more equity in educational opportunities;
- The use of test-based accountability as a means to evaluate schools against each other and to decide which ones should be retained or closed;
- The creation of an unregulated marketplace for teachers in lieu of professional expectations (which allows both standards and salaries to decline, especially in low-wealth communities).

In this section, we briefly describe the history of U.S. education reforms that advanced elements of this agenda between 1980 and 2015, along with the alternatives also advanced at the federal level and in various states.

Vouchers

In the education sphere, calls for publicly funded vouchers for private education began in the 1980s, during the Reagan years. Most voucher proposals did not succeed initially due either to a lack of public support or to lawsuits that opposed initiatives based on separation of church and state. Ultimately, the city of Milwaukee, Wisconsin established the nation's first large-scale voucher program in the early 1990s. We describe the outcomes of that program in the next section.

Standards-Based Reform

In a contrasting strategy aimed at public investment in public schools, the Clinton administration initiated new public education reforms in the 1990s. Clinton's reforms encouraged states to adopt standards of learning for students and to organize systemic changes around those standards. These "standards-based reforms" included creating standards for professional preparation and practice linked to the new student standards, investing in professional learning and curriculum materials, and, in many states, increasing and equalizing public school funding. These investments were justified in legislation and litigation by the need to enable students to achieve the new standards. However, while some states used "standards-based reform" to stimulate more equalized funding, others merely adopted standards and high-stakes testing, without investing.[13]

As we describe later, states such as Massachusetts and Connecticut undertook a holistic approach to standards-based reform and made strong gains in achievement as a result of their interlocking efforts.

Charters

Meanwhile, the idea of "chartering" schools was planted, initially with support from progressive leaders, including teacher union leader Al Shanker. The head of the American Federation of Teachers, Shanker originally thought that charter schools could foster innovation in the public school sector. Wisconsin was one of the first states to authorize charters at the state level in 1995, although Milwaukee was the only district in that state that engaged in significant chartering. Following the first law allowing the establishment of charter schools in Minnesota in 1991, charter school legislation had been passed in 42 states and the District of Columbia as of school year 2012–13. From 2000 to 2013, the number of students enrolled in public charter schools increased from 0.3 million to 2.3 million, reaching 4.6 percent of all students in 2013.[14]

In 2000, with the advent of the George W. Bush Administration (son of the earlier president, George H.W. Bush), both vouchers and charters got a major boost. In 2004, Congress replicated the Milwaukee voucher experiment in Washington, D.C., administering the first federally funded voucher program.

It offered private school vouchers to low-income students, giving priority to those attending low-performing public schools. Federal support for charters was also enacted, as described below. Over time, the charter movement grew from individual schools mounted by groups with specific education ideas to chains of schools operated by charter management organizations, some of them operating as for-profit companies.

Test-Based Accountability

The younger Bush, previously governor of Texas, proposed major changes to ESEA, the major federal education act. He based these changes in part on the Texas approach to education reform, which emphasized school accountability in the form of rewards and sanctions tied to changes in test scores. Proponents claimed that the so-called "Texas education miracle" had boosted achievement and closed achievement gaps. Later analyses showed, however, that low-performing students were often kept out of testing or pushed out of school entirely so that their scores would not count in the accountability rankings.[15] Furthermore, apparent gains on the high-stakes tests were not reflected in other assessments that did not carry penalties.[16]

Nonetheless, the Texas scheme became the guiding framework for the 2002 No Child Left Behind Act that set targets for each school, associated with score gains needed to bring all students to "100 percent proficiency" on the tests by 2014. To achieve "adequate yearly progress" (AYP), each school had to meet targets for both annual increases in test scores and participation rates (95 percent of students must be tested) for each individual subgroup of students (by racial/ethnic group, income, disability status, and English learner status) every year. Diverse schools might have to meet as many as 30 separate targets each year.

Among the sanctions for schools that fail to reach all of their targets are redirection of portions of their funding to private "supplemental service" providers, options for students to transfer to other schools, reconstitution (replacing staff), and/or a range of programmatic interventions, replacement by charter schools, and school closure.

This law created a predictable perception of widespread failure for public schools since it was impossible to meet the goal of 100 percent proficiency for all students on the tests, and virtually all public schools had failed to reach AYP by 2014. Schools that served English learners were the first to be declared "in need of improvement" and then "failing," because of a Catch-22 in the law—as soon as English learners became "proficient" in English they were taken out of the subgroup calculations, so that the group as a whole could never reach 100 percent proficiency and the group could not show much progress from year to year.

This meant that many schools serving such students—as well as those with other high-need students—were on a steady march through a list of sanctions of ever-increasing severity, which eventually included closure and/or replacement by a charter school, under aspects of the policy that evolved over the subsequent decade.

The Intersection of Test-Based Accountability and Privatization

Vouchers were proposed as part of NCLB in 2002, but did not pass at that time. However, No Child Left Behind did provide federal funding for charter schools under Title V, which was redirected from its earlier purpose.[17] Having previously been focused on developing career readiness in public schools through a "National Skill Standards Board," Title V was refocused on "Promoting Informed Parental Choice and Innovation" under NCLB and devoted to the planning, design, and initial implementation of charter schools.[18]

In 2006, when NCLB was due to be reauthorized, President Bush again sought vouchers that could be used in private schools for students in all schools that had not made AYP and hence had been declared "in need of improvement." The law was not reauthorized in 2006, so this proposal did not move forward at that time. This proposal, however, which occurred as more and more public schools were being declared "failing," persuaded many that the punitive accountability consequences triggered by the law (which did not apply to private schools) was a Trojan horse for privatization.

Although the NCLB law was increasingly unpopular, President Obama did not seek to change it when he took office in 2009. Instead, he created a program called "Race to the Top," which allocated $5 billion to a competitive grants program for which states could apply if they met a set of preconditions and proposed reforms to boost test scores. The preconditions included were:

- Expanding the testing system so that all teachers would be evaluated based on student test scores.
- Proposing means to boost student scores and reduce achievement gaps.
- Expanding the use of alternative certification for teachers (i.e. pathways that do not require preservice preparation of teachers, generally used only in low-income communities that experience shortages), a strategy launched and expanded in the Reagan and both Bush Administrations.
- Expanding charter schools by requiring states to authorize charter schools and lift any caps they had imposed on the number of such schools.

Later, the Obama administration used these same preconditions as the price of admission for states wanting to secure innovation grants (under the "i3" program) and, later, so-called flexibility waivers under NCLB that allowed them to retrieve the 20 percent of funds schools had to spend on private supplemental services. The effect of the preconditions, along with funding for state reforms under these programs, was to expand the growth of charters and to expand the amount of testing, while deprofessionalizing teaching and positioning teachers—rather than addressing growing poverty and disparities in education funding—as the source of low achievement among needy students.

Federal funding for expanding charters was augmented by substantial funding from private foundations and private entrepreneurs, who also supported test-based teacher evaluation, the elimination of due process rights for teachers, and alternative certification, as well as the growth of programs like Teach for America, which offers two-year stints in low-income communities to elite college graduates who teach en route to jobs on Wall Street or in education policy.[19]

During the period from 2008 to 2015, a Great Recession caused huge cuts in most states' education budgets, which were visited most aggressively on schools serving poor children.[20] Meanwhile, the number of children and families in severe poverty grew, and the number of homeless children doubled. Public schools struggled to meet their needs with fewer and fewer resources. As Figure 6.2 shows, the pace of privatization has increased alongside public disinvestment in the schools serving the neediest students—which are now typically highly segregated by race and class—often more than 90 percent African American and Latino students, more than 90 percent of whom are low-income.

In recent years, sharp budget cuts by states have placed many of these segregated urban school districts into financial crisis that has subjected them to receiverships or state takeovers that have eliminated their school boards and led to widespread school closures, often with district-run public schools replaced by charter schools, and/or designation of private managers (charter operators and others) to run public schools. New Orleans, with its public school district largely eliminated after Hurricane Katrina in 2005, was just the first district to be reshaped under "crisis" conditions.

Friedman and others believed that the best way of privatizing was not through a long process but via economic shock therapy—a rapid economic shock across

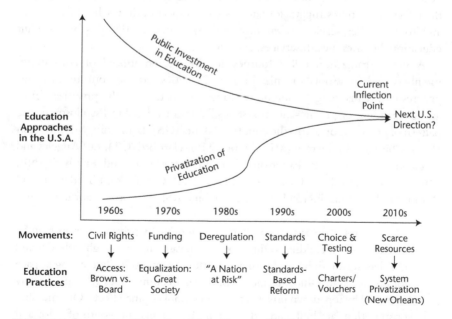

FIGURE 6.2 Competing Educational Paradigms in the United States

sectors that could change political control and institute neoliberal principles.[21] More recently, Naomi Klein argued in the *Shock Doctrine* that "disaster capitalism" variously creates or takes advantage of disasters for the benefit or profit of private operators.[22] Klein suggests that this process occurred in Chile and in New Orleans, among other places.

Other examples are more recent. For example, in the last two years, Detroit has been a site of manufactured disaster, as an economic downturn in the auto industry combined with state tax cuts to create fiscal challenges, lead to the installation of an emergency manager who has aimed to replace the entire school district with charters. In Pennsylvania, Governor Tom Corbett cut Philadelphia's budget by $500 million, throwing it into fiscal distress overnight. The local school board was eliminated, hundreds of educators were fired, and a manager was installed who carved up the school district and gave large sections to private operators.

With opportunity provided by financial crisis and the incentives provided under No Child Left Behind to close and replace low-scoring schools, coupled with influxes of funds from private foundations, more than 20 cities have experienced public school closures coupled with charter expansion, and the breakup of public school districts into components given to private organizations to run.[23]

While school changes may serve some students well, other students have to apply to schools that may not admit them (particularly if they have special education or language needs) and can be far from their homes, rather than having a neighborhood public school to attend. Schools may also start up and close down, which can create disruption and discontinuity. These changes often have the effect of creating struggles for families with respect both to school attendance and to the other services often provided by a neighborhood school—adult education, libraries, health services, and the like.

A new organization called Journey for Justice, comprised of community members and grassroots organizations in 21 cities, has set out to halt this progression, demanding "community-driven alternatives to the privatization of and dismantling of public schools systems."[24] Its membership list illustrates the pattern of privatization across the country: Atlanta (GA), Baltimore (MD), Boston (MA), Chicago (IL), Detroit (MI), Eupora (MS), Hartford (CT), Los Angeles and Oakland (CA), Newark, Patterson, Camden, Jersey City and Elizabeth (NJ), Minneapolis (MN), New Orleans (LA), New York City (NY), Philadelphia and Pittsburgh (PA), Washington D.C., and Wichita (KS). The organization explains:

> The policies of the last fifteen years, driven more by private interests than by concern for our children's education, are devastating our neighborhoods and our democratic rights.... Journey for Justice is intentionally creating a space for organized low-income and working class communities who are directly impacted by top-down privatization and school closing efforts. Our member organizations are built and led primarily by parents and youth of color and we fight unapologetically for community-driven school improvement...

Across our cities and school districts, our public schools are being closed. Students are being displaced and families are losing access to neighborhood schools. Sometimes, closure is based on student academic performance. Sometimes it is rationalized by under-enrollment or financial needs. But in every case—every time a neighborhood public school is closed—students' education is disrupted and communities are destabilized.[25]

The coalition notes that in every one of its districts, school closings disproportionately impact African American and Latino students, schools, and communities. As a consequence, a number of organizations have filed complaints under Title VI of the Civil Rights Act with the Department of Education's Office of Civil Rights, demanding that the department investigate the racial impact of public school closings in these cities.

Outcomes of Privatization in Education

That public education is now seen as a new and profitable market is certain. A 2013 report in *Education Week* called attention to the growing influence education companies were exerting on U.S. policymaking in their efforts to grow profits:

The online education provider K12 Inc.—a publicly traded company with $708 million in revenue in 2012—had 39 lobbyists around the country on the payroll last year to work for state and local policies that would help expand the use of virtual learning. Pearson Education—an offshoot of the publishing giant Pearson—has spent more than $6 million over the past decade lobbying at the federal level. And the charter school operator White Hat Management and its employees contributed more than $2 million in campaign support between 2004 and 2012 to mostly Republican politicians in Ohio, where the company, which runs 33 schools in three states, is the largest for-profit charter operator and has been under fire for poor performance.[26]

The performance of the fast-growing virtual school charter sector has been problematic elsewhere as well. A Stanford University report on Pennsylvania charter schools found that not only did most of them underperform traditional public schools serving similar students, but the on-line charter schools performed even worse than the other charters.[27]

Meanwhile, the for-profit school sector supported by public funds is growing rapidly. The National Education Policy Center found that, between 1995 and 2012, the number of for-profit education management companies running charter schools increased twentyfold, from 5 to 99, and the number of schools they operate increased more than one hundredfold, from 6 to 758.[28] Among other boosters, these companies have enlisted the help of the American Legislative Exchange Council, a conservative organization that writes and promotes legislation to privatize education, cut school budgets, and eliminate collective bargaining and teacher unions.[29]

A central example of the ongoing policy process is seen, once again, in Wisconsin, where Governor Scott Walker—a recent entrant into the Republican presidential primary—has proposed a budget, expected to pass both houses of the legislature. Walker's budget expands vouchers statewide with a $300 million increase while cutting $1.6 billion from public education budgets.[30] The budget expands programs promoting privately run charters, which are more segregated than public schools generally, while eliminating a metropolitan-wide program that allows students to choose public schools outside their district. Chapter 220, as the metropolitan program is called, is designed to reduce racial segregation and improve opportunities for students of color.

As Figure 6.3 below shows, these kinds of policies transfer resources from the public sector to a privately managed sector which adds middlemen—both non-profit and profit-making organizations—to the transactions between the tax-paying public and the recipients of education services. The policies also tend to increase segregation by race and class, as those with greater means (income, focus on education, access to transportation, etc.) are encouraged to choose schools which, by virtue of their admissions policies, costs, geographic location, or push-out policies, are less likely to serve higher-need students. This often leaves district-run public schools serving students who are disproportionately more disadvantaged. When programs that seek to decrease segregation are meanwhile eliminated (like Wisconsin's Chapter 220, described above), the segregating results are exacerbated.

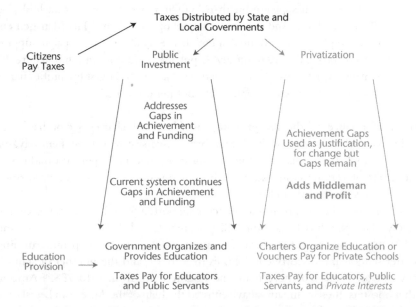

FIGURE 6.3 Education Taxes and Spending: Introducing the Privatized Middleman

Outcomes of Charters and Vouchers: National Data

A recent review of research on vouchers from the Center on Education Policy, including evidence about the impact of vouchers on student test scores from long-term studies about the publicly funded voucher programs in Milwaukee, Cleveland, and Washington, D.C., concluded that "studies have generally found no clear advantage in academic achievement for students attending private schools with vouchers," although voucher parents typically felt quite positively about their schools.[31]

The evidence about charter school effectiveness has also been decidedly mixed. As one review concluded:

> [S]ome researchers find insignificant or negative impacts of attending a charter school (Hanushek, Kain, Rivkin and Branch, 2007; Bifulco and Ladd, 2006; Sass, 2006; Zimmer and Buddin, 2003), while others find positive impacts (Booker, Gilpatric, Gronberg and Jansen, 2007; Hoxby and Rockoff, 2004; Solmon and Goldschmidt, 2004; Solmon, Paark and Garcia, 2001).... (W)e might conclude from these studies that the effect of charter schools on academic performance is, at best, unclear.[32]

Other research reviews report similarly mixed findings, noting that charters have had widely varying outcomes across different contexts.[33] Where charters have been poorly regulated, results for students have typically been negative. For example, in Ohio, where an unregulated market strategy created a huge range of for-profit and non-profit providers with few public safeguards, charter school students have been found to achieve at consistently lower levels than their demographically similar public school counterparts.[34] Students in charters in largely unregulated Arizona and Washington, D.C. have also been found to achieve at levels significantly below those of their similar peers in public schools.[35] In Minneapolis, Minnesota, where charters have proliferated, a recent study found that, on average, they produce significantly lower achievement relative to district public schools serving similar students.[36]

In California, charters have been more carefully regulated, with expectations for meeting curriculum, staffing, and financial standards. There, the differences in sectors appear more modest. In one study, students in elementary charters scored below their demographically similar counterparts, while those in middle school charters scored above. Students in high school charters did better in English language arts and worse in mathematics.[37] Students did particularly poorly in charters providing most of their instruction through home schooling, independent study, or distance learning.

A large-scale study of student data from 16 states, from the Center for Research on Education Outcomes at Stanford University, confirmed the mixed nature of the outcomes, finding that only 17 percent of charter schools produced academic gains that were significantly better than traditional public schools, while 37 percent of charter schools performed worse than their traditional public school counterparts serving similar students.[38] In 46 percent of charter schools, there was no significant difference between their students' achievement gains and those of their demographically similar peers in district-run public schools.[39]

An evaluation of Chicago's Renaissance 2010 initiative—which replaced a group of low-performing schools with charters and other schools of choice run by entrepreneurs and the district—found that the achievement of students in the new schools did not differ from that of a matched comparison group of students in their old schools, and both groups continued to have low performance.[40]

A troubling set of relatively consistent findings is that charters are more segregated than public schools generally, both racially and economically,[41] and they underrepresent English learners and special education students relative to public schools in their districts.[42] In some states, these socioeconomic differences also appear to translate into educational differences. For example, a Texas study found that the majority of white, Anglo students in the state's charters were in academically oriented schools, while most minority students were in vocational charters.[43]

Results of the Market-Based Reform Initiatives in Milwaukee

Milwaukee Public Schools (MPS) has had the longest-standing large-scale choice system in the nation, beginning with a voucher program launched in 1990, and expanded through charters and district-run schools of choice. Today the program allows over 20,000 low-income Milwaukee students to attend more than a hundred different schools with the assistance of a government voucher. Charter schools and a desegregation law known as Chapter 220, which aims for a racial balance among schools, have also fostered "school choice."

In 1998, the courts ruled that parochial schools could accept vouchers, expanding the pool of voucher schools and students. In 2011, the income eligibility criteria for the voucher program moved from 175 percent of the poverty level to 300 percent of the poverty level, providing access to additional families. The number of students using vouchers has steadily increased, from just over 300 in 1990 to a plateau just over the 20,000 student mark in 2008, where it has remained. Over these years, MPS enrollment dropped by more than 20 percent, from about 101,000 in 1998 to 78,363 in 2013.[44]

MPS officials responded to voucher competition by creating a portfolio of schools that offered students a range of choices, which include district-run traditional and alternative schools, partnership schools, contract schools, and more than 30 charters.

It is worth noting that state law treats Milwaukee differently from the rest of the state. Elsewhere in Wisconsin, chartering authority rests with local school boards, and, unless the school is a board-initiated charter, no school can be authorized without approval from 50 percent of the teachers in a school or 10 percent in a school district. Charter funds come to the district to be reallocated, as they normally would. In Milwaukee, a wider range of authorizers is permitted (including the City of Milwaukee and the University of Wisconsin-Milwaukee) and funding goes directly to those schools.

The Milwaukee educational marketplace has been highly volatile. For example, over the five years between 2007 and 2011, the district closed 59 schools and opened 24 new ones, with many of the most recent school closures occurring because of declining enrollment.[45] One district administrator explained that this deflected attention from building instructional quality to the logistics of opening and closing schools and moving students around. He added: "The vouchers are what caused us to be more market driven.... We deliberately created a culture of competition. There is no question about it."[46]

Despite the intensive competition, achievement has not improved in Milwaukee and achievement gaps have widened. Research has found little difference in achievement among similar students attending vouchers, charters, and district-run public schools.[47] Furthermore, achievement is low for all sectors, and has been stagnant for the last dozen years in which state test data have been available.[48] (See Figure 6.4, Table 6.1, and Table 6.2 below, showing data for the years in which Wisconsin maintained a common statewide test, which was launched to satisfy NCLB requirements.)

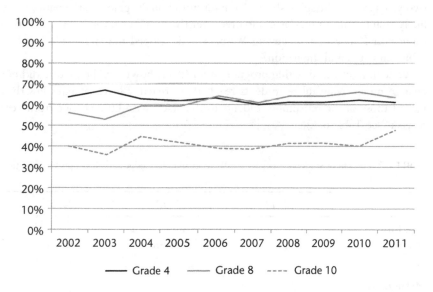

FIGURE 6.4 Percent of Milwaukee Students Proficient in Reading

TABLE 6.1 Percent of Milwaukee Students Proficient in Reading, 2002–2011

Grade	2002	2003	2004	2005	2006	2007	2008	2009	2010	2011
4	64%	67.1%	62.8%	62.3%	63.3%	60.8%	61.2%	61.4%	62.3%	61.1%
8	56%	52.9%	59.2%	59.4%	63.5%	60.1%	63.7%	64.2%	65.7%	63.7%
10	40%	36.4%	44.7%	41.9%	39.7%	39%	41.3%	41.7%	40.2%	47.8%

Source: Wisconsin Department of Public Instruction

TABLE 6.2 Percent of Milwaukee Students Proficient in Math, 2002–2011

Grade	2002	2003	2004	2005	2006	2007	2008	2009	2010	2011
4	47%	53.1%	46.4%	44.8%	53.1%	51.7%	60.2%	58.5%	56.7%	54.7%
8	35%	29.2%	36.4%	38.9%	41.2%	39.9%	50.2%	52.1%	47.5%	53.6%
10	28%	29.8%	31.2%	32.1%	29.7%	28.7%	28.8%	30.4%	31.6%	33.1%

Source: Wisconsin Department of Public Instruction

In 2011, the National Assessment of Educational Progress (NAEP) showed that Milwaukee was one of the lowest-achieving cities in the nation and students had actually lost ground in reading at both 4th- and 8th-grade levels from the assessment two years earlier, though it showed a slight uptick in 8th-grade mathematics,[49] the likely result of an instructional initiative over the previous several years.[50] During these years, once high-achieving Wisconsin developed the largest black–white achievement gap in the nation.[51]

Wisconsin changed testing programs after 2011; however, the picture did not change much. Milwaukee students reached proficiency levels at rates less than half of those of the remaining students in the state, with little change from year to year (see Table 6.3.).

TABLE 6.3 Percent of Students Proficient in Wisconsin Knowledge and Concepts Examination (WKCE), 2011–2013

	2011	2012	2013
Reading			
Milwaukee	14.1%	14.9%	15.1%
State	35.7%	36.0%	36.4%
Mathematics			
Milwaukee	20.7%	20.9%	20.6%
State	46.8%	48.3%	48.2%

In 2013, the *Milwaukee Journal Sentinel* reported that, although 95 percent of the state's 423 school districts met or exceeded the state's expectations for performance in 2012–2013, Milwaukee did not, and was assigned the lowest ranking.[52] A reporter noted:

> Despite having more freedom over curriculum, budgets and staffing than traditional public schools, the majority of Milwaukee's independent charter schools are not meeting performance expectations, according to statewide report card results for 2012-13. Of the 17 independent charters in Milwaukee that received a rating through the state's new school report card accountability system, 53% fell below expectations, with two schools authorized by the City of Milwaukee receiving a failing grade… The results raise questions about whether independent charters should be producing better results. The schools are publicly financed but privately managed, and are given freedom from bureaucratic restraints on school districts in exchange for upholding a promise to deliver on performance.[53]

The report also noted that, consistent with national trends, district-run MPS schools educated three times as many students learning English and twice as many students with special needs, as well as a greater share of students in poverty, compared with independent charters.

While the nation's most extensive educational market has not produced notable improvements in achievement over the 25 years it has been operating, it has produced a set of competitive responses from choice-based schools regarding getting and keeping the students who are easiest to educate and losing those who are more challenging. In a recent study, administrators described how this aspect of the marketplace operates.[54] As one explained:

> With enrollment changing, with district enrollment loss over the last number of years, schools really do compete for students.… We discovered, just as an example, that another school … was actually getting into the database and finding second grade kids with certain reading levels and above, and sending letters home to recruit those kids. There are many examples of that: schools do go after each other's students, with some vengeance.

Managing the enrollment of students of different kinds appears to focus on funding allocation and testing dates. Schools in Wisconsin receive their money from the state based on their student enrollment on the third Friday of the school year, and testing occurs in October. One principal described a neighboring school: "I know a school that promised [students] $50 and a TV if they stay for at least one month in the school. After that month, they're free to go."

For those schools that can compete for or manage the selection of the students they want, performance certainly has increased. However, for the system as a whole, which must educate those left behind in the marketplace, the end result of the grand experiment with choice appears to be greater segregation of students, an achievement gap that has grown to be the nation's largest, and little overall change in student performance.

Who Chooses? Results of System-Wide Charter Adoption in New Orleans

Whereas Milwaukee is the first U.S. example of a market-based portfolio of school choices, New Orleans is the first to completely privatize school operations at the district level. In 2003, *before* Hurricane Katrina, Louisiana established the "Recovery School District" (RSD) with the purpose of taking over schools designated as failing under federal law (NCLB). In the first two years of the RSD, the state provided charters for a few schools as one option for reconstituting schools under NCLB.[55] Then, in 2005, Hurricane Katrina ravaged the city, taking lives, destroying property, and displacing large numbers of people. Post-Katrina, the education landscape dramatically changed and New Orleans became the site of the first city in the United States ultimately to eliminate district-run public schools.[56]

The example of New Orleans is especially important, as privatizers have held it up as a grand experiment in education, providing a model that the nation's school districts should follow.[57] However, in the scientific world, experiments have the foundation of successful pilots, control groups, and opt-out options, none of which exist in this case. Children have been the captive subjects of a decision to eliminate their public school system. In addition to the fact that no deliberate process of controlled evaluation has thus far accompanied the radical reform process, the state of Louisiana has withheld publicly collected data about students and their outcomes from most researchers and the public, while providing it only to two institutions that collaborate with the reformers.[58]

While it is enormously difficult to identify the effects of chartering, given the dramatic transformation of the population in New Orleans after Katrina, and without student-level data that allows comparison of group analyses, it is clear that New Orleans continues to be a low-scoring district. As Table 6.4 illustrates, only 12 percent of students in the Recovery School District scored at the "mastery" level or above on the state tests in 2014, half the statewide rate of 24 percent. By contrast, in the Orleans Parish Schools—a now separate district that continues to operate public schools in New Orleans—the proportion was much higher, at 42 percent. (As we discuss later, many of the headlines announcing "success" in New Orleans have created it by combining the much higher results for the Orleans Parish district with those of the all-charter RSD.)

Publicly released data show that New Orleans RSD continues to be a low-scoring district—performing well below the Louisiana state average—and Louisiana continues to be a very low-scoring state.[59] In 2013, on the National Assessment of Educational Progress (the most recent data available at this writing),

TABLE 6.4 Percent of Louisiana Students Scoring at Mastery Level or Above, 2014

Statewide	24
Orleans Parish School Board (Not assigned to RSD)	42
RSD–New Orleans	12

Louisiana ranked 48th out of the 50 states in 4th and 8th grade reading, 49th in 8th grade math, and was tied for 50th in 4th grade math.[60]

Meanwhile, research on the ground, including some by the authors of this chapter, indicates that for many families, the application of a market-based competitive model in New Orleans has produced a system of winners and losers. It has increased stratification across schools and the exclusion of at-risk students from the most desirable options. This process has exacerbated already inequitable achievement outcomes. One New Orleans parent interviewed provided a dire view of the situation:

> There will be a [social] class here [in New Orleans] who will be educated and there will be a class here that will not be educated. That's just the reality that we're looking at now. I'm saying in a generation there'll be an underclass here like I don't know that we have an underclass anywhere else in this country, because there will be a part of the populous here that won't be educated, and if you have no educated populous, then you have no democracy and that is the problem.

In this parent's view, echoed by others, the privatization of education has diminished educational opportunities for many children, with serious long-term ramifications for the social and political future of New Orleans.

Transforming New Orleans' Public Schools Into Charters

As the "shock doctrine" would predict, those looking for means to privatize education viewed the crisis initiated by Hurricane Katrina as an opportunity. Shortly after the hurricane, the state board passed Act 35, which substantially expanded the definition of a failing school and provided the RSD with the legal mandate to take over or outsource the operation of failing schools.

ACT 35 increased the level of the School Performance Score (SPS) required for designating a school as failing from 60 to the state average of 87.4.[61] This means that half of the schools in Louisiana could be deemed failing, which seems like an extreme designation, especially considering that reconstitution or closure could be a consequence under NCLB. The law allowed the state to transfer any school with an SPS below 87.4 from the local school board to the RSD, with restrictions that, in essence, targeted the law specifically to New Orleans. Louisiana legislators passed Act 35 in an "extraordinary session" in 2005, without community input.

The Louisiana state board used Katrina and Act 35 to move control of the education system from New Orleans residents and locally elected officials to state officials and, often, unelected private boards of charter management organizations (CMOs). Louisiana, acting through the RSD, subsequently solicited nonlocal, charter organizations to manage New Orleans schools, a primary grievance of repatriated residents of the city. Indeed, one charter school principal we interviewed referred to the process as "stealing" the district.

During the ramp up to install the charter system, Louisiana engaged in the mass termination of more than 7,000 tenured teachers. These teachers did not receive due process and most did not have a chance to reapply for their jobs, even though their contract stipulated the creation and use of a teacher contact list for any rehiring. Instead, many charters contracted with Teach for America, importing young, inexperienced teachers on two-year commitments and administrators from other geographic backgrounds to institute, in many cases, a zero-tolerance model of behavior management in the charter schools. In 2012, the courts declared the mass teacher termination illegal, but the state supreme court reversed the decision in 2014.[62] The case is currently headed to the U.S. Supreme Court. However, the damage was already done for the city, and there was, by then, no district for teachers to return to if they had so desired.

From starting the RSD, taking over the New Orleans district using Act 35, firing tenured teachers, and installing a charter schools system, the state of Louisiana pursued a strategy that removed responsibility for public education from elected officials and placed it in the hands of privately selected charter boards and outside funders, disenfranchising students, parents, and teachers.

Flipped Choice: How Schools Choose Students

A primary assumption of market models is that consumers choose products from providers who compete for their business. The theory posits that pitting one school's performance against that of another will provide families with a measure for comparison, incentivizing the schools either to improve or risk losing students and eventually closing. Market proponents trust that this system will efficiently remove low-performing schools. However, this idealized situation assumes that all consumers are equally desirable customers for which providers will compete, as well as assuming perfect information for parents, the ability of students to switch schools at any moment, and the capacity of schools to adapt their approaches despite the previously discussed disparities in funding and the differential needs of students.

One particularly problematic aspect of the charter law in Louisiana is that it allows schools to set admissions standards rather than requiring them to accept all students who apply, or to use a lottery process when there are more applicants than slots, as in California's law. Until a recent regulation sought to constrain expulsions,[63] schools were also permitted to expel students for any cause without due process.

Because federal and state accountability systems center on student test scores, which are the primary factor in school ratings, each school's survival and competitive advantage depends on boosting scores. This creates incentives for attracting and retaining high-scoring students, and excluding those who would pull down the average—an approach called "cream skimming." As a consequence, instead of producing a perfect market of school competition and parental choice, the past decade in New Orleans has seen an increase in stratification between schools that further disadvantages the least advantaged students.

With the system set up to allow the most advantaged schools to "cream skim," three main tiers of schools have evolved in New Orleans. Because the state did not deem the highest-performing schools as failing, these "Tier 1" schools remained under the auspices of the Orleans Parish School Board (OPSB), either district-operated or chartered. They now employ several selective criteria for entry, including admissions tests and sibling and neighborhood preferences. These high-performing schools receive thousands of applications each year, from which they select only a small proportion.

As Figure 6.5 shows, the select schools serve the overwhelming majority of white students enrolled in New Orleans public schools. High schools in this tier have less than a third of African American or free/reduced lunch students, who comprise a majority in all other schools. The students identified as "special education" in the highest-performing schools are generally designated as "gifted"

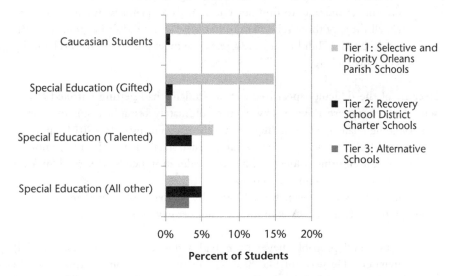

FIGURE 6.5 Differences in Ethnicity and Special Education Status, by School Tier in New Orleans, 2011–2012

or "talented," very different from the "emotionally disturbed" or "autism" designations found in lower-tier schools.

The second tier of New Orleans schools is the RSD charter schools. These schools engage in different skimming strategies to limit the number of students on the lower tail of the performance curve. Based on reports and interviews with parents and students who applied to RSD schools, these strategies include at least the following: (1) denying enrollment to low performers, students with discipline records, and special education students; (2) expelling students in October after receiving their annual funding from the state; and (3) having students arrested on school grounds and thereby eliminating them without having to expel them. A student explained, for example: "The other school wouldn't accept me because I failed the EOC [End-of-Course Assessment] by one point, so I signed up for [this school] and came here".[64]

A parent of a special education student described her experience:

> A person from the Recovery School District said that he would ... help me file a complaint because I was turned away from those schools at the high school fair ... in November. So early [in February] I went to the school expo, and ... of the four schools I talked to, two weren't gonna serve kids like Sam.[65] One of [the schools] was actually ... one of the same schools I spoke to in November. It was actually the same lady, in fact, she said, I remember talking to you at the high school expo in November. And I remember we talked about how we're full inclusion only ... we're not a good fit for you. So, then I started thinking, and well, I filed a complaint, I would have thought she would have been taught the law, so I contacted someone at the state to find out where my complaint went, and they said that all three of those schools said that what I said didn't happen, so it was just dropped ... I didn't deserve a response to let me know that I'd basically been called a liar, I guess."[66]

Because of the difficulty special education students had getting enrolled at any school, the Southern Poverty Law Center ultimately brought a suit in court.[67] The ongoing challenge was highlighted by the Cowen Institute's 2013 report on the *State of Public Education in New Orleans*, which stated that, "No single entity is responsible for ensuring students with special education needs are served, making it difficult to track students across schools."[68]

Some students have been turned away by so many schools that they have given up trying to attend. A community member gave this example:

> [This child] probably never even had a notice [for a particular school] anywhere. He was just like floating out there. We came across him. He wasn't enrolled in school. We got him a place at [a school]. We went in with the placement letter saying, "Here's the placement letter." We have

the mom with us. We're here to fill out the paperwork. And they had a meeting that was specifically meant to be intimidating towards this child and parent ... bringing things up like, "Now that you're enrolled in school, if you miss more than blah, blah, blah days then we're gonna refer you to municipal court." [They were] bringing up truancy, bringing up discipline policies before he's even attended a day of school, ... saying, "If you do this, then we're gonna do this. If you come here, we need you to know that we have hired an OPD [Orleans police department] as our security guard so you're gonna go straight to jail." That is what they said to this child.

Another community member confirmed that the use of local police in the schools often operates as an exclusion strategy:

Towards the end of last school year, they said that they were going to have an OPD on campus so that if anything happened, it's straight to jail. "Don't cross 'Go', don't collect $200." So the kid of course is like, "I don't want to go back there."

Two school administrators described the exclusion strategies used to eliminate struggling students from the rolls of many schools:

What they did was ... they figured out a way that would get the NFP money, which is the money that follows the Title I students, and then just before testing, which would be October. ... there were a lot of kids moving around suddenly around that date.... They would literally go and recruit kids out of schools that were scoring better if they could figure out a way to find them and get them into theirs, you know to transfer, and then pushing kids out with disabilities or low scoring [on] tests, so that they wouldn't bring the scores down. And they would do that in various ways. Some of them were more blatant than others. It could be saying to the parents, "We don't have the special ed staff support for your child's needs and we think you would be better supported in another school and we'll help you find one, or not" or suspensions and expulsions. The rate of expulsions in various schools is just startling, but it was one way [for schools] ... to say "We have an 85 percent graduation rate at our high school or 90 percent." But, that figure doesn't represent how many students left in the [previous] 4 years or 2 years or whatever.... If they have half the number that came in but they have a 90 percent graduation rate, they're just not mentioning that. So there are a lot of other ways, but those were the ones we saw.

So, on October 1 you have your kids, you get your check, you go "wow." You can make projections about spending and you're good.... So what happens is there's a purge. After October 1 it lasts about a month. After that month you're holding on to [those kids] for that February money. So we rarely get students who come in after let's say November. If you do, they just moved into the city, they're returning to the city. They've been at another school and have been expelled or about to be expelled and they realize [this school] will take me and that's when we get kids … We don't see a lot of mobility between November and February."

The third, and lowest, tier of the RSD is the alternative schools segment. These schools represent the last stop for students before being forced out of the school system entirely, or as a re-entry point from the correctional system. In fact, a corporation that operates correctional institutions in other states operates one of the alternative charter schools. This blurring of the lines between the three-tiered system of education and the state correctional system shows how the charter system in New Orleans is part of a school-to-prison pipeline for the most disadvantaged students.

We describe the organization of schools in New Orleans as stratified because students change schools primarily on a one-way ticket to lower performing schools. A student cannot decide to take an admissions test midway through the year and enter the highest-performing, predominantly white, public school. Students can, however, be expelled from a modestly performing charter and sent to an alternative school in the lowest tier of the RSD. Figure 6.6 shows how student performance declines at each tier of schooling, showing consistent decreases even between schools with different types of access within those tiers.

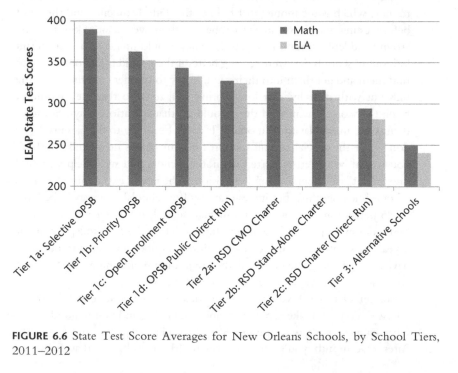

FIGURE 6.6 State Test Score Averages for New Orleans Schools, by School Tiers, 2011–2012

In 2012, in response to many parent complaints, the RSD instituted uniform citywide student transfer and expulsion policies. Between 2005 and 2012, RSD schools had their own individual discipline, reporting, and transfer policies, making monitoring virtually impossible. Principals could expel students for a variety of offenses, many unworthy of such a drastic measure, ranging from sleeping in class or being absent to disobeying a teacher.[69] In most RSD charters, principals meted out suspensions and expulsions as a result of "zero-tolerance" policies, the education equivalent of the "no broken windows" approach to crime. In some schools, students have to walk on lines in silence between classes, have silent lunches, track teachers with their eyes, and obey other measures at the risk of entering the demerit, detention, suspension, and expulsion cycle.

An observer sees stark differences in student populations and educational practices between the first and second tiers of schools. In a high–performing school, welcoming signs point to the principal's office, and students, most of whom are white, chat as they move from class to class. By contrast, it is almost impossible to walk into an RSD charter school because of the security guards and metal detectors stationed at the entrance. Once inside, lines on the floor show the direction students must walk. Between classes, mostly African American students walk in single file, enacting a silence that is eerie for adolescents, overseen every 20 feet by young teachers. To an outsider, the situation quickly brings to mind previous generations of racial discrimination.[70]

The logic of choice proposed by market-based proponents assumes the consumer, or student, chooses. In New Orleans, however, the schools make most of the decisions about students they will serve, resulting in a "flipped choice" system. To be sure, the system has implemented some forms of choice within the different tiers above. The RSD instituted the OneApp system, which includes most schools in New Orleans. In the OneApp, parents select a list of up to eight schools, to which they are then assigned by lottery, although the challenges we noted above can still enter in when students go to enroll or seek to stay.

Because only some (usually only a few) win in a lottery, the flip side of the choice coin is the inability to get one's choices. The Cowen Institute recently produced a report detailing the layers of decisions that families must make,[71] illustrating that choosing schools in New Orleans is a competitive enterprise that requires a lot of luck, as well as savvy. As we found, only lower-performing schools are available to most minority students and to those with the greatest needs, reproducing stratification more often than mitigating it.

In this tiered system, as schools made available to struggling students show low performance, they are closed and students are sent to other schools. Increasingly, reports suggest that these students are ending up in similarly failing schools.[72] It is important to note that increased stratification does likely produce benefits for those students lucky enough to attend a top-tier privileged charter school.

Is the Experiment Working?

Difficult methodological challenges confront studies seeking to make causal claims about the effects of post-Katrina reforms, since none can fully account for factors such as the loss of thousands of families who never returned to the city after the hurricane, the dramatic change in student demographics, or the resources available to some schools that now receive considerable private money. Census data show that not only has the city become smaller since 2000, it disproportionately lost low-income black families and those who did not own homes,[73] thus representing a more advantaged population today than previously.

Numerous claims have been made about the success of charter schools in New Orleans as proponents have put it forward as a model for other jurisdictions to follow.[74] The narrative often includes an account of how the system was underperforming before Katrina—something about which most people would agree—and data suggesting that school performance has improved since. For instance, one charter proponent, former CEO of New Schools New Orleans, a charter support organization, says that New Orleans schools have gone "from an F to a C," pointing to higher graduation rates and ACT scores as evidence.[75] Another study by the CREDO institute at Stanford showed positive impacts for students attending charter schools in Louisiana.[76]

Aside from not accounting for changes in student population and the fact that Louisiana has changed the metrics for designating what constitutes a failing grade for a school twice since the pre-Katrina days,[77] a number of issues need to be unpacked to evaluate such claims. Fully 79 percent of RSD charters were still rated D or F by the Louisiana Department of Education in 2013;[78] further analysis shows that even the gains "from an F to a C" depend on what data are used and what schools are included in the analysis. For example, when data are examined for the Recovery School District alone, little improvement is evident in test scores or graduation rates. The appearance of strong improvements typically relies on a comparison between the old New Orleans district with data from the RSD combined with Orleans Parish, although Orleans Parish is a separate district within the city that has long been higher performing and was not taken over by the state. ACT data referenced in that statement and many others are also influenced by how many and which students take the tests; those in RSD alternative schools are not required to do so, thus eliminating the lowest-performers from the calculations.

Researchers have questioned data released about the effects of the reforms on a number of occasions on various grounds:

- Purported gains for special education students included "gifted and talented" students, rather than limiting the category to students with disabilities.[79]
- Analysis of gains for RSD charters ignored the fact that many children were turned away from or pushed out of RSD charters into the RSD direct-run

schools (when they existed), thus biasing the comparisons because of differences in school composition.[80]
• Some charter school organizations touting large student achievement gains were found to achieve gains in part through extraordinary rates of attrition, disproportionately representing the lowest performing students.[81]

Unsurprisingly, high school graduation rates are also the subject of contentious debate. The governor of Louisiana, Bobby Jindal, claimed an improvement in graduation rates over time, citing data used by pro-charter school organizations:

> Right before Katrina, during the 2004–2005 school year, New Orleans had a graduation rate of 54.4 percent. The graduation rate for New Orleans is now 77.8 percent—which tops the statewide average for all students (which just reached an all-time high at 72.3 percent)—and the national average for African-American students.[82]

However, these graduation rate data are not supported by evidence. First, the pre-Katrina figure cited by Jindal is unsubstantiated by the Louisiana Department of Education, which says that such a statistic was not collected or published at that time.[83] The data that have been unearthed by determined researchers who have looked through state and district archives does not support the claim. Data unearthed for Orleans Parish in the pre-Katrina years (which then included what is now both RSD and OPSB) show graduation rates hovering at 78 to 81 percent between 1999 and 2002.[84] Since currently published data make it clear that the later statistic (77.8 percent) must be a combination of RSD and OPSB data, it would appear that graduation rates have declined slightly, rather than increased.

Another possibility is that the pre-Katrina statistic was using a cohort graduation rate, which is a different way to calculate graduation. Schneider explains that this calculation yields a 2001–2002 OPSB graduation rate of 52 percent, close to the number cited by the Governor. Louisiana state data show that, for the first RSD graduating cohort post-Katrina (2009–2010), the comparable rate was 49.7 percent. In 2013, the most recent year, it was 59.5 percent,[85] a modest improvement from the 2002 rate, but nowhere near the 78 percent claimed.

Similar concerns have been raised about claims regarding test score gains. For instance, one report cited data from the Louisiana Department of Education that the percentage of students performing "at grade level or above" rose from 23 percent in 2007 to 51 percent in 2012.[86] However, a different research organization presented data on student proficiency rates between these years that showed marked declines in as many years as gains occurred between 2007 and 2011 at the school level, raising questions about whether the calculations could be accurate.[87]

As we noted earlier, when data from RSD and OPSB are disaggregated, it is clear that a substantial difference in performance exists between students in the state-run recovery district and those in the top-tier schools still operated by the

Orleans Parish. Table 6.4 shows that only 12 percent of RSD students demonstrated "mastery" of English or math on the Louisiana state test (LEAP) in 2013 and 2014, while 42 percent of students in the OPSB schools did.[88] Only 15 percent of Louisiana districts scored lower than RSD on this measure.

Despite the fact that many of the charters identify themselves as college prep, few of their students meet a benchmark that would suggest they are approaching college readiness. For example, although more students in the RSD perform at the basic level (57 percent) than at the mastery level, the Louisiana Department of Education notes that, "basic achievement does not correspond with community college or university success. While 69 percent of students [statewide] hit this mark, for example, only 28 percent complete a university or community college degree."[89] This is very close to the proportion that reaches the mastery level on the state tests.

On the opposite side of the education spectrum from college admissions rest exclusion, crime, and the juvenile justice system. One research organization cites the longstanding research connecting lower educational attainment and higher crime rates and shows how that situation plays out in New Orleans.[90] The report states:

> Since the years following the [school] takeover, crime has increased dramatically, with more and more crimes involving juveniles and young adults. For the 2011 year in New Orleans, crime jumped 10 percent from the previous year, with significant spikes in murders, rapes, and armed robberies.[91]

The authors connect the issue of crime to the preponderance of school closings and exclusions. Both strategies simultaneously raise scores for schools (reopened schools are not required to readmit previous students) while pushing "low-performing" students either to schools further down the tier system, or more likely, out of the system altogether. The report authors find that the variety of exclusion tactics employed by charter schools, including those outlined above, correlate with the increased crime rate and require remedies to ensure that students can have access to high-quality educational opportunities.

In summary, the New Orleans case shows that adopting policies of privatizing education by installing charter schools has increased competition between schools; it has also (1) increased stratification and segregation in schools, (2) reduced options for high-need students and created an undesirable sector—often referred to as "dumping ground schools"—for these young people, and (3) encouraged exclusions of struggling students from school altogether. For those students who are not profitable, the market does not appear to offer choice. One parent, also an educator, remarked:

> I feel like advocates and parents and other people having problems around the education system as we're seeing it right now assume that you want to

set up a system to educate children well.… But if you [understand that] this is not about educating children, this is not about developmentally appropriate curriculum, or any of that, and this is profit driven, this is about the market, this is about making money, simple and pure—it's just purely about taking a public institution and making it a private one so that people can make money, it has nothing to do with educating children—then it's very simple. You no longer have to strain and hurt your mind to try to figure out why their boards and CEOs and people who are running schools have no education background and why the discipline system is the way it is. It's not rocket science: they want a population of low-wage workers who don't challenge the system, period. You know, they want people to come out of these factories already conditioned to work in these jobs and not push it, and not create unions, and not recreate unions as they bust unions. So, if you look at it from every level of profit, it makes complete sense, so it's really simple.

An Alternative to Privatization: Public Investment in Massachusetts

Interestingly, the highest achieving states in the United States—Connecticut, Massachusetts, New Hampshire, New Jersey, and Vermont—are among those that have had the least engagement with market-based reforms. The pro-charter Center for Education Reform (CER), which ranks states on their openness to charters, gives all of them a grade of "C" or "D."[92]

Massachusetts is a particularly instructive case. For more than a decade, since about 2002, Massachusetts has led the states in student achievement in every subject area on the National Assessment of Educational Progress. Massachusetts compares favorably with the top-scoring nations on PISA, ranking alongside Finland, Singapore, and others.[93]

This is not because of a widespread privatization movement: the CER complains that there is only one authorizer for charters, the Massachusetts State Board of Education, with an immovable cap on the number of charters, restricting the total to 72 Commonwealth charters, plus 48 Horace Mann (conversion) charters, run by districts. This represents only 6 percent of the approximately 1,850 schools in the state. Virtual charters are not allowed, although a new option for an "education collaborative" may allow the operation of a virtual learning component by two existing schools. New regulatory requirements put in place in 2014 tightened up charter school accountability and made it difficult for schools to exclude students.

The central story of Massachusetts' meteoric rise to excellence long preceded these recent, tiny charter school developments, which were responses to the federal Race to the Top incentives. The story began in 1992 with a court decision in *Hancock v. Driscoll* requiring an overhaul of school funding in the state. The school finance formula adopted in 1993 as part of Massachusetts' Education Reform Act stimulated substantially greater investments in needier schools through a weighted student formula which aimed to equalize funding and local effort simultaneously and which added funding increments based on the proportions of low-income students and English-language learners in a district.

This progressive approach helped boost educational investments and achievement as the state undertook a comprehensive reform, featuring new standards and assessments demanding more intellectually ambitious teaching and learning. In addition to much greater and more equitable funding to schools, the initiatives included statewide standards for students, educators, schools, and districts; new curriculum frameworks to guide instruction and state assessments; expanded learning time in core content areas; investments in technology; stronger preparation and licensing requirements for teachers; and more access to high-quality learning opportunities for teachers and school leaders.

In 1994, the state adopted a state plan for professional development, the first in Massachusetts' history, which led to the establishment of intensive summer institutes in content areas like math and science, dedicated funding to districts to support professional development for every teacher, requirements for recertification based on continuing education, and a new set of standards and expectations for local evaluation. The Attracting Excellence to Teaching program was created to subsidize preparation for qualified entrants into teaching.

In addition, the level of state funding for local early childhood programs increased by 500 percent in the first four years of the reform, and by more in the years thereafter. A Commission on Early Childhood Education was launched to create a plan for an early education and care system for the state. Demonstration sites were established for model preschool programs, and hundreds of Community Partnerships for Children grants were awarded to expand access to early education for children in need.

By the year 2000, Massachusetts had underwritten these reforms with more than 2 billion new state dollars to its public schools, greatly expanding the state share of funding and enhancing equity. University of Chicago economist Jonathan Guryan examined the effects of these investments and found that increased educational funding for historically low-spending districts led to improved student achievement in all subject areas, especially for traditionally low-scoring students.[94] By the year 2002, the state had dramatically improved overall achievement and sharply reduced its achievement gap.

It has maintained a lead over other states in all the years since then by continuing this program of investments. Studies have found that other states which have made similar long-term gains, such as Connecticut, New Jersey, and Vermont, have followed a comparable course of action—with equalizing shifts in funding, investments in high-quality standards and professional development, and support for child health, welfare, and early education.[95] Massachusetts and these other states demonstrate how investments in public education spent wisely and in concert with a systemic approach to reform can make a stronger difference in educational outcomes.

Conclusion

This chapter has linked the logic of neoliberal economics to the competing reform ideas advanced in the U.S. education system over the last 40 years, demonstrating how the United States arrived at an inflection point in education. It concludes that, despite considerable effort devoted in selected cities and states to market-based reforms, and the emergence, with federal support, of a larger number of privately managed schools, little evidence supports systemic improvement associated with these initiatives.

While some high-performing charter schools certainly exist—and undoubtedly some have acquired that distinction without creaming and cropping their student populations—the most consistent evidence indicates that market-based reforms have led to greater stratification and segregation, and to considerable effort on the part of schools to finding and keeping the students who are easiest to teach while finding ways to exclude those with greater needs. By contrast, states that have made strong, long-term gains in performance and have reduced achievement gaps have made strategic public investments in equity, improved educator preparation and instruction, and stronger supports for children.

The fundamental question at this juncture is whether the United States will continue down the privatization path by intensifying the corporate charter movement and expanding voucher programs, or will it seek to reclaim public education with reforms that will preserve it as a public good?

Notes

1   Carnoy, M., Adamson, F. Chudgar, A., Luschei, T., and Witte, J. (2007). *Vouchers and Public School Performance: A Case Study of the Milwaukee Parental Choice Program*. Washington, D.C.: Economic Policy Institute; Center for Research on Education Outcomes (2009). *Multiple Choice: Charter School Performance in 16 States*. Stanford, CA.

2   Elmore, R., and Burney, D. (1997). *Investing in Teacher Learning: Staff Development and Instructional Improvement in Community School District #2, New York City*. New York: National Commission on Teaching & America's Future; Darling-Hammond, L., Hightower, A., Husbands, J., LaFors, J., Young, V., and Christopher, C. (2005). *Instructional Leadership for Systemic Change: The Story of San Diego's Reform* (No. 3). Lanham, Maryland: The Rowman & Littlefield Publishing Group, Inc; Jackson, C. K., Johnson, R., and Persico, C. (2014). *The Effect of School Finance Reforms on the Distribution of Spending Academic Achievement and Adult Outcomes* (No. w20118). Cambridge, MA: National Bureau of Economic Research.

3   Adamson, F. (2010). How Does Context Matter? Comparing Achievement Scores, Opportunities to Learn, and Teacher Preparation Across Socio-Economic Quintiles in TIMSS and PISA (unpublished doctoral dissertation). Stanford University, Stanford, CA.

4   Any synopsis of American economic history is contested turf. This condensed version highlights the major policy shifts and actors, while Chapter 1 offers more discussion of different types of economic and political systems.

5   Indeed, the title of the final chapter of this book questions whether Smith's "Invisible Hand" can actually function like a magic wand over the economy or whether different

sectors, including education, require public investment to thrive. Results in the United States and other countries suggest the latter option.

6 Voting Rights Act of 1965, Public Law 89-110, 79 Stat. 437; *Brown v. Board of Education of Topeka*, 347 U.S. 483, 74 S. Ct. 686, 98 L. Ed. 873 (1954).

7 Freeman. Richard B. (1981). Black Economic Progress After 1964: Who Has Gained and Why? In S. Rosen (Ed.), *Studies in Labor Markets* (pp. 247–294). Chicago, IL: University of Chicago Press, accessed online at http://www.nber.org/books/rose81-1.

8 Darling-Hammond, L. (2010). *The Flat World and Education: How America's Commitment to Equity Will Determine our Future.* New York: Teachers College Press.

9 Jones, Stedman (2012). *Masters of the Universe: Hayek, Friedman, and the Birth of Neoliberal Politics.* Princeton: Princeton University Press.

10 Steger, Manfred and Roy, Ravi (2010). *Neoliberalism: A Very Short Introduction.* Oxford: Oxford University Press (p. 17).

11 Saez, Emmanuel and Zucman, Gabriel (2014). *Wealth Inequality in the United States since 1913: Evidence from Capitalized Income Tax Data.* NBER Working Paper, October 2014, accessed online at http://gabriel-zucman.eu/uswealth/.

12 Saez, Emmanuel and Zucman, Gabriel (2014). *Wealth Inequality in the United States since 1913: Evidence from Capitalized Income Tax Data.* NBER Working Paper, October 2014, accessed online at http://gabriel-zucman.eu/uswealth/.

13 Darling-Hammond, L. (2004). Standards, Accountability, and School Reform. *Teachers College Record*, 106(6), 1047–1085.

14 National Center for Education Statistics (2015). *The Condition of Education: Charter School Enrollment*, accessed online at http://nces.ed.gov/programs/coe/indicator_cgb.asp.

15 Heilig, J. V., and Darling-Hammond, L. (2008). Accountability Texas-Style: The Progress and Learning of Urban Minority Students in a High-Stakes Testing Context. *Educational Evaluation and Policy Analysis, 30*(2), 75–110.

16 Klein, S. P., Hamilton, L., McCaffrey, D. F., and Stecher, B. (2000). What Do Test Scores in Texas Tell Us? *Education Policy Analysis Archives*, 8(49); Haney, W. (2000). The Myth of the Texas Miracle in Education, *Education Policy Analysis Archives*, 8(41); Heilig, J. V., and Darling-Hammond, L. (2008). Accountability Texas-Style: The Progress and Learning of Urban Minority Students in a High-Stakes Testing Context. *Educational Evaluation and Policy Analysis*, 30(2), 75–110.

17 No Child Left Behind Act of 2001, 20 U.S.C. § 6319 (2008). *Title V—Promoting Informed Parental Choice and Innovative Programs*, Sec. 5101, accessed online at http://www2.ed.gov/policy/elsec/leg/esea02/pg57.html.

18 No Child Left Behind Act of 2001, 20 U.S.C. § 6319 (2008). *Subpart 3—Local Innovative Education Programs*, Sec. 5131, accessed online at http://www2.ed.gov/policy/elsec/leg/esea02/pg60.html.

19 Ravitch, D. (2013). *Reign of Error: The Hoax of the Privatization Movement and the Danger to America's Public Schools.* New York: Vintage.

20 Hall, D., and Ushomirsky, N. (2010). *Close the Hidden Funding Gaps in Our Schools. K-12 Policy.* Washington, D.C.: Education Trust.

21 Marangos, J. (2004). Was Shock Therapy Consistent with Democracy? *Review of Social Economy*, 62(2), 221–243.

22 Klein, N. (2007). *The Shock Doctrine: The Rise of Disaster Capitalism.* London: Macmillan.

23 For examples in Philadelphia and Detroit, see respectively: Gabriel, T. (June 16, 2013). *Budget Cuts Reach Bone for Philadelphia Schools*, accessed online at http://www.nytimes.

com/2013/06/17/education/budget-cuts-reach-bone-for-philadelphia-schools.html?_r=0; Pedroni, T. (2014). *Another Lost Year: Children in State-Managed Detroit Schools Lose Even More Ground to State Peers*, accessed online at https://sites.google.com/site/detroitdataanddemocracyproject/ANOTHER-LOST-YEAR.

24 Accessed online at http://www.j4jalliance.com/whoweare/.

25 Accessed online at http://www.j4jalliance.com/whoweare/.

26 Davis, M. (2013). Education Companies Exert Public Policy Influence, *Education Week*, 32(29).

27 Center for Research on Education Outcomes (2011). *Charter School Performance in Pennsylvania*. Stanford, CA, accessed online at http://credo.stanford.edu/reports/PA%20State%20Report_20110404_FINAL.pdf.

28 Miron, G., Urschel, J. L., Aguilar, Y., Mayra, A., and Dailey, B. (2012). *Profiles of For-Profit and Nonprofit Education Management Organizations: Thirteenth Annual Report, 2010–2011*. Boulder, CO: National Education Policy Center, accessed online at http://nepc.colorado.edu/publication/EMO-profiles-10-11.

29 The Center on Media and Democracy (nd), accessed online at http://www.alecexposed.org/wiki/ALEC_Exposed.

30 Peterson, B. (2015). Scott Walker's Budget Undermines Public Education, with Bull's-eye on Milwaukee. *Portside*, accessed online at http://portside.org/2015-07-10/scott-walkers-budget-undermines-public-education-bulls-eye-milwaukee.

31 Usher, A., and Kober, N. (2011). *Keeping Informed about School Vouchers: A Review of Major Developments and Research*. Washington, D.C.: Center on Education Policy.

32 Imberman, S. A. (2011). Achievement and Behavior in Charter Schools: Drawing a More Complete Picture. *The Review of Economics and Statistics*, 93(2), 416–435.

33 Miron, G., and Nelson, C. (2004). Student Achievement in Charter Schools: What We Know and Why We Know So Little. In Bulkley, K., and Wohlstetter (Eds.), *Taking Account of Charter Schools: What's Happened and What's Next* (pp. 161–175) New York: Teachers College Press; American Federation of Teachers (2002). *Do Charter Schools Measure Up? The Charter School Experiment After 10 Years*. Washington, D.C.: American Federation of Teachers.

34 Miron, G., Coryn, C. L., and Mackety, D. M. (2007). *Evaluating the Impact of Charter Schools on Student Achievement: A Longitudinal Look at the Great Lakes States*. Tempe, AZ: Education Policy Research Unit, College of Education, Arizona State University; Messina, I. (2005). State to Review Charter School Concerns, acessed onlineathttp://oh.aft.org/index.cfm?action=article&articleID=d2bd2915-42dd-487c-84ed-c311811bf95a.

35 Carnoy, M., Jacobsen, R., Mishel, L., and Rothstein, R. (2005). *The Charter School Dust-up: Examining the Evidence on Enrollment and Achievement*. Washington, D.C.: Economic Policy Institute.

36 Institute on Race and Poverty (2008). *Failed Promises: Assessing Charter Schools in the Twin Cities*. Minneapolis, MN: University of Minnesota, Institute on Race and Poverty.

37 EdSource (2008). *California's Charter Schools: 2008 Performance Update*, Palo Alto, CA: EdSource.

38 Center for Research on Education Outcomes (2009). *Multiple Choice: Charter School Performance in 16 States*. Stanford, CA.

39 Center for Research on Education Outcomes (2009). *Multiple Choice: Charter School Performance in 16 States*. Stanford, CA.

40 Young, V. M., Humphrey, D. C., Wang, H., Bosetti, K. R., Cassidy, L., Wechsler, M. E., Rivera, E., Murray, S., and Schanzenbach, D. W. (2009). *Renaissance Schools Fund-Supported Schools: Early Outcomes, Challenges, and Opportunities*, Menlo Park, CA: Stanford Research International and Chicago: Consortium on Chicago School Research, accessed online at http://ccsr.uchicago.edu/publications/RSF%20FINAL%20April%2015.pdf

41 Frankenberg, E., Siegel-Hawley G., and Wang, J. (2010). *Choice Without Equity: Charter School Segregation and the Need for Civil Rights Standards*. Los Angeles, CA: The Civil Rights Project/Proyecto Derechos Civiles at UCLA, accessed online at www.civilrightsproject.ucla.edu.

42 Miron, G., Urschel, J. L., Mathis, W. J., and Tornquist, E. (2010). *Schools Without Diversity: Education Management Organizations, Charter Schools and the Demographic Stratification of the American School System*. Boulder, CO and Tempe, AZ: Education and the Public Interest Center, University of Colorado, Boulder & Education Policy Research Unit, College of Education, Arizona State University, available at http://epicpolicy.org/publication/schools-without-diversity.

43 Wamba, N. G., and Ascher, C. (2003). An Examination of Charter School Equity. *Education and Urban Society* 35(4), 462–476.

44 *Milwaukee District Report Card 2012-13*, accessed online at https://apps2.dpi.wi.gov/sdpr/spr.action.

45 *Milwaukee District Report Card 2011-12*, accessed online at https://apps2.dpi.wi.gov/sdpr/spr.action.

46 Montgomery, K., Darling-Hammond, L., and Campbell, C. (2011). *Developing Common Instructional Practice Across a Portfolio of Schools: The Evolution of School Reform in Milwaukee*. Stanford, CA: Stanford Center for Opportunity Policy in Education.

47 Wolf, Patrick J., (2010). *The Comprehensive Longitudinal Evaluation of the Milwaukee Parental Choice Program: Summary of Third Year Reports*. School Choice Demonstration Project, Fayetteville, AR, accessed online at http://www.uaedreform.org/SCDP/Milwaukee_Research.html; Zimmer, R., Gill, B., Booker, K., Lavertu, S., Sass, T. R., and Witte, J. (2009). *Charter Schools in Eight States: Effects on Achievement, Attainment, Integration, and Competition* (Vol. 869). Santa Monica, CA: Rand Corporation.

48 Montgomery, K., Darling-Hammond, L., and Campbell, C. (2011). *Developing Common Instructional Practice Across a Portfolio of Schools: The Evolution of School Reform in Milwaukee*. Stanford, CA: Stanford Center for Opportunity Policy in Education.

49 D'Andrea, C. (2011). *Milwaukee Public Schools Rate Amongst Worst U.S. Urban Districts When it Comes to Reading*. McIver Institute, accessed online at http://www.maciverinstitute.com/2011/12/milwaukee-public-schools-rate-amongst-worst-u-s-urban-districts-when-it-comes-to-reading/.

50 Montgomery, K., Darling-Hammond, L., and Campbell, C. (2011). *Developing Common Instructional Practice Across a Portfolio of Schools: The Evolution of School Reform in Milwaukee*. Stanford, CA: Stanford Center for Opportunity Policy in Education.

51 Anderson, T. (2014). *Wisconsin Panel to Target Racial Achievement Gap*, accessed online at http://www.twincities.com/education/ci_25541424/panel-target-racial-achievement-gap

52 *Milwaukee District Report Card 2012-13*, accessed online at https://apps2.dpi.wi.gov/sdpr/spr.action.

53 Richards, E. (2013, September 23). Many Independent Charter Schools Miss Mark on State Report Card, *Milwaukee Journal Sentinel*, accessed online at http://www.jsonline.

com/news/education/many-independent-charter-schools-miss-mark-on-state-report-cards-b99102550z1-224814982.html.

54 Montgomery, K., Darling-Hammond, L., and Campbell, C. (2011). *Developing Common Instructional Practice Across a Portfolio of Schools: The Evolution of School Reform in Milwaukee*, Stanford, CA: Stanford Center for Opportunity Policy in Education.

55 The chronology of events reveals how the U.S. education system and certain states fostered privatization as an education solution. Louisiana started the Recovery School District (RSD) *before* Hurricane Katrina in response to Federal (NCLB) accountability policy. Thus, the word "recovery" does not refer to New Orleans recovering from the hurricane but to schools recovering from designation as "failing" under NCLB, as discussed previously in the chapter.

56 The entire story of the emergence of a charter school system in New Orleans is too extensive and complex for this book. Therefore, we focus on how this particular situation incorporates the rationales of privatization and the results.

57 See, for example: Osborne, D. (2012). Born on the Bayou: A New Model for American Education. *Third Way,* accessed online at http://content.thirdway.org/publications/579/Third_Way_Report_-_Born_on_the_Bayou-A_New_Model_for_American_Education.pdf; Smith, N. (2012). *The Louisiana Recovery School District: Lessons for the Buckeye State*. Washington, D.C.: Thomas B. Fordham Institute; The Mind Trust. (2011). *Creating Opportunity Schools: A Bold Plan to Transform Indianapolis Public Schools*, accessed online at http://www.themindtrust.org/files/file/opp-schools-full-report.pdf; Hill, P., Campbell, C., Menefee-Libey, D., Dusseault, B., DeArmond, M., and Gross, B. (2009). *Portfolio School Districts for Big Cities: An Interim Report*. Seattle, WA: Center on Reinventing Public Education.

58 After five years of repeated requests for data by New Orleans-based researchers concerned about the effects of the reforms were denied by the Louisiana Department of Education, an organization called "Research on Reforms" brought a lawsuit against the state. The suit was, after many years, decided in their favor in 2015 (see: http://www.researchonreforms. org/html/documents/AppealCourtReversesDistrictCourt.pdf). However, this organization has not been able to get data sets even after the favorable ruling. The authors of this chapter made similar requests and ultimately received limited data from the Louisiana Department of Education, inadequate for a complete analysis of student outcomes by race, class, disability, and language status, and have been unable to secure the remaining necessary data. Meanwhile, the state of Louisiana provided complete data sets to CREDO, at the Hoover Institution at Stanford University, and to the Cowan Institute at the University of Tulane, neither of which has been willing to share the data with others.

59 Ferguson, B. and Hatfield, C. (2014). *RSD High School Test Scores Remain Below State Average*. New Orleans, LA: Research on Reforms, accessed online at http://researchonreforms.org/html/documents/RSDHighSchoolTestScoresRemainBelowStateAveragePDF.pdf.

60 National Center for Education Statistics (2013). *How are States Performing? The Nation's Report Card: 2013 Mathematics and Reading* (Data file), accessed online at http://www.nationsreportcard.gov/reading_math_2013/#/state-performance.

61 The SPS is used in Louisiana to measure the relative success of schools. The primary component is performance on state tests, although the ingredients and the scale (100, 150, or 200 points) have changed in the past decade, leading to difficulties in comparisons over time.

62 The Associated Press. (2015). *Fired New Orleans School Workers go to U.S. Supreme Court.* accessed online at http://www.nola.com/education/index.ssf/2015/03/fired_new_orleans_school_worke.html.

63 The expulsion regulation went into effect for the 2014–2015 school year, pursuant to Louisiana administration code, Title 28:CXXXIX, Bulletin 126: Charter Schools, §2701, Section K, accessed online at http://doa.louisiana.gov/osr/lac/lac28.htm.

64 *Author's note:* While low performance is certainly a reason for excluding children, it is illegal (except in the highest-tier selective schools, which represents another method of reinforcing stratification). Therefore, many schools focus on exclusion of students likely to have lower test scores, but for other reasons, such as behavioral issues.

65 Pseudonyms used for all participants and schools in this research.

66 Public schools, under the federal IDEA act, are required to provide seats and necessary accommodation for every student, including special education students. Because of the expense and lower test scores of special education students, many students are discouraged from attending, in violation of the federal IDEA law.

67 Southern Poverty Law Center (n.d.). Case docket: *P.B., et al. v. Pastorek* (summary of legal case). Montgomery, AL. Accessed online at http://www.splcenter.org/get-informed/case-docket/new-orleans-special-education/.

68 Scott S. Cowen Institute (2013). *The State of Public Education in New Orleans: 2013 Report.* New Orleans: Scott S. Cowen Institute, Tulane University, accessed online at http://www.coweninstitute.com/wp-content/uploads/2013/07/2013_SPENO_Final2.pdf.

69 Ferguson, B. (2011). *New Orleans RSD Charter Schools Can Expel Unwanted Students—Making Test Results Questionable.* New Orleans, LA: Research on Reforms, accessed online at http://www.researchonreforms.org/documents/CharterSchsCanExpelUnwantedStudents.pdf.

70 For a more complete description of the experiences of students in the New Orleans system, see: Adamson, F., Cook-Harvey, C., and Darling-Hammond, L. (forthcoming), *Whose Choice? Student Experiences and Outcomes in the New Orleans School Marketplace,* Stanford, CA: Stanford Center for Opportunity Policy in Education; Buras, K. L. (2014). *Charter Schools, Race, and Urban Space: Where the Market Meets Grassroots,* New York, NY: Routledge.

71 Scott S. Cowen Institute (2015). *The State of Public Education in New Orleans: 10 Years After Hurricane Katrina.* New Orleans, LA: Scott S. Cowen Institute, Tulane University, accessed online at http://www.speno2015.com.

72 Williams, J. (2013, June 11). Most students leaving RSD's 4 closed, failing schools are headed to other substandard schools. *The Lens,* accessed online at http://thelensnola.org/2013/06/11/most-students-leaving-from-rsds-4-closed-failing-schools-are-headed-to-other-substandard-schools/. See also Scott S. Cowen Institute (2013). *The State of Public Education in New Orleans: 2013 Report.* New Orleans: Scott S. Cowen Institute, Tulane University, accessed online at http://www.coweninstitute.com/wp-content/uploads/2013/07/2013_SPENO_Final2.pdf.

73 Robertson, C. (2011, February 3). New Orleans shrank after Hurricane Katrina, census shows. *The New York Times,* accessed online at http://www.nytimes.com/2011/02/04/us/04census.html/.

74 See, for example: Osborne, D. (2012). Born on the Bayou: A New Model for American Education. *Third Way,* accessed online at http://content.thirdway.org/

publications/579/Third_Way_Report_-_Born_on_the_Bayou-A_New_Model_for_ American_Education.pdf; Smith, N. (2012). *The Louisiana Recovery School District: Lessons for the Buckeye State*. Washington, D.C.: Thomas B. Fordham Institute; The Mind Trust (2011). *Creating Opportunity Schools: A Bold Plan to Transform Indianapolis Public Schools*, accessed online at http://www.themindtrust.org/files/file/opp-schools-full-report.pdf; Hill, P., Campbell, C., Menefee-Libey, D., Dusseault, B., DeArmond, M., and Gross, B. (2009). *Portfolio School Districts for Big Cities: An Interim Report*, Seattle, WA: Center on Reinventing Public Education.

75 Emma, C. (2015, April 16). The New Orleans Model: Praised but Unproven, *Politico*, accessed online at http://www.politico.com/story/2015/04/the-new-orleans-model-praised-but-unproven-116982.html.

76 Center for Research on Education Outcomes (2013). *Charter School Performance in Louisiana*. Stanford CA, accessed online at http://credo.stanford.edu/documents/la_report_2013_7_26_2013_final.pdf.

77 After Katrina, Louisiana changed the cut-point for failing schools from an SPS score of 60 to the state average of 87.4. In the decade since, Louisiana has altered the cut-point, the scale of the SPS (from 100 to 200), and the metrics used to calculate the SPS. These changes prevent longitudinal understanding of the impact of charter schools on New Orleans students if the measure is the number of failing schools. Combined with the failure to release the individual data so that researchers can create indices that are comparable over time, the changes in SPS scores make it difficult to ascertain whether and where performance in improving or declining and how students are being served.

78 Andrea Gabor (2013, Sept. 20). The Great Charter Tryout, *Newsweek*, accessed online at http://www.theinvestigativefund.org/investigations/politicsandgovernment/1848/the_great_charter_tryout?page=entire.

79 Ferguson, B. (2013). *CREDO Report is Biased Evaluation*, New Orleans, LA: Research on Reforms, accesed online at http://www.researchonreforms.org/html/documents/CredoIsBiasedEvaluation.pdf.

80 National Economic and Social Rights Initiative and Families and Friends of Louisiana's Incarcerated Children (2010). *Pushed Out: Harsh Discipline in Louisiana Schools Denies the Right to Education (A Focus on the Recovery School District in New Orleans)*. New York.

81 Miron, G., Urschel, J. L., and Saxton, N. (2011). *What Makes KIPP Work? A Study of Student Characteristics, Attrition, and School Finance*, New York: National Center for the Study of Privatization in Education, Teachers College, Columbia University; and Kalamazoo, MI: Study Group on Educational Management Organizations, Western Michigan University. See also Tuttle, C. C., Teh, B., Nichols-Barrer, I., Gill, B. P., and Gleason, P. (2010). *Student Characteristics and Achievement in 22 KIPP Middle Schools*, Washington, D.C.: Mathematica Policy Research.

82 Jindal, B. (2014, September 13). New Orleans is Leading the Way in Education Reform. *Nola.com*, accessed online at http://www.nola.com/opinions/index.ssf/2013/09/louisiana_is_leading_the_way_i.html. See also Educate Now, which is likely the original source for the claim: Jacobs, L. (2011, November 11). *Historic Gains in Four-Year High School Graduation Rate*. Educatenow.net, accessed online at http://educatenow.net/2011/11/01/historic-gains-in-four-year-high-school-graduation-rate/.

83 Johnson, A. (nd). *Charter Schools' Katrina Memory Hole*. Citationsneeded.com, accessed online at http://citationsneeded.com/2014/05/24/charter-schools-katrina-memory-hole/.

84 Schneider, M. (2015, June 11). *Info on New Orleans Graduation Rates Pre-Katrina*, Deutsch29. wordpress.com, accessed online at https://deutsch29.wordpress.com/2015/06/11/news-info-on-new-orleans-graduation-rates-pre-katrina/.

85 The data can be found here: Louisiana Department of Education (nd). *District and State Graduation Rates (2005–2006 to 2012–2013)*. Louisianabelieves.com, accessed online at http://www.louisianabelieves.com/docs/data-management/cohort-graduation-rates-%282006-2012%29.pdf?sfvrsn=2.

86 Osborne, D. (2012). Born on the Bayou: A New Model for American Education, *Third Way*, accessed online at http://content.thirdway.org/publications/579/Third_Way_Report_-_Born_on_the_Bayou-A_New_Model_for_American_Education.pdf.

87 Hatfield, C. (2011). *Annual Percent Proficiency Changes in ELA by RSD Schools and Grade*. Accessed online at http://researchonreforms.org/html/documents/RSDGainsLosseswithCover.pdf

88 Louisiana Department of Education. (nd). *2014 and 2013 Percentile Ranks for Percent of Students Mastery and Above and Percent of Students Basic and Above (LEAP and iLEAP)*. Louisianabelieves.com, accessed online at www.louisianabelieves.com/docs/default-source/test-results/district-percentile-ranking-comparison-2013-to-2014-(mastery-above).xlsx?sfvrsn=2.

89 Louisiana Department of Education (nd). *Results Steady on Transitional LEAP and iLEAP Tests*. Louisianabelieves.com, accessed online at http://www.louisianabelieves.com/newsroom/news-releases/2014/05/27/results-steady-on-transitional-leap-and-ileap-test.

90 Ferguson, B. (2012). *New Orleans Schools Should Not Serve as a National Model: Omissions and Errors in the Report Used by Senator Mary Landrieu in Promoting New Orleans Schools as a National Model*. New Orleans, LA: Research on Reforms (accessed online at http://www.researchonreforms.org/html/documents/NOSchoolsNotServeasNatModel.pdf.

91 Ferguson, B. (2012). *New Orleans Schools Should Not Serve as a National Model: Omissions and Errors in the Report Used by Senator Mary Landrieu in Promoting New Orleans Schools as a National Model*. New Orleans, LA: Research on Reforms (p. 3). Accessed online at http://www.researchonreforms.org/html/documents/NOSchoolsNotServeasNatModel.pdf

92 Center for Education Reform (2015). *Charter school laws across the states: 2015 rankings and scorecard*. Edreform.com, accessed online at https://www.edreform.com/wp-content/uploads/2015/07/CharterLaws2015.pdf.

93 Kelly, D., Nord, C. W., Jenkins, F., Chan, J. Y., and Kastberg, D. (2013). *Performance of US 15-Year-Old Students in Mathematics, Science, and Reading Literacy in an International Context. First Look at PISA 2012*. NCES 2014-024. Washington, D.C.: National Center for Education Statistics.

94 Guryan, J. (2001). *Does money matter? Regression-discontinuity estimates from education finance reform in Massachusetts* (No. w8269). Cambridge, MA: National Bureau of Economic Research.

95 See, for example, Darling-Hammond, L. (2010). *The Flat World and Education: How America's Commitment to Equity will Determine our Future*. New York, NY: Teachers College Press; Murnane, R. J., and Levy, F. (1996). *Teaching the New Basic Skills. Principles for Educating Children To Thrive in a Changing Economy*. New York: Free Press.

7

DEVELOPING HIGH-QUALITY PUBLIC EDUCATION IN CANADA

The Case of Ontario

Michael Fullan[1] and Santiago Rincon-Gallardo

Canada, and in particular Ontario, offers an illustrative example of a high-quality public education system. Since the launching of its whole system reform strategy in late 2003, Ontario continues to demonstrate that significant improvements in student achievement and equity can be made in a large and diverse public education system. Sustained improvement in the province has been the result of a thoughtful and evolving strategy based on three key principles: a relentless focus on a few ambitious goals, collective capacity building linked to results, and a progressive partnership with the teaching profession. Specific initiatives have embodied these key principles, based on continuous learning from implementation.

We have organized this chapter into four main sections. First we consider the promise of high-quality public education. Second, we report on Ontario's educational accomplishments between 2003 and 2014. Third, we consider the policies and strategies that were used to reach a high degree of success. Finally, we take a retrospective look at the political shifts in Ontario between 1995 and 2015. The chapter emphasizes how a large public education system can achieve widespread and possibly sustainable success through deliberate policy means and strategic actions to build capacity and ownership across the system.

The Promise of High-Quality Public Education

Privatization and public investment are the larger themes of the book. With its passionate advocates and fierce critics, privatization has taken an important place in debates on how to achieve improved outcomes for children and youth. Simply put, privatization consists of transferring ownership of an enterprise or service from the public sector (government) to private hands. Its advocates argue that privatization spurs improved performance and efficiency in ways that governments cannot. This is, essentially, a theory of action: that is, a statement that proposes a causal relationship between actions taken (privatization) and desired results (improved performance and efficiency).

The key argument for privatization goes more or less as follows: unlike governments, private companies have a profit incentive, and thus are more likely to cut costs and improve efficiency. Unlike governments, private companies are not motivated by political pressures, and thus can make better and sounder decisions to improve efficiency and make long-term investments. Unlike governments, private firms have pressures from stakeholders and competition from other providers to improve the quality of their services.

A core assumption of the theory of action of privatization is that a publicly run system cannot substantially improve its performance. In this chapter, we present the case of education reform in Ontario as evidence that proves this core assumption wrong. We do so by examining the continuous improvement in student performance achieved in Ontario's public education system over the past 12 years. We also show that these outcomes provide a stark contrast to the rather stalled outcomes, low teacher morale, and public dissatisfaction that prevailed under the antecedent Conservative rule, which sought to advance an aggressive market-oriented agenda between 1995 and 2003. But more than simply proving a core assumption of privatization wrong, we offer in this chapter evidence to build a theory of action that causally connects the provision of and investment in public education with improved quality and equity of educational opportunities and outcomes for students. The power of this theory of action lies in its being built from a deliberate and successful attempt to improve an entire educational system. At the core of this theory of action is a firm belief that education, with its central role in promoting and improving moral, social, economic, and societal wellbeing, should be the direct responsibility of the state.

We don't assume that all systems can do what Ontario did. Every context has a different starting point and set of conditions. But the themes of success are similar. All education systems from around the world can learn these lessons and apply their own versions to get much better results than they do now.

Structural and Political Context: Canada and Ontario

Canada has a total population of 33.6 million, which includes people with over 200 ethnic origins and almost 20 percent with a mother tongue other than English or French. As a federal system and with the second-largest territory in the world, Canada includes ten provinces and three territories. Each provincial government is headed by an elected premier, similar to a governor in the United States. The premier, in turn, appoints a cabinet, made up of ministers who are drawn from elected members of the provincial legislature.

In Canada, education is the responsibility of each province and territory; there is no national or federal department or ministry of education, although there is some involvement of the federal government in education in various indirect ways. Each province has a ministry or department of education responsible for funding schools, making policies, setting curriculum, etcetera. Provincial departments of education are headed by deputy ministers, who are civil servants appointed by the government. Canadian provinces have local school districts with elected boards.

Virtually all funding for schools in the country comes from provincial governments, not local sources. Canada's vast scale, diverse populations, and provincial jurisdiction over education create many different contexts for education. Because the provinces function in similar ways to states, they serve as valuable sources of comparison for the United States.

Canada offers universal publicly funded schooling from kindergarten through grade 12, with attendance being compulsory up to the age of 16 in every province, except for Ontario and New Brunswick, where attendance to school is compulsory up to the age of 18 or until high school graduation, whichever comes first. Education in the country is generally divided into elementary (primary and middle school), secondary (high school), and post-secondary (college and university). Across the country, where the population warrants it, education is available in the two official languages, English and French.[2]

The priority given to education in Canada is evident in its relatively high percentage of GDP (7 percent) spent on this sector, representing a significant public investment. This overall percentage of GDP is mostly driven by post-secondary education. The GDP for elementary and secondary education (4 percent) is around the OECD average of 3.8 percent.[3] Teacher wages in the country, although not as high as in Japan or Korea, are higher than in the United States. In the case of Ontario, teachers' salaries range from CN $42,000 to CN $92,000 within a 12-year salary grid. Teachers can move along salary categories by completing a specific number of Additional Qualification Programs. Teachers who undertake responsibilities beyond regular classroom duties (such as acting as department head) can also receive additional remuneration.[4]

The methods of investment have evolved over time. Over the past three decades, all Canadian provinces but Manitoba changed to provincial-level funding, creating equitable and successful education systems. These provinces transitioned from funding methods similar to U.S. states (local boards setting tax rates) to provincial-level funding, offering an important lesson that viable alternatives to local funding do exist.[5] Throughout this transition, each province has maintained its autonomy, structuring their systems differently and maintaining some local control over spending and allocation.

Ontario is the most populous province in Canada, with approximately 38 percent of the country's estimated population of 35.7 million.[6] In 2013, Ontario received about 40 percent of the roughly 260,000 new immigrants to Canada.[7] The province has the largest, most diverse student population in Canada. Of the more than 2 million students attending Ontario public schools, 27 percent were born outside of Canada and 20 percent are visible minorities. Toronto, the capital city of Ontario, is considered one of the most diverse cities in North America and the world.[8]

The publicly funded education system in Ontario serves 95 percent of the school-age children in the province. Based on preliminary 2013–2014 figures, Ontario has nearly 4,000 elementary schools, over 900 high schools, and employs roughly 129,000 full-time teachers, administrators, and early childhood educators.[9] To put things in perspective, Ontario's system is larger than those in 45 U.S. states.[10] Ontario's schools are organized in 72 school districts, each belonging to one of four provincially operated education governance systems: English public, English Catholic, French public, and French Catholic.[11] The operational funding of Ontario's educational system in 2013 was about CN $22.5 billion.

Canada and Ontario's Educational Accomplishments

Canada is considered one of the highest-performing and most equitable educational systems in the world. The country has consistently performed well on international assessments, including the Programme for International Student Assessment, PISA.[12] In 2012, Canada scored 24 points above the OECD average in mathematics literacy (the primary domain tested) and similarly well on science and reading literacy.[13] While the average math and reading scores have declined slightly over time (science has been consistent), Canada remains well above the OECD average.

Furthermore, Canada is one of the few countries with higher than average performance *and* below-average disparities between students, measured by score differences between the 90th and 10th percentile of student scores. The score differences remain over 200 points (about 2 standard deviations) but show that Canada's system simultaneously prepares students at different ability levels better than most countries. Ontario in particular has been identified as one of the most improved education systems, both within Canada[14] and internationally,[15] and as one of the best school systems in the English-speaking world.[16] We start with the performance of the Ontario education system.

Student achievement in Ontario has increased steadily since 2003—more noticeably in literacy than in numeracy, where improvement has stalled over the past few years. Figure 7.1 shows the percentage of students in grades 3 and 6 achieving the provincial standard in literacy and mathematics: that is, the proportion of students achieving at level 3 or above in the tests developed and administered by the Education Quality and Accountability Office (EQAO) between 2003 and 2014. It should be noted that this standard is higher than the PISA standard, and as such represents very high performance. In this period, overall student achievement has increased from 54 percent to 72 percent (Figure 7.1). At the same time, the number of elementary students at or below level 1 on EQAO grade 3 and 6 assessments has fallen by over 50 percent.

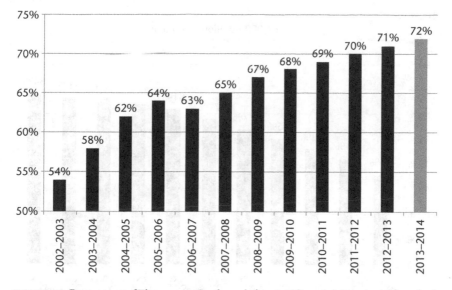

FIGURE 7.1 Percentage of Elementary Students Achieving Ontario's Provincial Standard, 2002–2003 to 2013–2014

Between 2003 and 2014, high school graduation rates in Ontario have increased by 16 percentage points, bringing the province's 900 secondary schools to an 84 percent graduation rate in 2014 from its starting point of 68 percent in 2003, as shown in Figure 7.2. The figures reported here reflect a five-year graduation rate from a 4-year program, so it includes an extra year for many students.

The accomplishments of Ontario's Whole System Reform Strategy can also be expressed as follows: over 180,000 more elementary school students have reached higher proficiency in reading, writing, and mathematics by grade 6 than would have been the case without the strategy. Because of the strategy, 163,000 more students have graduated from high schools.

Furthermore, important student achievement gaps have been reduced. For example, since 2002–2003, Ontario has reduced the gap between grade 3 and 6 English (ELL) and French (AFL) language learners and the rest of the population by 83 percent, coming very close to eliminating the differences. Also, during this period, the gap between the performance of students with special education needs and their peers has decreased by over eight percentage points. Especially in writing, significant learning gains among these students have been achieved and achievement gaps reduced, thanks to the use of assistive technologies and other interventions advanced by Ontario districts through a project known as "Essential for Some, Good for All."[17]

In addition to these overall improvements in student achievement, the number of low performing schools has declined dramatically over time, even though the

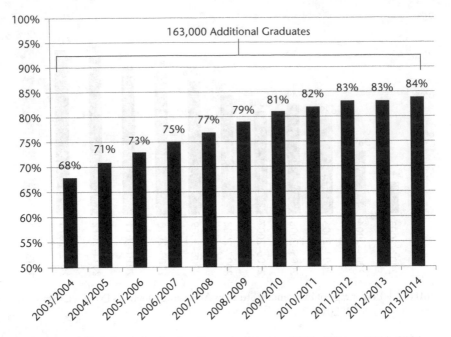

FIGURE 7.2 High School Graduation Rates in Ontario, 2003–2004 to 2013–2014

bar to determine low-performing status was raised in 2009–2010. The Ontario Focused Intervention Partnership (OFIP) was launched in 2006–2007 to offer targeted support to low performing schools.[18] Initially OFIP schools were included where 33 percent or fewer of their students were achieving levels 3 or 4 in grade 6 reading for two of the previous three years; whereas in 2009–2010 to present, schools are identified for intervention where 50 percent or fewer students reached provincial standard in at least two of reading, writing and/or mathematics assessments (or four or more of six assessments for schools with primary and junior students) for two consecutive years. From more than 700 schools qualifying for OFIP in 2004, based on the original criterion of one-third of the students achieving the provincial standards, in 2014–2015 only 63 schools were targeted for OFIP support based on the more demanding criterion of half of the students achieving the provincial standards.

Public confidence in Ontario's education system has also improved. According to the 18th edition of the *Public Attitudes Toward Education* survey conducted by the Ontario Institute for Studies in Education,[19] at the end of the Conservative Administration in 2002, the percentage of people who reported to be satisfied or very satisfied with the public education system was 43. As the Ontario whole system reform unfolded, satisfaction climbed to an all-time high of 65 percent in 2012.

The Council of Ministers of Canada (CMEC), the body representing all the provinces and territories in Canada, recently conducted its own PISA-like assessment of students in a nationwide sample of grade 8 students. This standardized set of tests known as PCAP (Pan-Canadian Assessment Program) assessed students in the areas of reading, science, and math in 2013.[20] The provinces of Alberta, British Columbia, Quebec, and Ontario showed high scores compared to the other provinces, while Ontario was well ahead of other provinces on reading (a mean score of 524 compared to the other three provinces that were grouped around 500), second in math, and a close third on science. Ontario's aggregate score (combining the three tests) was also well ahead of the others: 1544 compared to 1517 in Alberta, 1512 in Quebec, and 1504 in British Columbia—the latter three provinces have also done well, but in this chapter we focus on Ontario.

As one of us has argued elsewhere,[21] behind the obvious achievements of increased literacy, numeracy, and high school graduation rates lies the real accomplishment of the last decade in Ontario: the deep, widely shared ownership of the reform agenda on the part of teachers, schools, and district leaders. At least three prominent international agencies have studied Ontario, including the Organization for Economic Cooperation and Development,[22] the McKinsey group,[23] and the National Center for Education and the Economy (NCEE) in the United States.[24] All three agencies identify Ontario as an example of a government deliberately setting out to improve the whole system, and having the results to show for it. Numerous external researchers and others who have visited Ontario from other countries have noticed the high coherence of the educational system, understood as consistency of good practice and a shared understanding of the priorities and reform strategies across all levels of the system, from district leaders and unions to teachers, principals, and parents.[25] Overall, when visitors ask teachers, principals, or district leaders to explain what they are doing and why, answers are specific and widely shared across the system. We call this the shared ability 'to talk the walk' in accurate and consistent ways. The big question is: how was this achieved? Getting inside the policies and processes of change can offer important lessons for other countries.

During the past two decades, Ontario has undergone an important transition from an aggressive neoliberal agenda focused on budget cuts, financial accountability, and external accountability for outcomes, to a more collaborative orientation based on financial stewardship, partnerships among stakeholders, and shared accountability for student success.[26] The outcomes of these two approaches have been remarkably different: from stagnant performance, labor disruption, and public dissatisfaction with Ontario's public education system in the former approach, to improved performance, mostly vanished labor disruption (except for a blip in 2011–2012), and improved morale and confidence in public education in the later approach. We add parenthetically that in the summer of 2015 there was a current set of difficulties relative to the negotiation of the next contract with teachers, although recent breakthroughs have occurred with some of the unions. Time will tell, but we would say more generally that union-management partnerships focusing on the student learning agenda are much needed in Ontario and elsewhere. This does not gainsay the deep capacity that is currently built into the system with teachers, principals and districts, but does say that when it comes to labor relations nothing can be taken for granted.

In 1995, Conservative candidate Mike Harris was elected premier of Ontario. His "Common Sense Revolution" platform was an aggressive program of deficit reduction combined with lower taxes and cuts to government programs. A first priority of Harris's government was to reduce the costs of education, and it moved aggressively to cut spending and downsize school board budgets.[27] In November 1995, the provincial government announced expenditure reductions of CN $400 million for the following year, which represented a CN $1 billion cut from the education sector on an annualized basis. In late 1996, Bill 104, the *Fewer School Boards Act*, reduced the number of school boards from 129 to 72. Since the reform, the education system in Ontario looks more like Florida, with 75 school districts and 2.6 million students, and less like New York, with 727 school districts and 2.7 million students.[28]

Bill 160, the *Education Quality Improvement Act,* introduced the following year, removed taxation powers from local districts and established centralized financial control at the provincial level. The bill made it illegal for boards to operate on a deficit, introduced penalties for trustees who were unable to balance their budgets, and tightened financial accountability by requiring boards and the ministry to publicly disclose their spending. In June 2002, three of the largest public school boards—Toronto, Ottawa, and Hamilton—refused to balance their budgets, arguing that provincial funding was insufficient to deliver programs and services to students. In response, the province took over governing authority from the three boards and installed supervisors to oversee budget cuts and board operations.[29]

Despite promises to protect classrooms from the impact of the aggressive spending cuts enacted through the "Common Sense Revolution," funding cuts led school boards to lay off staff and reduce or eliminate many programs and services. Taking place in the context of sharp reductions in many social support programs such as housing and youth services, budget cuts reduced the ability of schools to support students, especially the most vulnerable, at a time when support was most needed.

As it pushed these drastic changes, the Conservative government was fiercely critical of schools and teachers, publicly portraying them as overpaid and underworked. This view of teachers and schools translated into policy decisions such as budget cuts and staff reductions, increased workloads for teachers, compulsory testing of new teachers, compulsory professional development for all teachers, reduction of the number of days for teacher professional development from nine days to five, and more intensive teacher evaluation.[30]

In schools, low morale and dissatisfaction prevailed. Andy Hargreaves and his colleagues[31] tracked the impact of Harris's reforms in nine Ontario high schools over a five-year period. The following quote illustrates the sharp decline in teacher morale during the Harris era:

I love teaching, and I go home every day [...] feeling energized by my students, believing that I am helping them to improve [...] and looking forward to what [my classes and I] will do next, but I am tired of being bashed by the Premier. So I have relinquished my headship for next year and will take retirement on before my date. [...] That is something I never thought I would ever contemplate, let alone plan to do. That says something. You have no idea of the feeling of betrayal I experience—and I know I'm not alone.[32]

The Harris government encouraged private schooling in two major ways. First, private schools were largely deregulated. Second, late in the government's tenure, a tax credit was offered for tuition at private schools, described elsewhere as a key neoliberal strategy to expand market choice and increase competition between schools by putting pressure on schools considered low performing.[33]

The aggressive changes to the education sector advanced by the Harris government encountered strong opposition and led to substantial labor disruption, including strikes and work-to-rule campaigns. In 1998, a public poll conducted by the Ontario Institute for Studies in Education revealed that a significant proportion of Ontarians felt that the quality of education had declined in the previous five years.[34]

Not surprisingly, student performance wasn't very strong. According to data from the Literacy and Numeracy Secretariat, in 1998, only 54 percent of elementary school students in Ontario were meeting the provincial standard in grades 3 and 6 literacy and mathematics, and 68 percent of high school students were graduating in five years.

A decade of low teacher morale, bitter labor-management relations, and decreasing investment in education set the stage for the provincial election of 2003. Dalton McGuinty, leader of the Ontario Liberal Party, ran on a platform that made the renewal of public education one of its highest priorities and announced an ambitious set of policy commitments to improve public education. The Ontario Liberal party took 72 of 103 seats, with 47 percent of the vote, becoming a majority government. McGuinty was re-elected four years later, largely due to his government's record in education (and to a mistake by the leader of the opposition who proposed full funding of private schools), giving the Liberal Party a second majority. The Liberal Party continues to lead the province of Ontario to this day, having lost majority by one seat in 2011, when Dalton McGuinty was reelected, but gaining majority back in 2014 under Kathleen Wynne who, among other roles, had served as Minister of Education under McGuinty's leadership.

Ontario's Improvement Strategy

Governments typically have educational visions but are less clear about implementation strategy. Ontario paid close attention to *how* to achieve progress.

Thus, in addition to the policy perspective, we want to emphasize the strategy that was central to implementation, leading to better performance after the political shifts of the 2000s. The question is what specific strategies and policies contribute to "whole system improvement." While this is by no means an easy matter, we will see that it involves focusing on a small number of key factors and pursuing them relentlessly through focused implementation, learning from experience, refining, and so on. In the four years prior to 2003, Michael Fullan was a lead member of a Toronto-based team that evaluated England's "literacy–numeracy" initiative. Tony Blair and his chief strategist Michael Barber had committed to improving literacy and numeracy across England—over 20,000 primary schools.

Blair said that they would use "knowledge about change" to accomplish this feat. The Toronto team conducted the evaluation over a four-year period, and filed its report in 2002.[35] The overall view was that early results in effect achieved by the strategy were obtained because a relatively loose system had been tightened up, but that these results would most likely wane because they did not develop enough ownership and conditions for innovation at the school and local authority levels.

More specifically, four conclusions were drawn: two negative and two positive. The two negative conclusions were that "strong (punitive) accountability" on balance had negative effects and that "obsession with targets" (specific targets had been set by local authorities for literacy and numeracy that were monitored and reported publicly in the media) was a dysfunctional distraction. The two positive forces were "focus" (naming the direction and maintaining the focus), and "capacity building" (investing in coaching, excellent curriculum, and teaching resources) that built pedagogical and leadership competencies of educators at all levels.

Fortunately by way of timing, the final report for England was completed in 2002, just as Dalton McGuinty was preparing for the election that resulted in his becoming Premier of Ontario in October, 2003 (more about politics in the final section of this chapter). We do not want to minimize the depth of the policy shift, but we can say that initially the guiding components were expressed in one page:

- focus on a small number of ambitious goals (raise the bar in literacy, numeracy and high school graduation, close the achievement gap, and increase public confidence in education);
- pursue a high trust "peace and stability" partnership with the school districts and the unions;
- invest in capacity building at all levels with a focus on instructional practices linked to results;
- foster learning from implementation laterally (across schools and districts), and vertically (between schools and districts); and
- build the capacity of the ministry to work in partnership with the sector.

The primary mechanism used to focus on capacity building involved the creation of a new unit—the 'Literacy and Numeracy Secretariat' (LNS)—within the ministry. The first leader was Avis Glaze, a prominent director (superintendent of one of the school districts). The LNS consisted of approximately 100 combined staff of existing ministry personnel and secondments from the field—lead practitioners on loan from school districts. The head of LNS was called the "Chief Student Achievement Officer."

The Ontario Strategy has always had a strong research and evidence base. Heavily action oriented, it bases these actions on existing and ongoing research and evidence. Indeed, Ontario committed to conducting and commissioning research on its own strategy, feeding such research back into the process, and publishing and participating in the international policy arena about the knowledge and practice base relative to "whole system improvement."[36]

When the Ontario strategy was launched in 2003, some school districts were several steps ahead of the provincial government with effective working policies for literacy and numeracy. The LNS intentionally searched for the most effective district practices to improve student performance in literacy and numeracy, as well as schools across the province that had significantly improved student outcomes in a two-year period. Once these schools and systems were identified, reports and case studies were created and key findings disseminated across the system.[37] A similar strategy is currently being pursued to improve mathematics performance.

Through continuous cycles of identifying and spreading effective practices in districts and schools, the LNS has operated as a learning organization able to gain an increasingly deeper understanding of the strategies and conditions under which improvement takes place, develop and refine its own support strategies, and become a trusted ally to districts and schools in their improvement efforts.

As the strategy got underway, Ontario leaders expressed the strategy as consisting of eight interrelated factors. The most recent rendition has been presented by Mary Jean Gallagher,[38] Avis Glaze's successor as Chief Student Achievement Officer of the province (see Table 7.1 below).

Note that this is not the typical starting list. Most systems lead with accountability, standards for students, teachers, and administrators, curriculum, and ad hoc policies. Ontario did incorporate these elements, some of which had already been put in place by the former government (for example, curriculum

TABLE 7.1 Levers to Successful Whole System Improvement

1. A small number of ambitious goals
2. Leadership at all levels
3. High standards and expectations
4. Investment in leadership and capacity building related to instruction
5. Mobilizing data and effective practices as a strategy for improvement
6. Intervention in a nonpunitive manner
7. Supporting conditions/reduce distractions.
8. Being transparent, relentless and increasingly challenging

and standards for students), but they did not *lead* with them. Instead, the strategy focused on leadership that mobilized capacity building by increasing instructional and change competencies in individuals and, especially, collectively.[39] In the following sections we examine the nature and evolution of the Ontario education reform strategy, first in the 2003–2011 period that was one of stable political conditions, and then in the 2011–2014 period of initial disruption and regaining stability.

The 2003–2011 Period

Almost immediately after taking office in 2003, the Liberals reversed some of the more contentious programs under Harris. They announced an additional investment of CN $1.6 billion in education spending by 2006. Local governance was restored to elected trustees in the districts of Toronto, Hamilton, and Ottawa. The tax credit for private school tuition was revoked. Two of the five eliminated teacher professional activity days were reinstituted. And teacher testing and recertification were cancelled and substituted by a new teacher induction program.[40] The provincial government developed a whole system improvement strategy based on partnership, capacity building, focus on results, and a relentless commitment to keep going deeper and deeper.

Using Table 7.1 as a guide, we will start with a small number of ambitious goals. Three goals guided the 2003–2013 period: high levels of student achievement (75 percent high proficiency in literacy and math; 85 percent graduating from high school);[41] reduced gaps in student achievement; and increased public confidence in education. Defining a small number of ambitious goals has been a crucial strategy to develop focus and system coherence across the entire educational system in Ontario. At the same time, as Andy Hargreaves and Dennis Shirley[42] point out in *The Global Fourth Way*, the persistent focus of the provincial government on achieving its target goals can sometimes produce unintended consequences. These include efforts to "game the system" through calculative concentration of some schools to meet the targets by focusing interventions on students who score only a few decimal points below the provincial standard (see Hargreaves and Shirley, pp 33–39). In concert with the other seven levers discussed here, however, the risk of provincial tests becoming a major driving force in schools and districts are greatly diminished.

Second, leadership at all levels consisted of a "guiding coalition" and leadership development with a focus on improving teaching and learning for district leaders, principals, and teachers. The guiding coalition included the Premier, the Minister of Education, the Deputy Minister, the Chief Student Achievement Officer, and a Senior Policy Adviser, Michael Fullan, one of the authors of this chapter. The strong leadership by McGuinty was especially critical at the beginning of the reform, from 2003–2007. He declared education as his top priority, chairing meetings of the "guiding coalition" every six weeks to review progress, reinforce strategies, and help to generate additional ideas and strategies. This kind of persistent "feet to the fire" drive and support from heads of state is rare in education.

Third, high standards and expectations included a standards based curriculum related especially to literacy and numeracy, a transparent standard of performance, and independent assessment of student achievement by the Education Quality and Assessment Office (EQAO).

Fourth, a variety of activities focused on leadership and capacity building related to instruction and its link to student achievement. At the elementary level (approximately 4,000 schools in 72 districts) these included: coaching, collaborative inquiry, online video and other supports related to instructional practices, networking school and districts around effective practices, targeted interventions, and various forms of collaborative professionalism. All these activities developed and spread capacity. Additional "tools" for leadership and teacher development were used to reinforce (but not drive) capacity building—a point that we will return to toward the end of this section. Organized teams, consisting of staff of LNS called "Student Achievement Officers," worked with sets of districts to identify, develop, and spread capacity.

At the 900 high schools, two of the most powerful leadership and capacity building strategies revolved around the "student success teachers" (SSTs) and a new initiative called "Specialist High Skills Major". SSTs were school-based teachers who worked directly with students in coordination with school leaders and teachers to help students at risk of not graduating as early as in grades 9 and 10. Their intervention included a focus on literacy, credit recovery, tutoring, re-engagement in school, and the like. The Specialist High Skills Major (SHSM) was an innovation for grade 11 and 12 students that enabled schools to develop programming for students who needed to see more vividly the relevance of what they were learning to a future career option. This initiative commenced in 2006–2007 with 600 students in 27 programs in 44 schools. Programs included construction, hospitality, manufacturing, forestry, etc. SHSM programs expanded rapidly and by 2014, 40,000 students enrolled in 1,600 programs in 660 schools. New programs were included such as Information and Communication Technology, Justice, Aviation and Aerospace, Sports, and the Non-Profit Sector. In addition to the work of SSTs and the new SHSM programs, other capacity building activities focused on literacy and math, differentiated instruction, and professional learning cycles.[43]

Factor five, mobilizing data and effective instructional strategies, involved building a data base for assessments, tracking data, and correspondingly developing and spreading precise teaching to meet student needs. For the first time, the province was in a position to identify and disseminate evidenced-based examples in all core areas: what effective literacy instruction looked like, who was being successful in addressing the needs of English-language learners, what practices in which high schools were most effective at engaging students and reducing dropouts, and so on.

The sixth element was intervention in a nonpunitive manner through a program for elementary schools called the Ontario Focused Intervention Partnership (OFIP). Nonpunitive means that you identify schools not doing well or that are stagnant (the new database made that easy to do), and assume that the first order of business is capacity building, not blame. This strategy is the opposite of the punitive accountability approach often associated with privatization efforts. Intervention strategies were developed between LNS and specific schools and their districts that included needs assessment, support, co-development of an action plan, participation in school-based learning communities and learning from other schools through formal and informal networking.

At the secondary level, a Student Success School Support Initiative provided support and development for the lowest achieving 20 percent, or about 180 schools. Activities primarily involved building the capacity of the principal and teachers as instructional leaders in order to enhance instructional practices resulting in improved student achievement.

Seven, a number of supporting conditions essentially reinforced the core capacity building strategy or paved the way for new initiatives. These included policies and programs related to: safe schools, full-day kindergarten, equity and inclusivity, mental health, the Ontario leadership strategy, and others. Policymakers and educators maintained focus on the three core goals in order to avoid the distractions of ad hoc and multiple initiatives, and to integrating additional elements into the overall strategy. We will illustrate this later concerning full-day kindergarten, the leadership strategy, and well-being.

The final component was called "being transparent, relentless, and increasingly challenging" about the core goals. The belief that *all children can learn* was kept front and center with a focused sense of urgency that the work is never entirely done, and an eye to sustaining and extending the reforms which we will take up relative to the strategy for 2014 and beyond.

In terms of policy statements or documents about the strategy, it is worth noting that there was no formal policy document in the first term (2003–2007). This is an important lesson on whole system change. Ontario got started by getting started. Instead of spending a year getting input from the sector, Ontario launched into action. In effect, leaders predicted that the core goals would resonate with schools and communities. The three core goals were informally and explicitly stated and restated. The strategy was to partner with districts and schools, constantly reiterating the goals, and engaging in focused capacity building. It was not until 2007 when the government was reelected that the overall strategy was extended and committed to paper in a publication called *Energizing Ontario's Education*[44]—a 15-page policy document. It reiterated and extended the three core goals of improving student achievement in literacy, numeracy, and high school graduation; reducing achievement gaps in these three domains; and increasing public confidence in the public school system.

The "Energizing" document also identified a number of "supporting conditions" that we referred to above under item seven (Table 7.1). One of these ideas was major: "early childhood learning" that was acted on in 2010 when legislation was passed to provide full-day integrated day-care kindergarten to all four and five year olds, phased in over a four-year period. This initiative became known as Full Day Kindergarten (FDK). Starting with 35,000 children in September 2010 (15 percent of the total) increases were made each September until 2014 when full implementation was achieved (285,000 children). In 2008, Ontario was in a large budget deficit position. Years of research and analysis by economists had demonstrated that investing in early learning (and implementing it well) would yield at least a 7-1 return on investment in economic terms, not to mention social benefits. In a move that is rarely seen in state leaders, McGuinty chose to add to the deficit in the short run, predicting that the investment would result in a high-yield return in the future. McGuinty appointed Charles Pascal as Early Learning Commissioner who made major recommendations in his final report.[45] Nearly all of Pascal's recommendations were acted on beginning in 2010.

In full-day kindergarten classrooms, certified teachers and registered early childhood educators work together in educator teams to deliver a full day of inquiry, play-based learning, guided by the principles set out in The Full-Day Early Learning–Kindergarten Program. FDK also involves integrated before- and after-school programs delivered in schools by school boards or licensed childcare providers. Before- and after-school programs are intended to be a support for working parents and to parents interested in returning to the workforce and/or the pursuit of further study. There is no other jurisdiction in North America that provides such programming for four- and five-year-olds.[46]

It is still early in the development of FDK to draw firm conclusions. The first evaluation was conducted by researchers from Queen's and McMaster Universities who were able to compare children in FDK with those who had not been in FDK. They found that overall students in FDK were better prepared once they entered grade 1, and that this progress was evident in every area of development (social competence, language and cognitive development, and communication skills). These are only early results. Much more research and development will be needed with respect to the nature and quality of implementation, and its impact on the development of all children.

Keeping with the theme of integration of initiatives (as distinct from ad hoc initiative overload), FDK was introduced as a way of strengthening the further development of teaching and learning capacity. The play-based inquiry curriculum and related practices is a catalyst in several ways. It prepares children better as they enter grade 1. Since teachers in the elementary level have been working in improving pedagogy since 2004, they were better prepared to receive the children that had gone through FDK. And interestingly, since the FDK pedagogy focuses more on the whole child, it feeds forward in elementary schools by challenging primary teachers to adequately serve these newly prepared six-year-olds. We don't have the space to take up the latter issue in detail, but there is a healthy (creative) tension between teaching the whole child, and the place of literacy and numeracy (the too broad—too narrow debate). All this creates conditions for continuous improvement and innovation in pedagogy.

Let us return to the matter of "tools" such as those relating to leadership, and to teacher development. The Ontario Leadership Framework contains a school effectiveness framework, a district effectiveness framework, and a leadership development framework–developing leadership in one's own district (www. education-leadership-ontario.ca). Developed by the leadership branch of the Ministry of Education in partnership with the Literacy and Numeracy Secretariat (itself an example of co-ordinated leadership), these documents mirror the capacity building elements in Table 7.1.

There are some very important lessons about change here. The frameworks have been co-developed with the sector over time; they are not compulsory, yet virtually everyone uses them. This phenomenon reflects a critical finding from our own work: an effective change process shapes and reshapes good ideas as it builds capacity and ownership.[47] Through an iterative process of shaping and reshaping ideas, the following programs have been created to develop leadership capacity in Ontario:

- a Principals' Qualification Program, which all principals and vice-principals are required to complete to attain principal qualifications;
- funding and support provided to every school district in Ontario to develop and implement a Board Leadership Development Strategy, aimed at developing the leadership capacity of current and aspiring school and system leaders;
- a mentoring program for all principals and vice principals over the first two years in each role, which includes training, a learning plan co-developed between mentor and mentee, and a transparent matching and exit process to ensure a good mentor-mentee match; and
- a Principal Performance Appraisal process, which includes setting a small number of challenging yet achievable goals in consultation with the supervisor, developing strategies to meet these goals, appraisal according to the progress in meeting these goals, developing an improvement plan and timeline if the appraisal is unsatisfactory, and intervention of the district in cases of insufficient improvement. Performance appraisal is required for all principals and vice principals every five years.[48]

Teacher development contains similar lessons—integration with the overall strategy and focus on growth and development through partnerships. Housed in the Teacher Policy and Standards branch of the Ministry of Education, the teacher development framework covers induction, annual learning plan, and teacher appraisal (www.edu.gov.on.ca/eng/teacher/appraisal.html). The first lesson is that the framework and its activities are aimed at growth and "enhancing the teaching profession." Second, the teacher education branch at the ministry has as its centerpiece the three core goals of improving student achievement

K–12, closing gaps, and increasing public confidence. As before, teacher development tools have been designed in partnership with the sector, and with other ministry departments, they are voluntary (except for statutory requirements), and virtually everyone uses them.

Another change lesson for whole system reformers: you cannot get widespread change by using teacher appraisal as a driver. It is not intense enough and becomes immediately contentious once you try to use it to judge all teachers. The Ontario strategy in our view actually generates greater accountability through the eight components we have discussed here.[49] Pervin and Campbell offer a comprehensive account of Ontario's approach to teacher preparation and professional development.[50] A combination of resources, strategies, and incentives has been used to attract, retain, and develop highly skilled teachers across the province. These include:

1. Initial Teacher Education, which requires teacher candidates to complete a minimum of three or four years of undergraduate study and further university-based teacher pre-service education to obtain a certificate from the Ontario College of Teachers. Starting in the fall of 2015, the length of the pre-service program is doubled to a four-semester university program, with an enhanced focus on preparing teachers on diversity, special needs, mental health for young people, and integrating technology and pedagogy;
2. the Building Futures program, launched in 2004 to assist teacher candidates in understanding the core education priorities of the province;
3. the mandatory *New Teacher Induction Program* (NTIP) which provides orientation, mentoring, and professional learning opportunities specific to the needs of beginning teachers, as well as two performance appraisals by the school principal;[51]
4. the provision of multiple supports for the ongoing professional learning of teachers, such as direct program supports, professional learning sessions and materials, time built into the school schedule for teacher collaborative inquiry, and release time to attend professional learning activities to support their ongoing teaching duties;
5. multiple resources that offer information about existing and emerging successful practices, such as case studies of "Schools on the Move" and webcasts and online videos of effective classroom practice in Ontario;
6. the *Teacher Learning and Leadership Program* (TLLP), designed for experienced teachers to model and share best practices with other teachers through self-directed, job-embedded professional learning projects funded by the Ministry of Education;[52] and
7. Additional Qualifications Programs accredited by the Ontario College of Teachers, and Summer institutes sponsored by the Ministry of Education and the Ontario Teachers' Federation that offer teachers opportunities to upgrade their qualifications and enhance their practice.

Finally, we will discuss briefly the political relations with directors (superintendents) of education, and with the teacher federations. The districts have been strong partners all the way through. In addition, one of the actions that the ministry took was to grant the directors' organization CN $25 million to help implement the special education (and it turned out all students) component of the literacy-numeracy strategy. This turned out to be a great move. A team led by Andy Hargreaves was commissioned to evaluate the project. They did that by studying a representative sample of 10 districts (of the 72). Hargreaves and Braun found a good deal of success in the districts, and they also uncovered a new strategy that they called "leadership from the middle" (the districts being the middle between the government and the schools).[53] This is a strategy we are using in other parts of our work.[54] Leadership from the middle represents another powerful source of capacity building and commitment.

There are four independent teacher unions in Ontario—the Elementary Teachers Federation of Ontario, the Ontario Secondary School Teachers Federation, L'Association des Enseignantes et des Enseignants Franco-Ontariens, and the Ontario English Catholic Teachers Association. Since 2013 there have been strong but not necessarily deep partnerships with the unions, featuring two four-year agreements. In addition, as with the directors, the government has funded teachers to work on the overall agenda—one through a grant of CN $25 million for the federations to conduct summer workshops on literacy and numeracy; and the other through an ongoing initiative developed in partnership with the Ontario Teachers Federation called the Teacher Learning and Leadership Program (TLLP). In TLLP, teachers can apply individually or in small groups for grants to develop innovations, and are required to report back on what they did and found. Teams of two to four teachers lead the majority of TLLP projects. The program has been evaluated favorably.[55] For a deeper analysis of the present and future of the teaching profession see Hargreaves and Fullan's *Professional Capital*.[56]

The 2003–2011 period, characterized by stable political conditions, allowed the provincial government to launch and deepen Ontario's improvement agenda. Between 2011 and 2014, the loss of majority government for the Liberal Party, a 12-month conflict between parliament and the teacher federations, and McGuinty's resignation resulted in little political leadership at the provincial level for Ontario's educational improvement agenda. Over the previous seven years, however, the system had built strong capacity to continue to develop. In the fall of 2014, when interim Premier Kathleen Wynne won back a majority government for the Liberal Party, the education sector and the provincial government re-established a common agenda to continue and deepen Ontario's trajectory of sustained improvement.

The 2011–2015 Period

In October 2011 McGuinty ran for a third term and fell short of majority government by one seat. The politics become complicated at this point, but in an attempt to be tough with teachers with respect to a new collective agreement, McGuinty imposed a wage freeze and suspended the collective bargaining rights of the federations. Major conflict erupted, along with other troubles for the government, the largest concerning a gas plant scandal. There followed 12 months of contentious times within parliament between the government and the teachers that resulted in McGuinty's abrupt resignation in October 2012. Former Minister of Education Kathleen Wynne became interim premier in January 2013 and led a tentative minority government until a general election in June 2014 in which she won back a majority government for the Liberal Party.

There are two lessons here—one obvious, and the other encouraging. Relative to the former, no matter how much you invest in relationships and trust building it can be destroyed overnight by yourself or others. The other lesson is that once you build strong capacity across the system, including in the Ministry of Education (the LNS as a case in point), it can keep going in the absence of political leadership. Stated another way, there was little leadership from the political center from the summer of 2011 (when electioneering started for the third term) to the fall of 2014 when the new government settled in—*but the system continued to develop*. We wouldn't say this is ideal, but most districts continued to see improvement, and thus were ready for re-engagement with a government who embraced the same agenda.

After wide consultation with the sector and the public, the Wynne government issued a new education policy document, *Achieving Excellence: A Renewed Vision for Education in Ontario*.[57] This policy recommitted to the previous three core goals and added a fourth, "well-being." In the language of the document the four core goals are: achieving excellence (high student achievement), ensuring equity, promoting well-being, and enhancing public confidence. The new plan also called for a two-year initial teacher education program (in effect changing it from a five-year to a six-year program). The new two-year teacher education program and curriculum is now under development.

Overall, from the initial reform in 2003 to the present, persistence around the core goals has combined with a watershed development to broadening the learning focus to include well being and attention to the whole child, academically and socio-emotionally. This integrated focus on excellence and equity for all subgroups is intended to reach those students and subgroups not yet effectively served by the system.

As we take stock in 2015, the goals remain the same: (1) reaching 75 percent of students with high levels of literacy and numeracy skill by age 12 and (2) 85 percent of students graduating from high school within five years of starting. Originally, these had been set in 2003 as target goals for 2008. The fact that the goals have not yet been met 12 years after may raise questions about the degree to which Ontario's reform has been successful. At the same time, almost every year the government has been able to announce overall gains—in literacy more than in mathematics. The 85 percent graduation goal has been virtually achieved with commitments to keep on going. What is indisputable is that the work of systemwide improvement in Ontario is deeply embedded.

Beyond this, the original achievement and equity goals have been extended to include higher order skills and well-being. The overall goal is to develop students who are personally successful, economically productive, and actively engaged citizens. Part of the work in the next phase of Ontario's reform involves developing precision in the definition of the new priorities of deep learning and of well-being, operationalizing them in practice; developing measures to mark success, monitor progress, and identify areas of improvement; and identifying and spreading what works. Several school boards are already taking steps in this direction. As has been the case over the past decade, it is to be expected that the knowledge and expertise gained by school districts as a result of their work in this area will be tapped into, spread across the entire system, and refined in ongoing cycles of implementation and evaluation.[58]

Fulfilling the Promise of High-Quality Public Education

The emergence over the past 15 years of examples of high-quality public education systems such as Ontario stands in stark contrast with the relative failure of advocates of privatization to provide conclusive evidence that market-oriented approaches can simultaneously improve quality and equity of educational opportunities and outcomes for all students across entire educational systems. Recall the third key goal: public confidence in the public education system. This is strong now in Ontario but not to be taken for granted.

The next phase in Ontario is to go deeper in learning, both in terms of student and teacher engagement, and in the use of digital to change pedagogy and accelerate and deepen learning and well being for all students. Several districts are engaged in an initiative called New Pedagogies for Deep Learning (www.newpedagogies.org). New pedagogies consist of learning partnerships between and among teachers, students, and families. Deep learning refers to the outcomes of new learning—essentially the 21st century learning skills (character education, citizenship, collaboration, communication, creativity, and critical thinking). The strong collective capacity foundation puts Ontario in a good position to move rapidly into the new pedagogies' agenda to make learning irresistibly engaging to students and teachers.[59] As successful as Ontario has been, we believe that the deep learning revolution has not yet happened. The immediate future requires inclusive innovative learning environments, student and teacher engagement, a powerful teaching and school leadership profession, collaborative and transparent action, digital depth and acceleration, and immersion in the 6Cs—education that produces great citizens for tomorrow by becoming great citizens today. Ontario is well positioned, and indeed is already immersed in this radical transformation of learning that if successful will go far beyond what it has already accomplished.

The Ontario Reform experience not only illustrates that public education can achieve high levels of performance across an entire province. Its key features of progressive partnerships, sustained focus, and collective capacity building also point to a more robust view of public education. In this more robust view, the "public" in public education does not merely refer to a prevailing funding mechanism but, more importantly, to a renewed partnership of high expectations, trust, and collaboration between an educational system and its actors in a way that serves simultaneously the educational needs of the population, the economic needs of the states, social cohesion, and democracy.

In this chapter, we outlined eight key levers for system improvement that explain the relative success of the Ontario strategy. We also derived some key change lessons for policymakers, which include: "Getting started by getting started" and refining strategies through constant interaction with the field, co-developing interventions, frameworks and tools with the sector; maintaining focus and staying the course around a small number of ambitious goals connected to student learning; integrating new initiatives with the overall strategy; using capacity building and leadership development as the key driver of the improvement effort, keeping a growth orientation. We are confident that the key levers and change lessons presented here are applicable to a wide range of educational systems but require ongoing refinement and adaptation in order to work effectively in specific political, cultural, and social contexts.

There is a very important lesson about system coherence in the Ontario case. Coherence is achieved through three deeply interrelated factors. The first is to have an uplifting agenda that is based on the moral imperative of raising the bar and closing the gap for all children while focusing on a small number of ambitious goals. Second is to lace the system with purposeful vertical and lateral interaction that develops capacity, disseminates good ideas, and builds a shared sense of purpose and know how. Coherence is a mindset and system coherence is a shared mindset among the vast majority of members that can only be achieved through continuous interaction, improvement, and sharing. Third, and this is what most systems fail to do, the different policies and units at the state level must consciously and deliberately serve the same integrated purpose. Let's call this third factor "system cohesion."

We have already described system cohesion. There is a *core* that focuses on the student achievement goals and agenda—in this case exemplified by the "Chief Student Achievement Officer." Coupled with this center of gravity, again unlike most other cases we know, *all* other policy units, and their leaders describe their responsibilities as acting to serve and integrate with actions designed to accomplish the core agenda. To be specific, each of the following ministry departments publicly and privately articulates their work in relation to the core student achievement goals, and in relation to each other: finance, leadership development, curriculum, early learning, teacher education, assessment. The result is a shared sense of purpose, capacity, clarity, and commitment among system leaders, and correspondingly among vast numbers of participants at all levels of the system. In turn, this establishes enormous depth and consistency within the system that serves the immediate agenda and establishes a base for sustainable growth and innovation in the future. System coherence and system success go hand in hand.

High-quality, equitable public education is possible and the keys to attaining it increasingly clear and precise. The next phase of reform in education around the world promises to be contentious and action packed. Leaders would do well to consider the "whole system improvement" lessons from Ontario.

Notes

1 Michael Fullan was special policy adviser to Premier Dalton McGuinty from 2003 to 2013, and currently serves, along with Andy Hargreaves, Carol Campbell, and Jean Clinton as an adviser to Premier Kathleen Wynne, and the Minister of Education, Liz Sandals.

2 Gambhir, M., Broad, K., Evans, M., and Gaskell, J. (2008). *Characterizing Initial Teacher Education in Canada: Themes and Issues*. Ontario: OISE/University of Toronto.

3 OECD (2014). *Education at a Glance 2014: OECD Indicators*. Paris: OECD Publishing. Retrieved from http://dx.doi.org/10.1787/eag-2014-en.

4 Pervin, B., and Campbell, C. (2015). "Systems for Teacher and Leader Effectiveness and Quality: Ontario, Canada." In Darling-Hammond, L. and Rothman, R. (eds.) *Teaching in the Flat World: Learning from High-Performing Systems*. New York: Teachers College Press.

5 Herman, J. (2013). *Canada's Approach to School Funding*. Washington, D.C: Center for American Progress.

6 Statistics Canada (2014). *Quarterly Population Estimates, National Perspective—Population*. Retrieved from http://www.statcan.gc.ca/pub/91-002-x/2014003/t002-eng.htm.

7 Statistics Canada (2014a). *Quarterly Estimates of Demographic Components, National Perspective—Immigrants*. Retrieved from http://www.statcan.gc.ca/pub/91-002-x/2014003/t025-eng.htm.

8 OECD (2011). Chapter 3: Ontario, Canada: Reform to Support High Achievement in a Diverse Context, in *Strong Performers and Successful Reformers in Education: Lessons from PISA for the United States*. Paris: OECD. Retrieved from http://www.oecd.org/pisa/pisaproducts/46580959.pdf.

9 Ontario Ministry of Education (2014a). *Education Facts, 2013-2014 (Preliminary)*. Retrieved from http://www.edu.gov.on.ca/eng/educationFacts.html#enrol.

10 Herman, J. (2013). *Canada's Approach to School Funding, www.Americanprogress.org*, Washington, D.C: Center for American Progress.

11 Gallagher, M. J. (2014). *Ontario Education Improvement. Slide Deck for International Presentations*. Toronto: Ministry of Education; Glaze, A., Mattingley, R., and Andrews, R. (2013). *High School Graduation: K-12 Strategies that Work*. New York/Ontario: Corwin/Ontario Principals' Council.

12 Barber, M., and Mourshed, M. (2007). *How the World's Best-Performing School Systems Come Out on Top*. London: McKinsey and Company; OECD (2011). Chapter 3: Ontario, Canada: Reform to Support High Achievement in a Diverse Context, in *Strong Performers and Successful Reformers in Education: Lessons from PISA for the United States*. Paris. Retrieved from http://www.oecd.org/pisa/pisaproducts/46580959.pdf;

OECD (2013). *PISA 2012 Results: Excellence through Equity, Giving Every Student the Chance to Succeed. Volume II.* Paris.

13 Brochu, P., Deussing, M. A., Houme, K., and Chuy, M. (2013). *Measuring Up: Canadian Results of the OECD PISA Study: the Performance of Canada's Youth in Mathematics, Reading and Science.* Toronto: Council of Ministers of Education, Canada.

14 Council of Ministries of Education, Canada (CMEC) (2013). *PCAP 2013: Report on the Pan-Canadian Assessment of Science, Reading and Mathematics.* Toronto.

15 Mourshed, M., Chijioke, C., and Barber, M. (2010). *How the World's Most Improved School Systems Keep Getting Better.* London: McKinsey and Company.

16 OECD (2011). Chapter 3: Ontario, Canada: Reform to Support High Achievement in a Diverse Context, in *Strong Performers and Successful Reformers in Education: Lessons from PISA for the United States.* Paris. Retrieved from http://www.oecd.org/pisa/pisaproducts/46580959.pdf.

17 Hargreaves, A., and Braun, H. (2013). *Leading for All.* Ontario: Council of Ontario Directors of Education. Toronto. Retrieved from http://www.ontariodirectors.ca/downloads/Essential_FullReport_Final.pdf.

18 Ontario Ministry of Education (2007). *Ontario Focused Intervention Partnership.* Toronto: Queen's Printer for Ontario. Retrieved from http://www.edu.gov.on.ca/eng/literacynumeracy/ofip.html.

19 Hart, D. (2012). *Public Attitudes Toward Education in Ontario 2012: The 18th Survey of Educational Issues.* Ontario: OISE/University of Toronto.

20 Council of Ministries of Education, Canada (CMEC) (2013). *PCAP 2013: Report on the Pan-Canadian Assessment of Science, Reading and Mathematics.* Toronto.

21 Fullan, M. (2013). Great to Excellent: Launching the Next Stage of Ontario's Education Agenda. Retrieved from http://www.michaelfullan.ca/media/13599974110.pdf.

22 OECD (2011). Chapter 3: Ontario, Canada: Reform to Support High Achievement in a Diverse Context, in *Strong Performers and Successful Reformers in Education: Lessons from PISA for the United States.* Paris. Retrieved from http://www.oecd.org/pisa/pisaproducts/46580959.pdf.

23 Mourshed, M., Chijioke, C., and Barber, M. (2010). *How the World's Most Improved School Systems Keep Getting Better.* London: McKinsey and Company.

24 Tucker, M. (2011). *Standing on the Shoulders of Giants: An American Agenda for Education Reform.* Washington, D.C: National Center on Education and the Economy.

25 Fullan, M. & Quinn, J. (2015). *Coherence: The Right Drivers in Action for Schools, Districts, and Systems.* Thousand Oaks, CA: Corwin.

26 Herman, J. (2013). *Canada's Approach to School Funding, www.Americanprogress.org,* Washington, D.C: Center for American Progress.

27 Gidney, R.D. (2002). *From Hope to Harris: The Reshaping of Ontario Schools.* Ontario: University of Toronto Press. (Original work published 1999); Sattler, P. (2012). Education Governance Reform in Ontario: Neoliberalism in Context. *Canadian Journal of Educational Administration and Policy,* 128.

28 Herman, J. (2013). *Canada's Approach to School Funding, www.Americanprogress.org,* Washington, D.C: Center for American Progress.

29 Sattler, P. (2012). Education Governance Reform in Ontario: Neoliberalism in Context. *Canadian Journal of Educational Administration and Policy,* 128.

30 Gidney, R. D. (2002). *From Hope to Harris: The Reshaping of Ontario Schools.* Ontario: University of Toronto Press. (Original work published 1999); McCaffrey, V. (October

2008). Liberal government repeals Tory initiatives. *ETVO Voice*, Toronto. Retrieved from http://etfovoice.ca/wp-content/uploads/2014/01/V11N1_FALL_08.pdf.

31 Hargreaves, A., Moore, S., and Fink, D. (2003). Teaching Despite the Knowledge Society, Part II. In Hargreaves, A. (2003). *Teaching in the Knowledge Society: Education in the Age of Insecurity*. New York: Teachers College Press: 96–126.

32 Hargreaves, A., Moore, S., and Fink, D. (2003). Teaching Despite the Knowledge Society, Part II. In Hargreaves, A. (2003). *Teaching in the Knowledge Society: Education in the Age of Insecurity*. New York: Teachers College Press: 96–126. (p. 117).

33 Lessard, C. and Bassard, A. (2009). Education Governance in Canada, 1990–2003: Trends and Significance. In Levine-Rasky, C. (Ed.) *Canadian Perspectives on the Sociology of Education* (pp. 255–274). Don Mills, ON: Oxford University Press.

34 Livingstone, D. W., Hart, D. J., and Davie, L. E. (1998). *The 12th OISE/UT Survey: Public Attitudes Towards Education in Ontario in 1998*. Toronto: OISE/University of Toronto.

35 Earl, L., Watson. N. Levin, B., Leithwood, K., and Fullan, M .(2003). *Watching and Learning 3: The Final Report of the OISE/UT External Evaluation of the National Literacy and Numeracy Strategies*. Department for Education and Employment, U.K.

36 Fullan, M. (2010). *All Systems Go: The Change Imperative for Whole School Reform*. Thousand Oaks, CA: Corwin.

37 Campbell, C., Fullan, M., and Glaze, A. (2006). *Unlocking Potential for Learning: Effective District-Wide Strategies to Raise Student Achievement in Literacy and Numeracy*. Toronto: Ontario Ministry of Education; Ontario Ministry of Education (2006, 2007, 2008, 2009). *Schools on the Move (Lighthouse Program)* Toronto: Queen's Printer for Ontario. Retrieved from http://www.edu.gov.on.ca/eng/literacynumeracy/onthemove.pdf.

38 Gallagher, M. J. (2014). *Ontario Education Improvement: Slide Deck for International Presentations*. Toronto: Ministry of Education.

39 Campbell, C. (In press) Leading System-Wide Educational Improvement in Ontario. In Harris, A., and Jones, M. S. (Eds.) (2015) *Leading Futures: Global Perspectives on Educational Leadership*. London: Sage.

40 McCaffrey, V. (October 2008). Liberal government repeals Tory initiatives. *ETVO Voice*, Toronto, Canada. Retrieved from http://etfovoice.ca/wp-content/uploads/2014/01/V11N1_FALL_08.pdf; Sattler, P. (2012). Education Governance Reform in Ontario: Neoliberalism in Context. *Canadian Journal of Educational Administration and Policy*, 128.

41 Hargreaves, A., and Shirley, D. (2012) *The Global Fourth Way: The Quest for Educational Excellence*. Thousand Oaks, CA: Corwin.

42 Hargreaves, A., and Shirley, D. (2012) *The Global Fourth Way: The Quest for Educational Excellence*. Thousand Oaks, CA: Corwin.

43 Glaze, A., Mattingley, R., and Andrews, R. (2013). *High School Graduation: K-12 Strategies that Work*. New York/Ontario: Corwin/Ontario Principals' Council.

44 Ontario Ministry of Education (2008a). *Reach Every Student: Energizing Ontario Education*. Toronto: Queen's Printer for Ontario. Retrieved from http://www.edu. gov.on.ca/eng/document/energize/energize.pdf.

45 Pascal, C. E. (2009). *With Our Best Future in Mind: Implementing Early Learning in Ontario*. Ontario: Government of Ontario.

46 Ontario Ministry of Education (2015). *Early Years Division Initiatives: 2010–2015*. Toronto.

47 Fullan, M., and Quinn, J. (2015). *Coherence: The Right Drivers in Action for Schools, Districts, and Systems*. Thousand Oaks, CA: Corwin Press.

48 Pervin, B., and Campbell, C. (2015). Systems for Teacher and Leader Effectiveness and Quality: Ontario, Canada. In Darling-Hammond, L., and Rothman, R. (eds.) *Teaching in the Flat World: Learning from High Performing Systems*. New York: Teachers College Press

49 Fullan, M., Rincon-Gallardo, S., and Hargreaves, A. (2015). Professional Capital as Accountability. *Education Policy Analysis Archives*, 23, 15.

50 Pervin, B., and Campbell, C. (2015). Systems for Teacher and Leader Effectiveness and Quality: Ontario, Canada. In Darling-Hammond, L,. and Rothman, R. (eds.) *Teaching in the Flat World: Learning from High-Performing Systems*. New York: Teachers College Press.

51 Ontario Ministry of Education (2010). *New Teacher Induction Program: Induction Elements Manual*. Toronto: Ministry of Education. Retrieved from http://www.edu.gov.on.ca/eng/teacher/pdfs/NTIP-English_Elements-september2010.pdf.

52 Campbell, C., Lieberman, A., and Yashkina, A. (2013). *Teacher Learning & Leadership Program. Executive Summary*. Toronto: Ontario Teachers' Federation; Ontario Teachers' Federation (2014). Teacher Learning and Leadership Program. Toronto: OTF/FEO. Retrieved from http://www.otffeo.on.ca/en/learning/teacher-learning-and-leadership-program.

53 Hargreaves, A., and Braun, H. (2013). *Leading for All*. Ontario: Council of Ontario Directors of Education. Toronto: Council of Ontario Directors of Education. Retrieved from http://www.ontariodirectors.ca/downloads/Essential_FullReport_Final.pdf.

54 Fullan, M. (2014b). *California's Golden Opportunity: A Status Note*. Retrieved from www.michaelfullan.ca.

55 Campbell, C., Lieberman, A., and Yashkina, A. (2013). *Teacher Learning & Leadership Program. Executive Summary*. Toronto: Ontario Teachers' Federation; Ontario Teachers' Federation (2014). Teacher Learning and Leadership Program. Toronto: OTF/FEO. Retrieved from http://www.otffeo.on.ca/en/learning/teacher-learning-and-leadership-program.

56 Hargreaves, A. and Fullan, M. (2012). *Professional Capital*. New York: Teachers College Press.

57 Ontario Ministry of Education (2014). *Achieving Excellence: A Renewed Vision for Education in Ontario*. Toronto: Ministry of Education. Retrieved from http://www.edu.gov.on.ca/eng/about/renewedVision.pdf.

58 Fullan, M. (2013). *Great to Excellent: Launching the Next Stage of Ontario's Education Agenda*. Retrieved from http://www.michaelfullan.ca/media/13599974110.pdf.

59 Fullan, M. (2013). *Great to Excellent: Launching the Next Stage of Ontario's Education Agenda*. Retrieved from http://www.michaelfullan.ca/media/13599974110.pdf.

8

PRIVATIZATION AND PUBLIC INVESTMENT

Is the Invisible Hand a Magic Wand?

Linda Darling-Hammond and Frank Adamson

As we have seen in these country cases, economic philosophies and education policies are often entangled, and both can change as they are contended over time. We examined three pairs of countries across the world that have taken very different approaches to structuring their education systems in ways associated with distinctive economic paradigms. We have seen that these different approaches produce—at the system level—quite disparate results. We summarize these approaches and outcomes in this chapter and evaluate the implications of these findings.

The market-based approaches taken up seriously in three of the countries are founded on the neoliberal economic ideas that the "invisible hand", that is the expression of individual interests will produce social benefits as individuals pursue their own goals in private markets. In 1759, Adam Smith articulated this idea in *The Theory of Moral Sentiments* when he argued that an appreciation of self-interest on the part of the wealthy would lead to the same distribution of basic goods to the people as a regulatory approach focused on equity:

> The rich…are led by an invisible hand to make nearly the same distribution of the necessaries of life, which would have been made, had the earth been divided into equal portions among all its inhabitants, and thus without intending it, without knowing it, advance the interest of the society.[1]

As it has evolved in economic theory, the invisible hand metaphor suggests that freedom of consumer choice and of producer offerings will trigger a set of supply, demand, and quality adjustments that result in an equilibrium that benefits each individual and the community as a whole. In Adam Smith's imagination, this equilibrium would also assure equity. The question we have explored is whether and to what extent this notion of how markets operate appears to produce both quality and equity in education. We contrast the policies and outcomes in jurisdictions that have embraced this view with those in nearby jurisdictions that have taken a public management approach in which they seek to improve education systems by investing in stronger curriculum, teaching, and other resources.

Chile was among the first to institute a strongly market-based education system, under the right-wing Pinochet dictatorship, vastly different from the public investment approach taken by Cuba under Castro's version of communism. Sweden followed Chile's lead with a strong turn to market approaches in the 1990s, while nearby Finland undertook a strategy to redesign and improve its public education system around the same time. The larger and more complex cases of the United States and Canada feature variation both within and across countries: The United States has experienced a tug-of-war between market ideas—planted firmly in a few cities like Milwaukee and, later, New Orleans—which have recently spread to a number of others—and strategies pursued in other states and districts to improve public education systems through capacity-building strategies. Meanwhile, next door Canada flirted briefly with privatization ideas in locales such as Ontario, and then rejected those initiatives in favor of a strong public investment strategy.

The market-based reforms have featured a variety of ways to provide public funding to privately managed schools, through vouchers, charters, contracts, and other tools. They have also typically featured test-based accountability (arguably, providing the information by which consumers can make choices), and market-based strategies for organizing the teaching force—usually eliminating requirements regarding preparation and licensing governing who can enter teaching and what knowledge base they must possess, and thereby deprofessionalizing the teaching force. Sometimes the reforms have also weakened collective bargaining or other negotiating capacity for teachers and other public school employees.

The public investment strategies have typically sought to create an equitable platform of funding for public schools and an equitably distributed, high quality curriculum and teaching force. These strategies generally entail policies that professionalize teaching through stronger preparation and professional development and that prepare educators to teach a rich curriculum to diverse learners. These jurisdictions use tests or assessments for different purposes: to inform investment and improvement strategies at the state and local level, rather than to guide parent choice or to determine which schools to close. Finally, these jurisdictions see education as a public good and schools as owned by their communities, with a strong two-way relationship between the two.

Educational Outcomes

There are success stories about individual schools that can be identified in both the private and public sectors in any of these countries. Some of this is likely the result of genuine education innovation and use of productive educational and management techniques. Some of these results, the evidence shows, are also the result of "creaming," or recruiting in, the highest-performing students and "cropping," or pushing out, the lower performing students where schools have the leverage to do so. At the system level, however, little evidence shows that jurisdictions that adopted market-based reforms improved overall achievement or attainment for students, and substantial data suggests that, over time, they have lost ground with respect to both educational equity and quality.

One lens is provided by the scores of students on the Program for International Student Assessment (PISA). As Figure 8.1 shows, Chile and Sweden—countries that have long pursued privatizing reforms—perform well below OECD averages in mathematics, reading, and science, even though they are wealthy countries in their respective regions.[2] Sweden's performance is particularly shocking, since it was once considered the most educated country in the well-educated region of Scandinavia, and it suffered an alarming drop on PISA from well above the OECD mean in 2000 to well below the mean in 2012. Chile's scores have been improving somewhat in recent years, as equalizing reforms have been established to undo some of the damage of Pinochet's approach, but Chile remains very far below the norms, ranking between 47th and 55th across the content areas tested.

The United States, once the world's undisputed education leader during the 1970s, also ranks below OECD averages in mathematics and science, and just above the average in reading. Lower scores in the United States are primarily due to great disparity in student performance, with under-resourced and underserved students performing significantly lower than their peers in other OECD countries. Data in the U.S. case study show that the highly privatized districts of Milwaukee

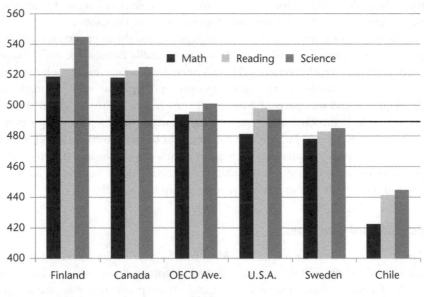

FIGURE 8.1 PISA Scores by Country, 2012

and New Orleans perform at the very bottom of their respective states and below other urban districts nationally on state and national achievement tests. These districts exhibit enormous achievement gaps, as do the three nations, and these disparities are closely tied to socioeconomic status.

Meanwhile, Finland and Canada perform among the most highly ranked nations in mathematics, reading, and science and have been in the top ranks since PISA began in 2000. Finland's high standing was a particular surprise when PISA results were first reported, because the Finns were once among the least-educated populations in Scandinavia. They eschewed the fancy market-based reforms going on next door in Sweden, opting instead to invest in a more equitable system of funding and curriculum and to create a highly professionalized teaching force. In 2012, they ranked third among countries in science, fourth in reading, and eighth in mathematics. Canada ranked in the top ten on all of these areas as well.

Also shocking is the standing of economically disadvantaged and long-boycotted Cuba, which does not participate in PISA but led the country rankings on SERCE (Second Regional Comparative and Explanatory Study), a Latin American regional assessment (Figure 8.2). Whereas the *average* student in Cuba performed at the highest proficiency level on the SERCE (more than 50 percent of students in grade 6 reading and math as well as 3rd grade math, plus 44 percent in 3rd grade reading), the proportions for the region and for Chile were generally well under

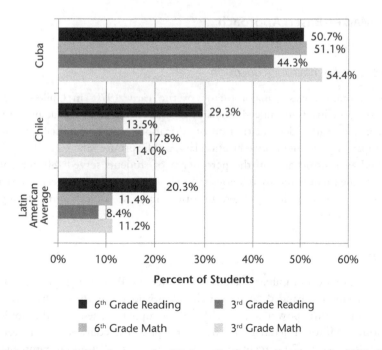

FIGURE 8.2 Percent of Students at the Highest Proficiency Level on the 2005–2006 SERCE Test, by Content, Area, and Grade Level

half that number. For example, whereas Cuba places 54 percent of its students in the top tier in 3rd grade math and 51 percent in 6th grade math, Chile has only 14 percent in this highest tier in both grades.[3] These massive differences exist across every tier of performance, content area, and grade level. When compared with every other Latin American country, Cuba's student performance is literally off the charts. This success suggests that, despite its economic challenges, Cuba's substantial public investment in its students' education has paid off well, especially when compared with Chile's privatization model.

The Strategies in Action

Of course the full story is much more complex, and there are not straight-line causal relationships among any single action and outcome. In addition, the stories are different in each country and have evolved over time. In this section, we examine what these general precepts looked like in each of the distinctive country contexts and how they unfolded. We briefly summarize the history of reforms that took place, illustrating the political processes and forces that enacted these ideas and the outcomes that ensued. We begin with an analysis of the evolution of market-based approaches in Chile, Sweden, and the United States. We then turn to the public investment strategies of Cuba, Finland, and Canada.

The Market-Based Approach

Chile

A Press for Democratic Education

Democratization was a major theme of the early 1970s in Chile—one that extended to education. Indeed, Socialist president Salvador Allende pronounced 1971 as the year of democratization of education. With substantial investments accompanying a compulsory education law, public primary and secondary schools reached an historic high in the percentage of students served (80 percent) by 1974, while private, mostly religious schools, served about 20 percent. Teachers' salaries experienced their greatest historical increase in real terms during the 1960–1972 period.[4]

Privatization

In 1973, however, a military takeover put General Pinochet in power, and the situation rapidly changed, as he sought to privatize enterprises that had been public and return power and wealth to the upper classes. On the advice of economist Milton Friedman, he began to privatize education. For teachers, salaries dropped by 70 percent in real dollar terms as inflation ran rampant. The teachers' union was dissolved and many of its members were imprisoned or killed. Many teachers left the profession, and schools suffered both financially and in terms of their human resources.

Several years later, with the military occupying every city in the country, citizens approved the dictatorial Constitution of 1980. This paved the way for privatization in all sectors of government. Starting in 1981, a series of measures that completely transformed the educational system was put into place. These included seven "modernizations" to institutions (including education) enacted by the Military Junta, including:

1. Tuition charged for education, except for high-poverty students
2. State subsidies provided to private schools
3. Vouchers attached to student attendance
4. Tertiary education subject to fees
5. Decentralization of administration to municipalities
6. Implementation of national student testing (the SIMCE assessment)
7. Teachers no longer treated as public servants, but subject to general labor laws.

Teaching was deprofessionalized: following the steep decrease in salaries, education training no longer required a bachelor's degree or the completion of an undergraduate thesis, and enrollment in teaching programs dropped by 30 percent between 1983 and 1990. When Pinochet was finally unseated in 1988, the educational system had changed dramatically. The private sector had grown substantially, and the system as a whole was much more segregated by class and unequal in quality, less grounded in professional norms and knowledge, and more driven by standardized tests.

In the early to mid-1990s, as Chile sought to regain a democratic system, over 25 percent of the population lived in extreme poverty, fewer than 50 percent of students finished high school and fewer than 15 percent of high-school graduates enrolled in tertiary education. The country invested only $360 per pupil per year in education, as public spending on education accounted for only 2.4 percent of the GDP. Subsequent efforts to redress some of these problems in the 1990s introduced relatively small, incremental changes from time to time to address equity issues, but they did not uproot the privatized system in place and were inadequate to change the dramatic inequalities in access to education.

Growing Inequality

Over the three decades, the proportion of public schools dropped from 72 percent in 1980 to 46 percent by 2012, and the number of voucher (publicly subsidized, tuition-charging private) schools increased from 18 percent in 1980 to 49 percent in 2012. The remaining small share of schools (about 5 percent) is the unsubsidized private school sector. These schools are deeply stratified. All of the private school students are from the highest socioeconomic group, while the public schools are nearly entirely comprised of low-income students: three-fourths of the lowest SES students are in public schools; and two-thirds of the next poorest group of students are in public schools. None of these students are in private schools, and only a few are in privately subsidized (voucher) schools, where three-quarters of the students are middle to upper class.

These class stratifications are accompanied by dramatically different funding and resource levels for schools in the three sectors, which offer strikingly disparate educational quality. This—along with high tuitions and little student aid for higher education—is the source of student-generated revolts, which began in 2001, increasingly involving more and more students, with a crescendo in 2006 with the so-called Penguin Revolution (named because of the black-and-white uniforms worn by municipal high school students who boycotted and marched by the hundreds of thousands). The student protests have re-gained momentum at different times, with another massive set of marches and boycotts in 2011 which gathered over hundreds of thousands of people from all sectors, not only education.

Outcomes

The protests are directed at the fact that, after 32 years of having applied the regulations dictated by the Military Junta, public schools declined tremendously in quality while families had to pay for private schools to gain even marginally better quality. Of course, the private schools serving the wealthiest students score most highly on the national tests. However, despite the common perception that private schools are superior to public schools, recent data show that—controlling for socioeconomic status—both the lowest-income students and those who are upper middle class do better in public schools, on average, than similar students in the subsidized private schools.

Even the wealthiest and highest-performing students in Chile, however, fall far below international norms on assessments like PISA—and below the performance of most students in tiny, economically disadvantaged Cuba (which we discuss below). And despite recent investments that have tried to equalize opportunities, PISA scores showed a decline for nearly all SES groups between 2009 and 2012.

The results of the educational marketplace have been disappointing in relation to progress elsewhere in the world, while they have also reinforced economic segregation and contributed to a huge achievement gap, which has translated into differential opportunities for students to learn, graduate, attend college, and gain employment.

Deprofessionalization of Teaching

Even with some efforts to redress educational inequalities since the 1990s, the deprofessionalization of teaching has continued, including a teacher evaluation process for municipal schools (passed in 2004) that makes the results of evaluations public and compares them to students' test scores, leading many to conclude that the lower scores of students in under-resourced municipal schools, which cannot select students as the private schools do, are a direct consequence of the poor performance of teachers. These evaluation provisions do not apply to the private schools. Recent enactments (in 2009) have further lowered standards for entering teaching so that any degree in a professional field will suffice, even if it does not include substantial education training. Other initiatives have destabilized teaching by explicitly providing for school principals to lay off up to 5 percent of teachers each year if they choose. Authors Castro-Hildalgo and Gómez-Álvarez conclude that:

> In sum, since 1973, the teaching profession has systematically been degraded from being one of the most respected professions in Chile to having a very low social valoration. This has systematically and negatively impacted salaries, work conditions, and, especially, pre-service training.

Current Efforts

Recent governments have tried to ameliorate some of the negative effects of this legacy. Legislation passed in 2008 allocated large increases in spending per student in primary schools for low-income students and seems to have had a positive impact on achievement for students in high-poverty schools. Under continued pressure from student protests, recently joined by educators as well, the second-term Socialist government headed by Michelle Bachelet, elected in 2014, has been working to transform this entrenched system. Her government's reforms aim at reducing segregation, eliminating selective school admissions based on academic performance or socioeconomic status, banning government funding to profit-making schools, along with requirements for co payment, ensuring universal educational coverage, and securing quality and accountability at all levels. The jury is still out as to whether these initiatives will transform the Chilean education system, but it is clear than an effort is underway to increase public investment and reinstate a perspective on education as a social good, rather than a purely private one.

Sweden

Sweden has long been known for its social democratic approach to governance and public service provision. And indeed, during its most substantial social democratic era, from the 1950s until the 1990s, Sweden's educational system gained a prominent reputation worldwide,[5] as Swedish pupils were placed at the top of international rankings on the International Association for the Assessment of Educational Achievement (IEA) assessments of mathematics, science, and reading that preceded PISA.[6] However, current data show that PISA scores in

Sweden have plunged to an all-time low, dropping further and faster than those in almost any other country and now lagging other OECD countries. Furthermore, Sweden now has the most rapid growth of inequality.[7]

The Creation of a Democratic Education System

The market-based reforms that led to this decline were instituted in the 1990s, but they had a precedent in the system that existed in Sweden before the end of World War II, when the country's education system featured a mix of private and public institutions; early selection of students into different, parallel educational tracks; and high levels of inequality. Like Finland, which had a similarly tracked system, it replaced this unequal schooling system after the war with a unified, comprehensive model geared toward democratic ambitions and equality, with substantial success through the 1980s.

In the shadow of Nazism, the goal was to build an education system that would make citizens as equal as possible, to build a stronger society, and to secure endorsement of the democratic state. Thus, in 1950, Sweden created and piloted a comprehensive, mandatory nine-year school model shared by students from all social classes, which was finally fully implemented in the early 1970s. Educational equity was to be anchored in the common national curriculum and a uniform and equitable teacher education.

During this era, from the 1950s to the 1990s, the relatively few private alternatives were thought to be a source of positive influence on public schools, by demonstrating new or different ideas. However, when Sweden redesigned the welfare-based school model to create a market-oriented model based on individual choice, private alternatives and competition, the perceived role of private schools shifted from one of a potential positive *influence* to a role of *replacing* regular public schools.

Investment in Private Education

Major changes were precipitated by an economic crisis in the early 1990s, as the nation accumulated a large national debt from prior industrial crises coupled with the continual growth of the public sector. In the context of a general reform of the welfare state, the Swedish school system was also reformed around the themes of decentralization and deregulation, together with rationales of competition and freedom of school choice. The reforms, which resulted in a school market model and a sharp increase in private schools, reactivated elements of the unequal pre-war education system.

In 1992, Sweden decided that accredited private schools would be eligible for public funds. Choice was billed as a means to "break up the public school monopoly," overriding the post-war goals of shared school experiences and equitable opportunities. Meanwhile, Sweden ended the centralized funding of schools and allowed local jurisdictions to decide how much money to allocate to education, creating inequalities in public school resources. National contributions are small and marginal, and not targeted directly to student needs. The resulting disparities are now substantial, with expenditures across municipalities ranging from just over US $8000 per pupil to nearly US $14,000 per pupil, a level that is nearly 75 percent higher than the lowest-spending areas.

In 2006, another wave of school reforms created an expanded testing and grading system. As in Chile, the privatization strategy was accompanied by increased inequality in the allocation of public funds and the increased use of student testing and school rankings as a source of information for parent choice and an alternative to funding equity and educational quality standards for accountability. This metric also stimulates competition for the students who score well, which private schools can manage by where they locate (since transportation is not provided) and how they market their services.

A Swedish private school can today be organized as a joint stock company, private company/enterprise (limited partnership or sole proprietorship), cooperative, non-profit association, faith-based organization, or foundation. These schools receive the same funding as the municipality schools, so while there is inequality in school funding across municipalities, there is equal funding between public and private schools. Private schools cannot ask for additional tuition or fees from parents. However, private schools have the right to make a profit and, thus, the share of funding available for instruction may be less in the private schools than in public schools that are not trying to reimburse their shareholders. Because staff represents the main cost in schooling and national regulation of class sizes disappeared with deregulation in the early 1990s, large differences in student–staff ratios exist across public and private schools, with many fewer teachers or counselors per pupil in the private sector. The largest student–staff ratios are found in for-profit schools.

By 2010, more than 15 percent of the primary and lower secondary schools (grades 1–9) were private, along with 20 percent of preschools, and close to 50 percent of schools at the upper secondary level (grades 10–12). Overall, one in four Swedish schools is now private, with a growing number run by for-profit education companies that own a collection of schools. These school companies aim to accomplish economies of scale to feed substantial profits. In 2014, for example, the Swedish school company Academedia made a US $53 million surplus (EBIT) on its schools, half of which ended up as owners' profit.

The new marketplace has created a great deal of instability in the school system as a function of buy-outs, expansions, contractions, and closings. For instance, the rapid growth of the school company Fourfront earned it a famous industrialist prize, The Gazell, in 2006. Soon after, the owner sold the company to JB Education, a company at the time already owned by venture capitalists Axcel, which was, in fact, a buy-out enterprise. JB Education had a growth rate of 1,000 percent in four years prior to its collapse in 2013 due to bankruptcy, at which point all the schools were either sold or closed. Liquidating schools is a new phenomenon in Swedish history.

The business model can also drive the educational process. According to an article in *Economist,* one large chain of schools, Kunskapsskolan, which is expanding internationally, mirrors the IKEA concept in getting "its customers to do much of the work themselves." A representative of the chain, which does not mind being compared with McDonalds, stated: "If we are religious about anything, it is standardization." Consequently, students mainly work independently on web-based assignments, meeting with tutors only 15 minutes per week. They follow a standardized syllabus, are constantly monitored, and their performance is available for parents on a weekly basis.

Deprofessionalization of Teaching

As in Chile, the market-based approach has been accompanied by considerable deprofessionalization of teaching in both the private and public sectors. The decentralization of responsibility for teacher staffing coincided with the disappearance of stricter regulations for teacher qualifications. Since 1991, the overall proportion of qualified teachers has been reduced from about 95 percent to just slightly above 80 percent, with an even lower proportion in private schools. The differentials are quite large in preschools, where private school teachers meeting degree requirements have dropped to only 40 percent. For grades 1–9, the proportion of teachers meeting education requirements in 2012–2013 was significantly higher in municipality schools (86 percent) in 2012–2013 than in private schools (70 percent). Differences were also substantial in upper secondary schools (79 percent in municipality schools and 62 percent in private schools).

The declines in teacher qualifications are even more stunning if one looks at subject matter specializations. For example, in lower secondary schools, about 75 percent of teachers in French, German, and History are qualified to teach their subjects, while the rates in Physics, Social Studies, and Geography—and in mathematics in the southern part of the country—have declined to 50–60 percent. In addition, a 2014 OECD study raised concerns that experienced and qualified Swedish teachers are less equitably distributed among schools serving low-income students, that recurring teacher shortages impact on socioeconomically disadvantaged schools more, and that these shortages are further amplified by unequally distributed resources.

Increasingly severe teacher shortages may be in part a product of the declining working conditions for Swedish teachers—larger class sizes, lower salaries, and poorer working conditions in schools that are more poorly resourced or are seeking to eke out larger profits. According to the recent international TALIS surveys (2013), Swedish teachers were less likely than those in other countries to agree that the teaching profession is valued in their society, and they had the lowest level of job satisfaction.

Outcomes

As we saw earlier, Sweden's overall student achievement has declined sharply on PISA to well below OECD averages, while it has simultaneously become more unequal. While one Swedish study has argued that municipalities with more private schools have overall higher student grades and attainment than those that have fewer (suggesting that competition promotes quality), the research has been critiqued for failure to control adequately for socioeconomic differences across municipalities, and for evidence of grade inflation in private schools.

Current Efforts

Growing concerns about the outcomes of this experiment stimulated an intensified debate about private schools preceding the fall 2014 election. Since then, the new government has launched inquiries both on limiting profit in the welfare sector and on the possibility of a local veto-right regarding private school establishment, as well as a school commission for the improvement of schooling in Sweden.

United States

The United States has always experienced competing impulses—a press for equity in tension with a history of racial discrimination and forces favoring a concentration of wealth and power. The press for social equity has occurred in cycles, following eras where inequality has become extreme: reconstruction followed the end of slavery in the 1860s; Roosevelt's New Deal followed the 1929 economic crash that led to the Great Depression; and Johnson's Great Society initiatives, triggered by civil rights actions in the 1960s. Each of these eras was followed, in turn, by a pushback that reversed some of the equity gains.

An Era of Democratic Progress

During the 1960s, among other social investments, major new education legislation supported resources for schools serving low-income children, desegregation, education for handicapped children, curriculum reforms, teacher education and more equitable distribution of teachers, and higher education access. The largest reductions in the achievement gap between black and white students occurred during the 1960s and 1970s when these investments expanded educational opportunity. This period also saw near-elimination of the gap between minorities and whites enrolling in higher education, with the expansion of financial aid and affirmative action.

Pushback and Privatization

Most of the federal investments that produced these advances were reduced or eliminated in the 1980s during the Reagan Administration, when market-based ideologies were rekindled and government services dramatically curtailed at both the state and federal levels. Among the policies launched in the 1980s and further developed in the subsequent decades were:

- Support for public funding of privately managed schools through private school vouchers and, later, charter schools;
- Resistance to lawsuits and legislation seeking equalized funding of public schools;
- The use of test-based accountability as a means of evaluating students and schools;
- The creation of an unregulated marketplace for teachers by creating alternative certification pathways around professional preparation and licensing standards.

Courts struck down many early voucher initiatives on the grounds of separation of church and state. Ultimately, though, the nation's first large-scale voucher program was established in the early 1990s in Milwaukee, Wisconsin, which was also the site of one of the initial charter school initiatives in 1995. A small number of additional voucher plans have survived to enactment, but the charter movement has grown rapidly in a number of states, evolving from individual schools mounted by groups with specific education ideas to chains of schools operated by charter management organizations, some of them for-profit.

This movement was accelerated by Barack Obama's *Race to the Top* program in 2009, which required states competing for federal funding to lift caps on the number of charters, expand the use of alternative certification for teachers, and evaluate teachers based on their students' test scores. Substantial funding from venture capitalists and private foundations augmented federal funding for expanding charters.

Following the first law allowing the establishment of charter schools in Minnesota in 1991, charter school legislation had been passed in 42 states and the District of Columbia as of school year 2012–2013. From 2000 to 2013, the number of students enrolled in public charter schools increased from 0.3 million to 2.3 million, reaching 4.6 percent of all students in 2013.[8]

When Hurricane Katrina hit New Orleans in 2005, these funders collaborated with public officials to replace the public school district with a "Recovery School District," eliminate the school board, terminate the contracts of all teachers, and ultimately replace the teachers with non-unionized teachers and the district entirely with charter schools. This model has been advocated for other cities made vulnerable by large budget cuts since the Great Recession of 2008. In recent years, sharp budget cuts by states have placed many urban school districts serving largely low-income students of color into financial crisis that has subjected them to receiverships or state takeovers that have eliminated their school boards and led to widespread school closures, often with district-run public schools replaced by charter schools, and/or designation of private managers (charter operators and others, some of them for-profit) to run public schools.

Community advocates from 21 of these cities have recently banded together to fight these changes, and a number of groups have filed civil rights charges because the school closings and reconstitutions affect primarily African American and Latino students. In addition to the loss of public schools that serve communities in many ways, new charters that are opened may be geographically inaccessible or may not accept and keep high-need students. Much of the action community members are protesting is a result of the growing for-profit sector supported by public funds: the number of for-profit education management companies running charter schools increased 20-fold between 1995 and 2012, and the number of schools they operate increased more than 100-fold in that time, from six to 758. Virtual charter schools are also rapidly increasing, saving money on buildings and using a smaller number of teachers to offer on-line learning at a very substantial profit.

While considerable federal policy action has encouraged privately managed schools, the uptake in the field has been highly variable. Some cities and states are aggressively pursuing privatizing options while others have resisted the federal or state incentives and have relatively little engagement in private schools or charters. More headway has been made in urban districts serving low-income students of color than in more affluent areas. Overall, there has been little change in the longstanding fact that 90 percent of U.S. students attend public schools. Of these, about 5 percent attend charter schools, ranging from zero in some states to as many as 42 percent in the District of Columbia.

Outcomes

A recent review of research on publicly funded private school vouchers concluded there was "no clear advantage in academic achievement for students attending private schools with vouchers,"[9] although voucher parents typically felt quite positively about their schools. The evidence about charter school effectiveness has also been decidedly mixed, with studies finding no effects or negative effects of attending a charter school as often as they find positive effects. Where charters have been largely unregulated, as in Ohio and Arizona, results for students have typically been negative relative to similar students in district-run public schools. In states like California, where charters must meet curriculum, staffing, and financial standards, modest differences across sectors sometimes favor charters and other times favor district-run schools. However, in virtually all contexts, students do particularly poorly in charters providing most of their instruction through independent study or distance learning.

A troubling set of consistent findings is that charters are more racially and economically segregated than public schools generally, and they underrepresent English learners and special education students relative to public schools in their districts. In some states, these socioeconomic differences also translate into educational differences. For example, a Texas study found that the majority of white, Anglo students were in academically oriented charters, while most minority students were in vocational charters.

In Milwaukee, where charters and vouchers have the longest history, about 20 percent of students attend private schools on vouchers and about one-fourth of public school students are in contract or charter schools. Wisconsin also enabled the hiring of not-yet-prepared teachers in Milwaukee through alternative certification pathways, a practice not permitted in the rest of the state at that time. The Milwaukee educational marketplace has been a highly volatile one. For example, over the five years between 2007 and 2011, the district closed 59 schools and opened 24 new ones. The culture of choice and competition, in the context of test-based accountability under the major federal education law (No Child Left Behind) has caused schools to compete for the best-performing students and to seek to unload those that are viewed as more difficult to educate.

Despite the intensive competition and much opening and closing of schools, achievement has not improved in Milwaukee and achievement gaps have widened. Research has found little difference in achievement among similar students attending vouchers, charters, and district-run public schools, even though charters serve many fewer English learners and special needs students than the district as a whole. Achievement is low for all sectors, and has been stagnant for the last dozen years in which state test data have been available. National data show that Milwaukee is one of the lowest achieving cities in the nation, and that once high-achieving Wisconsin has developed the largest black–white achievement gap in the nation, largely because of the decline of its largest city.

Whereas Milwaukee is the first U.S. example of a market-based portfolio of school choices, New Orleans is the first example of a school district in which all schools are either private schools or privately operated charters. There have been a variety of competing studies and claims made about achievement in New Orleans, which have been hotly contended, as the U.S. chapter details. Because the Louisiana Department of Education will not share individual-level student data with most researchers (this refusal been the subject of a lawsuit), it is enormously difficult to identify the effects of chartering, given the dramatic transformation of the population in New Orleans after Katrina. (Those who returned after having been displaced were more likely to be property owners and wage-earning, which by itself would improve average school performance.)

What is clear is that the Recovery School District in New Orleans continues to be a low-performing district in a low-performing state. Only 12 percent of students scored at the "mastery" level or above in the state tests in 2014, half the statewide rate and far less than the separate Orleans Parish Schools that were not taken over by the state. The RSD ranks 69th out of the 70 districts in the state, and Louisiana ranks 48th to 50th among 50 states on national assessments of reading and math.

Meanwhile, the schools are highly stratified by race, class, and disability, with schools choosing students more than students choose their schools. A top tier of selective schools, which creates a great student competition, is the primary location for white students and those identified as gifted and talented. The charter law allows these schools to set admissions standards based on academic performance and other factors. A second tier in the RSD requires admission by lottery if there are more students than slots; these engage in competition for the more desirable students that are left over after tier 1 schools have chosen. A third tier exists for the students who are expelled from other schools, have returned from the corrections system, or are one step away from entering it (at least one of these schools is operated by a company that also operates prisons).

As in Milwaukee, there has been much opening and closing of schools from year to year. Because federal and state accountability systems center on student test scores, each school's survival and competitive advantage depends on boosting scores. This creates incentives for attracting and retaining higher-scoring students, and for excluding those who pull down the average. Researchers have found that exclusion strategies include: (1) denying enrollment to low performers, students with discipline records, and special education students; (2) expelling students in October after receiving their annual funding from the state; and (3) having students arrested on school grounds and thereby eliminating them without having to expel them. The difficulty special education students have had getting enrolled at any school has been the subject of another lawsuit. For those students who are not profitable, the market does not appear to offer choice.

Interestingly, the highest achieving states in the United States—Connecticut, Massachusetts, New Hampshire, New Jersey, and Vermont—are among those that have had the least engagement with market-based reforms. The pro-charter Center for Education Reform, which ranks states on their openness to charters, gives all of them a grade of "C" or "D."[10]

Massachusetts is a particularly instructive case: for more than a decade, since about 2002, Massachusetts has led the states in student achievement in every subject area on the National Assessment of Educational Progress. Massachusetts compares favorably with the top-scoring nations on PISA, ranking alongside Finland, Singapore, and others.[11] This is not because of a widespread privatization movement: the number of charters is small and tightly capped, while strong accountability systems regulate their quality and make it difficult to exclude students. Virtual charters are not allowed.

The central story of Massachusetts' rise to excellence began in 1992 with a court decision requiring an overhaul of school funding. The finance formula adopted in 1993 as part of Massachusetts' Education Reform Act stimulated substantially greater investments in needier schools through a weighted student formula which aimed to equalize funding and local effort simultaneously and which added funding increments based on the proportions of low-income students and English language learners in a district.

This progressive approach helped boost educational investments and achievement as the state undertook a comprehensive reform featuring new standards and assessments demanding more intellectually ambitious teaching and learning. In addition to much greater and more equitable funding to schools, the initiatives included statewide standards for students, educators, schools and districts; new curriculum frameworks to guide more equitable access to high-status knowledge, as well as stronger instruction; expanded learning time in core content areas; investments in technology; stronger preparation and licensing requirements for teachers; and more access to high-quality learning opportunities for teachers and school leaders. Investments in preschool education and health care for children were also part of the overall strategy.

The Public Investment Strategy

Massachusetts' success, and that of other high-achieving states and cities in the United States, stands as counter-evidence to the notion that the best or only way to achieve excellence is by emphasizing private provision of education in a competitive market over the improvement of public systems through investments in instruction and professional learning. The countries that we examined as regional contrasts to those discussed above offer examples of strategies for public investment that have common elements.

Cuba

Cuba is, by any standards, a lower-income country that has been subject to an economic blockade for more than 50 years. But the Cuban education system outperforms all other countries in Latin America, with higher achievement than many wealthier nations, including Chile. Chapter author Martin Carnoy summarizes the situation:

> Cuban children attend schools that are intensely focused on instruction and are staffed by well-trained, regularly supervised teachers in a social environment that is dedicated to high academic achievement for all social groups. Combining high-quality teaching with high academic expectations and a tightly controlled school management hierarchy with well-defined goals is what makes the Cuban system tick.... In essence, Cuban education gives most Cuban pupils a primary education that only upper-middle-class children receive in other Latin American countries.

Cuba invested heavily in education as part of its socialist program. In 1961, shortly after the revolution, Cuba embarked on a yearlong campaign to eliminate illiteracy. An estimated 250,000 volunteers spread across rural areas and helped over 700,000 people work on their literacy skills. This literacy campaign set the stage for ongoing public investment in education that eventually led to high achievement and a capable, professionalized teacher labor force.

Building a Democratic Education System

The Cuban government guarantees employment to adults, provides reasonably good health care to all, and enforces child labor laws, so that low-income children are well fed and do not have to work when they are not in school or instead of attending school. Poverty exists in Cuba, but even the very poor have access to food, shelter, health care, and education. Thus, there is a much more even start for schooling, which is provided in settings that are equally well funded and are economically integrated. Students also receive a common curriculum, which has been developed by the Ministry of Education, based in part on what it learned from other models in eastern Europe.

Schools in Cuba are small, designed as highly personalized for students, and very strongly connected to communities, involving families in a variety of ways. Cuban education and the preparation of teachers start from a developmental perspective on student learning, which is expressed both in the training teachers receive and the structure of schools. Primary teachers generally stay with their pupils for the first four years and even six years of primary school, developing a long-term relationship in which teachers get to know students well. This also enhances accountability, as there can be little finger pointing at other teachers if students do not make progress. Greater responsibility is placed on both teachers and supervisors to ensure that students are learning the curriculum as planned.

This approach was recently extended to lower secondary school (7th through 9th grades), where students now have one main teacher for all subjects except English and physical education, in order to provide stronger relationships and more guidance for students. This focus on teaching the child relies in part on teachers' preparation in child development and also on their preparation to skillfully teach the adopted curriculum.

Investment in Professional Learning

Cuba has invested in the professional learning of teachers to a much greater extent than most countries, and has done so in highly effective ways. The teacher education curriculum is developed with the Ministry of Education and constructed around teaching the official school curricula using well-developed teaching techniques grounded both in theory and practice. Cuba's future teachers study the ideas of Dewey, Vygotsky, and Makarenko, among others who have illuminated the learning process, and they connect these ideas to practice. They learn how to teach the Cuban national curriculum in ways that encourage student engagement in active, collaborative learning contexts where deep understanding of concepts, rather than rote memorization, is the goal.

Teacher educators in these institutes have generally been teachers themselves who have gone on for advanced degrees in education or specific subject matter. Prospective teachers are trained in cadres, with each cadre overseen by a mentor teacher who will follow them into and oversee their student teaching. Because training is focused on teaching the required curriculum, both content and pedagogical knowledge are taught using the curriculum students will teach. Candidates learn to apply teaching principles in specific content areas through a combination of study, practice, and reflection throughout their preparation.

Furthermore, teachers are intensively supervised during a long induction period once they start teaching. Cuba has developed a widespread system of administrative involvement in and vigilance toward the quality of instruction. School principals and vice principals share responsibility with teachers to assure high-quality instruction for students. They observe frequently in classrooms and offer constructive feedback. Beginning teachers are heavily mentored to ensure a "learning transition" into teaching.

Unlike market economies that have opened up a variety of pathways to teaching that do not require common strong preparation before entry, every teacher in Cuba is supported to become well prepared before he or she enters a classroom. Teachers have been well paid in Cuba, relative to other occupations, and teaching is an honored profession, so there have been incentives for able people to enter and stay. Because salaries are comparable across the country and all teachers are well prepared, Cuba has been able to ensure well-prepared educators across all communities, even rural areas.

The Use of Tests

Although there is periodic testing for students in Cuba, tests are used very differently than tests in Chile, Sweden, or the United States, where they serve as accountability measures for allocating rewards, sanctions, and informing the market. Cuban municipalities are responsible for testing sixth- and ninth-grade pupils to provide feedback to the Ministry of Education and to the schools on how well the system is doing. Whereas Chile provides incentives through school competition and monetary rewards for higher test scores, in Cuba test results are not released to the public. Tests are used to inform educators but not to "drive" teachers or schools. They are used to make organizational decisions, shaping actions aimed at more effective education in all schools. The assumption seems to be that teachers, rather than tests, drive improvement.

The Role of the State

In Cuba, the state takes on the role of a *guarantor* of quality education for all, taking public responsibility for children's success. This means that it takes responsibility for assuring high-quality instruction through the development of a shared curriculum, the creation of school designs that support its effective delivery, the management of universities' schools of education in their initial preparation of teachers, and a focus on improving instruction through effective supervision at the school level. Carnoy argues that, "By setting high standards for schools and teachers and enforcing them, the state reduces the need for parents to agonize over where they should send their children to school, as almost all schools would be delivering similarly and reasonably high-quality education. This is what the public wants in a democratic state, and this is what the public should get."

Finland

Against all expectations, Finland topped the world in the Program for International Student Assessment (PISA) in 2001 and remained one of the top-performing nations on PISA in all of the years since. Unlike its neighbor Sweden, Finland's educational investments are exclusively public: it operates only public schools and manages parent choice within the public sector; it keeps tight control of who can own or run a school; and does not allow individuals, foundations, or corporations to donate private money to schools.

Although Finland has a well-developed welfare state—offering strong health care, education, and social welfare benefits to its citizens—it has also been ranked as one of the most competitive market economies in the world. The country boasts a very high level of human capital, widespread use of information and communication technologies, and education and research institutions redesigned to foster cutting-edge research and development. It ranks at the top in innovation, prosperity, and the implementation of environmental policies.

The Creation of an Equitable School System

As in a number of other countries (including Chile and Sweden), democratic reforms took hold in the early 1970s. At that time Finland overhauled its education system to create a common system of schooling, which eliminated tracking and provided equal access to a thoughtful curriculum, and which invested heavily in well-trained teachers. The reforms also eliminated tuition-based private schools. While some countries did a U-turn that reduced public investments and equity commitments in the 1980s, Finland has stayed committed to these early ideals and reforms, even in the face of internal opposition at various points from elements in the business community and more right-wing political groups which wanted to reinstate tracking and private schooling, and introduce other market-based reforms.

All schools in Finland are now publicly funded, including about 75 "private" schools that operate under charters issued and funded by the government. Privately governed educational institutions are prohibited from collecting student fees for tuition, ensuring that education resources are not unfairly distributed and avoiding inequities in access and quality. The state subsidy system calculates funding on a per-person basis and ensures that more funds are allocated in ways that compensate for differential wealth at the local level.

Although the system has continued to evolve since then, more recent changes, which decentralize greater authority to local municipalities, preserve the values of public investment and collaboration among schools and teachers, instead of privatization and competition among educators and schools.

Decentralization with Equity

The Finnish version of decentralization is very different from the kind of decentralization that has occurred in jurisdictions pursuing privatization. The latter version of decentralization gives private operators control over decisions, usually by loosening public control over equity-related policies, which allows more differential spending on schools and more disparate standards for things like teacher qualifications. Private operators often want to hire less experienced and well-trained individuals because they are less expensive. The privatization approach then attempts to determine if teachers can do their job using high-stakes, often multiple-choice, exams.

In the case of Finland, equity-related policies around access to well-qualified teachers and adequate resources are maintained in the public sector. Decentralization of decision-making pertains to the opportunities schools have to design curricula—responsive to the national curriculum but tailored to their students and community values—and to create innovative school organizations. There are no external tests except for a sample-based assessment in primary school and a voluntary matriculation examination at the end of high school for students who wish to go to college.

Professionalization of Teaching and Personalization of Learning

Finland invests heavily in the knowledge and skills of its teachers—all of whom receive a five-year preparation for teaching, which ensures strong content and pedagogical training, resulting in both a bachelor's and research-based master's degree. As a consequence of this preparation, teachers are respected and trusted and the system can decentralize many decisions to local schools and maintain quality. In addition, because teachers are so well trained in child development and learning, as well as curriculum and teaching strategies, they can diagnose the learning strengths and needs of individual children and thereby personalize education, rather than having to use standardized tools that oversimplify the learning process. These kinds of tools are common in countries where teachers are less well prepared.

Educators are a well-educated, closely organized professional community in Finland, which has enabled them to make and justify well-grounded decisions for schools and to resist fly-by-night ideas that might have undermined trust in this public system.

Canada

Canada offers another example of a high-quality public education system. It has persistently ranked in the top 10 nations on PISA assessments, and the provinces of Alberta and Ontario have often been placed neck and neck with the highest-achieving jurisdictions in those rankings. Student performance is more equitable and less predetermined by socioeconomic status than in most other countries. Michael Fullan's chapter in this volume focuses especially on Ontario, which is Canada's most diverse province: a multiethnic, multiracial, and multilingual region that has a higher proportion of immigrants than the United States.

Since the launching of its whole system reform strategy in late 2003, Ontario has shown that significant improvements in student achievement and equity can be made in a large and diverse public education system. Ontario has been identified in studies by OECD and the McKenzie group as one of the most improved educational systems in that country and in the world, having dramatically improved its literacy rates, performance in mathematics and science, and graduation rates to levels that lead internationally and within Canada. Ontario has also nearly closed longstanding achievement gaps between English-speaking, French-speaking, and immigrant students who speak other languages, and has sharply reduced differentials between special education students and others. Fullan identifies three major reasons for this success:

- a relentless focus on a few ambitious goals: raise the bar in literacy, numeracy and high school graduation, close the achievement gap, and increase public confidence in education
- collective capacity-building among educators and schools aimed at improving instruction to achieve these results, and
- a progressive partnership with the teaching profession.

Government Disinvestment and Privatization Rebuffed

It was not always thus in Ontario. A conservative government put forth an aggressive market-oriented agenda between 1995 and 2003 that sharply cut funds to government schools while removing taxation powers from local districts so that they could not make up the difference. The provincial government took over several large school systems to exert financial controls on spending, cutting programs, and laying off staff, while also decreasing funding for housing and social services for children and families. Meanwhile, the government encouraged private schooling by, first, deregulating private schools, and then offering parents a tax credit for tuition at private schools.

Public school teachers were portrayed as overpaid and underworked; their workloads were increased and professional development days reduced from nine to five. Compulsory testing of new teachers and more intensive evaluation of teachers on-the-job accompanied the discourse of distrust. The teacher-bashing tone and policies mirrored those seen in Chile and the United States during similar eras. This statement from a teacher quoted in an evaluation of the Harris reforms over a five year period is resonant with those in these countries and others struggling with similar policies:

> I love teaching, and I go home every day [...] feeling energized by my students, believing that I am helping them to improve [...] and looking forward to what [my classes and I] will do next, but I am tired of being bashed by the premier. So I have relinquished my headship for next year and will take retirement on before my date. [...] That is something I never thought I would ever contemplate, let alone plan to do. That says something. You have no idea of the feeling of betrayal I experience—and I know I'm not alone.[12]

The aggressive changes to the education system led to labor unrest and public dissatisfaction. A public poll in 1998 showed that a significant proportion of Ontarians felt that the quality of education had declined in the previous five years.[13] Meanwhile, student performance was poor: only about half of elementary school students in Ontario were meeting the provincial standard in grades 3 and 6 literacy and mathematics, and only two-thirds of high school students were graduating in five years.

In the provincial election of 2003, Dalton McGuinty, leader of the Ontario Liberal Party, ran on a platform that made the renewal of public education one of its highest priorities and announced an ambitious set of policy commitments to improve public education. The Liberal Party took a large majority of seats; furthermore, McGuinty was re-elected four years later, largely due to his government's record in education—and to the opposition leader's proposal to provide full funding of private schools, which was publicly rejected. This has allowed a substantial redirection of the schools, with a short-lived detour in 2011 that has since been returned to the path that has been so successful.

Reinvestment and Reform

The new government moved quickly to reverse the policies of the prior administration and to establish a public education reform strategy. Local governance was restored to elected trustees in the districts that had been taken over by the province; the tax credit for private school tuition was revoked; two of the five eliminated teacher professional activity days were reinstituted; teacher testing and re-certification were cancelled and replaced with a new teacher induction program and a streamlined teacher performance appraisal process. The cuts in funding were restored and augmented with an additional investment of $1.6 billion in education spending by 2006.

A whole system improvement strategy was developed, based on partnership between the provincial government, the districts, and the unions, as well as knowledge growth and capacity building for educators, schools, districts, and the ministry itself. Using new literacy and numeracy standards as a starting point, the ministry created a new unit, the "Literacy and Numeracy Secretariat" (LNS), that drew in part on leading practitioners on loan from school districts; it searched for and studied the most effective district and school practices used to improve student performance in literacy and numeracy and disseminated key findings across the system. A similar strategy is currently being pursued to improve mathematics performance. It helped build capacity to improve instruction through coaching, collaborative inquiry, online video, and other supports related to instructional practices, networking schools and districts around effective practices, targeted interventions, and various forms of collaborative professional learning. Organized teams, consisting of staff of LNS called "Student Achievement Officers," worked with sets of districts to identify, develop, and spread capacity.

In the high schools, in addition to strengthening literacy and mathematics teaching and differentiating instruction, "student success teachers" (SSTs) began to work directly with students and with educators to support literacy, credit recovery, and engagement for students at risk of not graduating. The Specialist High Skills Major (SHSM) created engaging and relevant instruction in a wide range of career pathways for grade 11 and 12 students. Finally, the ministry developed supportive policies and programs related to safe schools, full-day kindergarten for all four- and five-year-olds (fully implemented by 2014), before and after school programs and mental health to support the work in the schools.

Assessment and Accountability

In all of these areas, data and information were developed, disseminated, and tracked. The purpose was not to manage competition or to punish schools, teachers, or students but to analyze practices and outcomes, so as to spread knowledge. The province sought to identify and disseminate evidenced-based examples in all core areas to support collaborative learning across schools and classrooms: What did effective literacy instruction look like? Who was successful in addressing the needs of English-Language Learners and what did they do? What practices in which high schools were most effective at engaging students and reducing dropouts?

In addition, programs were developed to identify and support the lowest-performing schools, primarily by building the capacity of the principal and teachers as instructional leaders in order to enhance instructional practices resulting in improved student achievement.

Through continuous cycles of identifying and spreading effective practices in districts and schools, the ministry has increasingly operated as a learning organization able to gain an increasingly deeper understanding of the strategies and conditions under which improvement takes place, develop and refine its own support strategies, and become an ally to the field in its improvement efforts.

Professionalization of Teaching and Leadership

Instructional capacity building was grounded in a strategy to strengthen professionalism that was conducted in collaboration with the unions. The ministry invested in professional development, beginning teacher induction, and grants for teacher research and dissemination of practices, all aimed at growth and "enhancing the teaching profession." Teacher education was strengthened through standards passed by the Ontario College of Teachers and requirements for extended clinical practice to match the two-year master's degree programs for training found elsewhere in the country—and not unlike Finland's model.

A focus on building leadership capacity has included a required preparation program, which all principals and vice-principals are required to complete to attain principal qualifications, plus a mentoring program for the first two years of their practice; funding and support provided to every school district in Ontario to develop and implement a Board Leadership Development Strategy, aimed at developing the leadership capacity of current and aspiring school and system leaders; and a Principal Performance Appraisal process, which includes setting a small number of challenging yet achievable goals in consultation with the supervisor, developing strategies to meet these goals, and ongoing support and appraisal in relationship to the goals.

Finally, the Ontario Strategy has committed to developing and using a strong research and evidence base to support action, which is key to a professional system. Ontario conducts research on its own strategy and encourages teachers and leaders to conduct, disseminate, and use action research on what is working, in collaboration with a research community that is engaged with practitioners in improving the system.

Over the past decade, overall student achievement has increased from 54 percent to 72 percent of students meeting the Ontario standards, while the number falling in the least proficient category at grades 3 and 6 has fallen by over 50 percent. Eighty-three percent of students are now graduating from high school within five years, and the system has regained public trust, a sign that these strategies are likely to continue to be refined and deepened over time.

Discussion and Conclusion

In his chapter in this volume, Michael Fullan succinctly summarizes the theory of action associated with privatization as a government policy. To paraphrase his definition: privatization consists of transferring ownership or management of an enterprise or service from the public sector (government) to private hands. Fullan notes that advocates of privatization argue that it "spurs improved performance and efficiency in ways that governments cannot. This theory of action proposes a causal relationship between actions taken (privatization) and desired results (improved performance and efficiency)."

As we have seen in the cases of Chile, Sweden, and the United States, this theory of action has not produced the expected results. No case showed noticeably better systemwide results due to of reforms that transferred the ownership or management of education to private agents, and in each case growing segregation and inequality accompanied the reforms. In its most extreme form, in Chile, the long-term result of a privatized education system was a set of deep-seated inequalities that also set expectations and investments so low that the entire system suffered in terms of quality. We saw that Chilean students are left in the dust, achievement-wise, by students from Cuba's system of publicly managed schools, despite the greater economic challenges Cuba faces. Furthermore, Martin Carnoy suggests that, from a global perspective, rather than one that compares results only within a country, privatization does not even help the upper class that has escaped to the country's "best" schools. Based on international achievement data, he argues that:

> On an international scale, top 10 percent social class Brazilian and Chilean students—with all the advantages of a higher social class upbringing and most attending elite private schools—score about the same in math and lower in reading on international tests such as the 2009 Program of International Student Assessment (PISA) as middle-class students in the United States and considerably lower in math than lower-middle-class Canadian students. The bottom line is that elite private Brazilian and Chilean schools (and Latin America's elite schools more generally) gauge their students' performance against the poorly equipped, poorly staffed schools catering to their low social class students. This results in lower academic standards for all students, including the so-called academically elite.

Thus, Carnoy notes that, at least in primary and secondary school, market conditions in education do not appear to produce more learning across the society. "The negative aspects of inequality and markets, especially as they play out at the bottom of the social scale, seem to offset any positive effects of parents' 'freedom' to pick and choose among schools." This appears to have been the case in Sweden, as well, where overall achievement has dropped precipitously, leaving what was once one of the most highly educated countries in Europe performing well below the current OECD average on PISA.

The United States is a more complex case, with different policies across its 50 states and 15,000 local school districts. On average, demographically similar students educated in private schools (with or without vouchers) and those in charter schools perform about the same as those in traditional public schools—occasionally they do better and somewhat more often than that, they appear to do worse. (Interestingly, in Chile, data also suggest that, for several groups, demographically similar children are performing better in the government schools than in private schools in recent years.) The U.S. states with the highest overall performance have been least involved in chartering or privatization, while those with the most unregulated approaches to market-based reforms are lower performers overall, and have seen significantly worse outcomes for their students in charter schools than those in district-run public schools. In these cases, disadvantaged students rarely have access to schools worth choosing.

Individual School Versus System-Level Outcomes

These case studies suggest there may be several factors that could depress overall achievement in systems, even if some individual schools are doing well. One key factor may be the deprofessionalization of teaching: In Chile, Sweden, and the United States, as well as the shorter period in Canada before 2003, market-based reforms have often been accompanied by verbal attacks on teachers, in some cases mass firings (Chile and New Orleans), reduction of standards for entry into the profession and decreased investments in professional learning (all of the cases), and incentives for attrition rather than rewards for retention. The preference for inexperienced, less well-trained, and, consequently, less expensive teachers—and in some models, for larger class sizes to reduce costs (as noted in Sweden's for-profit schools)—could undermine the quality of education more broadly as teaching conditions worsen and expertise in the profession dwindles through increased attrition and lack of high-quality supply.

A second factor that could depress overall achievement is the focus on competition among schools for enrollments, rather than collaboration aimed at solving common problems and sharing best practices. Not only does competition create incentives to keep successful innovations secret, so as to be better positioned in the marketplace, it also often directs more attention to efforts to recruit the most able students and avoid or shed those who struggle than to developing stronger education, as educators described in both Milwaukee and New Orleans. Even as educators work to boost enrollments and scores—and succeed in doing so in some schools—the system as a whole must attend to the needs of all students, including those who are less economically or educationally advantaged. The evidence suggests systems may end up serving these students with fewer resources in more segregated settings, so the apparent successes of a few schools do not translate into the success of the system overall.

Finally, and ironically, the focus on test-based accountability in all of these systems could depress overall achievement, particularly when tests narrow the curriculum and focus on lower-level skills. Researchers have found that focusing instruction on such tests can reduce opportunities for developing higher order thinking and performance skills.[14]

A Public Theory of Action

Cases like those of Ontario, Finland, and Cuba—as well as states like Massachusetts in the United States—prove a core assumption of privatization wrong by demonstrating that publicly provided education can offer both high-quality and equitable education. Furthermore, as Michael Fullan notes, these cases provide evidence to build a theory of action that illustrates how deliberate policy actions can improve entire educational systems. The cases describe how each of these countries provided equitable resources for schools; invested in high-quality preparation and ongoing development for teachers; organized instruction around a common, core curriculum with little tracking; personalized instruction for students; and supported ongoing research, evaluation, and sharing of knowledge to support improvement. In these jurisdictions, collaboration among educators and sharing of knowledge and practice across classrooms and schools play a major role in a deliberate process of ongoing improvement.

Fullan notes that, "At the core of this theory of action is a firm belief that education, with its central role in promoting and improving moral, social, economic, and societal well-being, should be the direct responsibility of the state." Carnoy reinforces this point, suggesting that governments must take "full responsibility for improving instruction." He argues that, "the state has to be much more of a *guarantor* of quality education for all, [taking] public responsibility for children's success."

Can Markets be Managed?

While this volume offers examples of publicly managed systems of education that perform well and have substantially improved, it is also true that there are publicly managed systems that have not found pathways to quality and do not support the equitable education of all children—including, at various moments in history, some of those we have featured here. It is often when dissatisfaction with public systems emerges that privatizing options are most appealing. Indeed, one of the central concepts of choice-based systems is the possibility that they can offer better opportunities for some students and may spur reform in the system as a whole.

Choice is clearly better than coercion as a basis for education. Yet, as we have seen, choice, as it is pursued in privatized systems, raises knotty and profound issues. The systems we have reviewed here have not had well-developed answers to questions such as: what happens when choice initiatives create schools not worth choosing—schools that may even harm some students? Or when schools of choice will not "choose" students who are low-achieving, in need of special educational services, or otherwise viewed as not a "fit" for the school? What are the implications when publicly funded schools are allowed to exclude children? Or exacerbate segregation?

Can we design schools of choice that serve the broad purposes of public education? Interestingly, in both the United States and Sweden, the original choice or charter movements were viewed less as a marketplace and more as a means to stimulate innovation while maintaining the context of democratically accountable institutions. In the United States, state policies continue to differ in the extent to which they favor a competitive market ideology (e.g. Ohio, Florida, Louisiana, Milwaukee) or emphasize democratic values and the importance of strong oversight of public education providers (e.g. California, Massachusetts, Minnesota). Indeed, research in the United States has suggested that charter school outcomes differ across states, with relatively more positive outcomes in those with greater public oversight of these schools.

This raises the question as to whether better-managed markets might have better and more equitable outcomes overall than those that are left entirely unregulated. Author Björn Åstrand notes of the Swedish experiment that "the market model took a few years before expanding and turning into a mainly for-profit oriented business. A clearer set of regulations could have preserved and supported the "influencing" strategy of private school alternatives, possibly with positive influences on the Swedish schools."

Can Choice and Democracy Co-Exist?

What might the parameters be that would support a democratic system that incorporates productive choice? In a seminal article some years ago, noted school innovators Ted Sizer and George Wood, each of whom had launched schools of choice in both the traditional public and charter school sectors, described a democratic theory of action for choice.[15] They began with the principle that individuals should have the power to shape their public institutions by voicing their preferences and holding their leaders accountable through direct democratic processes. They then introduced the principles of equity, access, public purpose, and public ownership as critical to the demands of a democracy for an educated citizenry, and as standards to guide how schools of choice should be regulated.

Schools of choice aimed at democratic values would increase educational quality and equity, not by creating a competitive marketplace of successes and failures but by encouraging innovation and allowing more diversity among schools, thereby enabling students to find settings that support their learning styles and passions, and by giving parents a greater voice in school improvement.[16] When conceptualized in this manner, the primary objective of schools of choice is to enable educators and parents to work together more closely, while protecting students' rights of access and guarantees of basic educational quality.

To serve the public purpose, schools would need to serve all students equitably and help develop a citizenry that shares common values and knowledge and can live together productively in a pluralistic democracy. To accomplish this, public ownership would need to be conceptualized in a way that maintains proximity to the local community being served, and providing oversight from agencies that have both a commitment to the public goals of public education and a capacity for effective monitoring. Continuous improvement processes that share knowledge and help schools build capacity would be needed; to succeed, they would have to be based in a collaborative, rather than competitive, framework for school operations. Allowing for-profit entities to operate publicly funded schools would have to be questioned, given the inherent conflict of interest in an enterprise that, in order to maintain profit margins, must continually decide which services can be reduced or eliminated or which students will not be served because they are too expensive to educate.

A commitment to equity and access would demand open admissions policies and would disallow selective admissions that would separate schools by their ability to choose their students, rather than by the ability of all students and families to choose their schools. Schools of choice would need to be monitored to ensure that they do not push or counsel out students who present educational challenges. School funding would need to be equitable across all schools and pose no burdens to families for tuition, fees, or transportation. In short, the system would need to operate like a public system.

Ultimately, the challenge is to create a system filled with schools worth choosing in which all students have a genuine right to choose and be chosen. This can be and has been accomplished within public education systems without privatization.[17] There may be ways that a broader range of school types can contribute to such a system, if there are strong mechanisms to preserve commitments to equity, access, public purpose, and public ownership. Such efforts will not reap profits for entrepreneurs, but they could reap benefits for citizens, including both parents and those who have no children in the schools themselves.

At the end of the day, the public welfare—not just the individual's pocketbook —is best served when investments in schools enable all young people to become productive, responsible citizens prepared to participate effectively in the political, social, and economic life of their democracy. As John Dewey wrote more than a century ago in *The School and Society*:

> What the best and wisest parent wants for his own child, that must the community want for all of its children. Any other ideal for our schools is narrow and unlovely; acted upon, it destroys our democracy... Only by being true to the full growth of all the individuals who make it up can society by any chance be true to itself.[18]

Notes

1 Smith, A. (2010). *The Theory of Moral Sentiments*. Penguin. (Part 4, chapter 1).
2 OECD (2013). *PISA 2012 Results in Focus: What 15 Year Olds Know and What They Can Do With What They Know*. Paris: OECD.
3 Retrieved from http://unesdoc.unesco.org/images/0016/001610/161045e.pdf.
4 CENDA (Centro de Estudios Nacionales de Desarrollo Alternativo) (2002). *Estudio de Remuneraciones del Magisterio*. Santiago, Chile.
5 Esping-Andersen, G. (1990). *The Three Worlds of Welfare Capitalism*, Princeton: Princeton University Press.
6 Husén, T. (1972), *Skolans kris och andra uppsatser om utbildning*, Stockholm: Almqvist and Wiksell Förlag AB; Husén, T. (1979), *The School in Question: A Comparative Study of the School and its Future in Western Societies*, Oxford: Oxford University Press.
7 In PISA 2012, in "all subject areas, Sweden is the country whose performance has declined the most." Skolverket (2013), *PISA 2012, 15-åringars kunskaper i matematik, läsförståelse och naturvetenskap*, Stockholm: Skolverket. In a special report OECD highlights a decline in all "three core subjects measured in PISA", a "significant" increase in the proportion of students that do not "reach baseline of performance in mathematics" and the fact that the "share of top performers on mathematics roughly halved over the past decade." OECD (2014) *Resources, Policies and Practices in Sweden's Schooling System: An In-depth Analysis of PISA 2012 Results*. Paris.
8 National Center for Education Statistics (2015). *The Condition of Education: Charter School Enrollment*. Retrieved from http://nces.ed.gov/programs/coe/indicator_cgb.asp.
9 Alexandra Usher and Nancy Kober (2011). *Keeping Informed about School Vouchers: A Review of Major Developments and Research*. Washington, D.C.: Center on Education Policy.
10 Center for Education Reform (2015). *Charter School Laws Across the States: 2015 Rankings and Scorecard*. Edreform.com. Retrieved from https://www.edreform.com/wp-content/uploads/2015/07/CharterLaws2015.pdf.
11 Kelly, D., Nord, C. W., Jenkins, F., Chan, J. Y., and Kastberg, D. (2013). *Performance of US 15-Year-Old Students in Mathematics, Science, and Reading Literacy in an International Context. First Look at PISA 2012*. NCES 2014-024. Washington, D.C.: National Center for Education Statistics.
12 Hargreaves, A., Moore, S., and Fink, D. (2003). Teaching Despite the Knowledge Society, Part II. In Hargreaves, A. (2003). *Teaching in the Knowledge Society: Education in the Age of Insecurity*. New York: Teachers College Press: 96–126 (p. 117).
13 Livingstone, D. W., Hart, D. J., and Davie, L. E. (1998). *The 12ᵗʰ OISE/UT Survey: Public Attitudes Towards Education in Ontario in 1998*. Toronto: OISE/University of Toronto.
14 For research on the effects of testing on learning, see Darling-Hammond, L., and Adamson, F. (2014). *Beyond the Bubble Test: How Performance Assessments Support 21st Century Learning*. San Francisco: John Wiley & Sons.
15 Sizer, T. and Wood, G. (2008). Charter Schools and the Values of Public Education. In L. Dingerson, B. Miner, B. Peterson, and S. Waters (Eds.), *Keeping the Promise? The Debate over Charter Schools*, pp. 3–16. Milwaukee: Rethinking Schools.
16 This section draws on Darling-Hammond, L. and Montgomery, K. (2008). Keeping the Promise: The Role of Policy in Reform. In L. Dingerson, B. Miner, B. Peterson, and S. Waters (Eds.), *Keeping the Promise? The Debate over Charter Schools*, pp. 91–110. Milwaukee: Rethinking Schools.

17 See for example: Sergiovanni, T. J. (1994). *Building Community in Schools.* Jossey-Bass; Wasley, P. A., Fine, M., Gladden, M., Holland, N. E., King, S. P., Mosak, E., and Powell, L. C. (2000). *Small Schools: Great Strides. A Study of New Small Schools in Chicago.* Retrieved from http://files.eric.ed.gov/fulltext/ED465474.pdf; Darling-Hammond, L., Ancess, J., and Ort, S. W. (2002). Reinventing high school: Outcomes of the coalition campus schools project. *American Educational Research Journal,* 39(3), 639–673; Fine, M. (1994). *Chartering Urban School Reform: Reflections on Public High Schools in the Midst of Change.* New York: Teachers College Press; Fine, M., Stoudt, B., and Futch, V. (2005). *The International Network for Public Schools: A Quantitative and Qualitative Cohort Analysis of Graduation and Dropout Rates. Teaching and Learning in a Transcultural Academic Environment.* Retrieved from http://www.internationalsnps.org/pdfs/FineReport.pdf.
18 John Dewey (1907). The School and Social Progress. Chapter 1 in *The School and Society.* Chicago: University of Chicago Press, pp. 19–44.

INDEX